To Alan,

Help us get the truth out!

Steve Young
1/94

Alan, we really appreciate you!

Will Perkins

Alan, Thank you for your friendship

Kevin Tebedo

Josh 1:8

GAY POLITICS VS. COLORADO

The Inside Story of Amendment 2

GAY POLITICS
VS.

a n d A m e r i c a

The Inside Story of Amendment 2

by

Stephen Bransford

Sardis Press
Cascade, Colorado

GAY POLITICS VS. COLORADO
The Inside Story of Amendment 2

Printed in the United States of America.

1 2 3 4 5 6 7 8 9 10 11 12 13 14 15

Published and distributed by:

Sardis Press
PO Box 11
Cascade, CO 80809.

Editor/Project Manager: Phil Murdy
Jacket Design: Patrick J. McGuire and
Kim Fiedler/Sonlight Graphics

Library of Congress Catalog Card Number: 93-87440

ISBN (cloth): 0-9639465-0-1

For
the
53.4%

Table of Contents

1

Introduction

A cultural shift occurred in Colorado on Election Day '92. Against a tide of elite pressure the people voted for what the media called an "anti-gay" constitutional amendment. The *Washington Times* observed: "When Amendment 2 appeared on the ballot last year, critics dismissed it, saying it would never pass in live-and-let-live Colorado."[1] Opinion polls agreed, predicting its doom. But in the privacy of the voting booth, 53.4% of the electorate shocked the experts, banning gay rights laws statewide.

In a year that saw a president elected with far less than half of the popular vote, Amendment 2 provided a clear winner. The win tasted sweeter because the amendment had been a grassroots effort. The election surprise provided a classic David and Goliath drama in which the little people beat the political giants at their own game.

However, the people of Colorado paid an unfair price for their victory. In voting against gay rights laws they received the wrath of the political elite nationwide. This included a boycott and the mean-spirited label "State of Hate." Activists and the press further characterized the voters in terms of "religious right" bigotry—even though the question posed by the amendment had been about civil rights.[2]

Shrewd observers suspected that the explosion of hate rhetoric after the election revealed the shallowness of the gay lobby's civil rights position. Exposed by Amendment 2, and lacking better arguments, they had resorted to name-calling. The real surprise was to see how many Americans seemed willing to follow their lead.

The accusations of voter hatred had the effect of escalating a simple civil rights discussion into a major question of national values: Did the citizens of Colorado vote for hate? *Really*? If so, then, of course Amendment 2 deserved to be repealed. America should not tolerate a hateful law. On the other hand, if the election reflected a true standard of decency, the will of the people should be allowed to prevail.

Post election polls favored the latter interpretation of events. Colorado did not express bigotry. It was, as they said, a "live-and-let-live" state. Its voters revealed more, not less, tolerance toward homosexuality than the rest of the nation. Colorado was among the first states to abolish sodomy laws. Only 29% of its voters want such laws reinstated versus 54% nationwide. Fifty percent of Coloradans approved of gays in the military versus 43% nationwide.[3] Remarkably, 60% of Coloradans say homosexuals are no different from heterosexuals except in their choice of bed partners.[4] So how could it be claimed that Colorado had voted for hate?

Was the Colorado majority out of step with society at large? Apparently not. In April '93 a national Gallup Poll posed the question of extending civil rights laws to include homosexuals. Forty-eight percent agreed with Colorado's voting majority, 46% disagreed, while 6% remained undecided.[5] Colorado had expressed its opinions in roughly the same pattern before the election. It is quite possible that a national vote on Amendment 2 would match Colorado's results.

But another factor must be added to the election results: Amendment 2 won the undecided vote against the fierce opposition of the state's cultural and media powers. This surprising fact, more than any other, has thrown the political left into a panic of self-examination. Did they miscalculate? Were they blinded by Bill Clinton's momentum? Are they out of touch with political reality? Or was there something special about Amendment 2 that caused it to win against great odds? Perhaps some combination of reasons? The shock of losing the election after throwing the full strength of gay political power into the battle has caused many activists to lay blame on anyone and everyone—most unjustly, upon the good citizens of Colorado.

Within six months of the election, Colorado for Family Values (CFV), the Colorado Springs citizens group sponsoring Amendment 2, had received calls from would-be organizers in 34 states. These people wanted to follow the winning Colorado strategy against gay rights. All across the nation, state-by-state initiatives against homosexual laws and ordinances began to shape-up in the election's aftermath. The Colorado model continues to inform these son-of-Amendment 2 issues. A recent article in *The Blade*, a leading Washington, D.C. gay publication, bore the stark headline, WE ARE IN A LOT OF TROUBLE.[6] The article went on to describe those set to oppose their agenda as "inspired by the success of Colorado's Amendment 2."

During the April '93 homosexual parade in Washington, D.C., the Colorado delegation marched symbolically at the head. More specifically, the Colorado Springs' gay contingent (birthplace of Amendment 2) led all groups.[7] Immediately after the parade Torie Osborn, head of the National Gay and Lesbian Task Force, visited Colorado Springs, hailing it as "the epicenter of hate." She dramatically commiserated, "It's tough to be in the belly of the monster."[8] This level of rhetoric indicated a continuing loss of political equilibrium in the gay lobby.

Perhaps homosexuals remain out-of-touch because so many in government, education, business, religion, Hollywood, and the news media seem enamored by gay politics. It's trendy. All across the nation gay rights laws are being called "the public issue of the '90s," the leading battle of the culture war. The contest is engulfing the ballot box, political parties, private clubs, education, chambers of commerce, churches, businesses, board rooms, and the courts. It's dividing homes and families as well. The current occupants of the White House want to give the homosexual lobby everything it demands. No one is likely to escape the impending consequences, whatever they are.

First of all, the Colorado experience warns that whoever opposes the gay agenda will not win a quick and easy victory. Not even after winning an election. In today's courts, dominated by the ACLU (American Civil Liberties Union), any law—even a good one—can be challenged and sometimes held hostage for years. To enhance this possibility, activist judges are expanding the powers of the court so that they can, in effect, serve as America's social engineers. (A trend that must be stopped for the good of the nation.)

It is not surprising, then, that the rich and powerful homosexual lobby planned six months before the election to drag Amendment 2 into court. In May of '92 ". . . the group immediately created a national network of legal support, bringing in the American Civil Liberties Union, Lambda, private attorneys in California and New York, and city attorneys from Denver, Boulder, and Aspen."[9] (They knew exactly how to defeat an election—if they lost, of course.) True to form, a socially aggressive Colorado judge used his position to invent a new fundamental right based on homosexual orientation (a weird right never before seen in history). This unproven right he then used to quickly grant the gay lobby a temporary injunction, stopping Amendment 2 from being enforced.

Next, the state Supreme Court voted 6-to-1 to uphold this judge's eccentric ruling, saying that the amendment would "probably" be found unconstitutional. They followed a unprecedented line of reasoning to reach this conclusion, claiming Amendment 2 would deny homosexuals as a group the right to petition government for protection from discrimination. (To understand how far afield the court has gone to rule against the people of Colorado, read Appendix D, *Brief Amicus Curiae of Colorado for Family Values* by The National Legal Foundation.)

Finally, in an unprecedented effort to defeat the amendment, the state's highest court cited untested and unproven case law to make a further defense of Amendment 2 in Colorado courts futile. (For a full treatment of this topic, see MEET ME AT THE INJUNCTION on page 183.)

Colorado's Attorney General subsequently appealed to the U.S. Supreme Court, asking them to intervene to stop the inevitable courtroom loss under the Colorado rules. At the U.S. Supreme Court level, court precedent favors Amendment 2. But the high court seldom hears a case that has not been argued and appealed through the entire lower court process. Not surprisingly then, the Supreme Court denied this early appeal. The will of the people of

Colorado must thus remain under a Colorado judge's injunction until Amendment 2 passes through its obligatory court losses, then follows a costly appeals process all the way to the high court again.

What has been lost here? First of all, judicial activism has created a wrong impression. The court rulings suggest to the people that a difficult petition process and campaign for votes no longer count in America. A small group of loud protestors can be given a privileged—and unwarranted—place in line ahead of 53.4% of the state's voters. Even worse, judicial activism implies that a vote against gay rights is insupportable in court. This has put a damper on the democratic process itself. In order to do this damage, the Colorado courts were obliged to stretch the law to its limits (and perhaps beyond) in favor of the gay lobby. Their rulings appear to have been made on flimsy legal ground. A court that truly served a constitution "of the people" would have erred in the other direction.

The Colorado court action on Amendment 2 indicates that the time has come for voters to hold political candidates' feet to the fire regarding judicial appointments and approvals. A candidate should reveal whether he will support judges who believe in the constitution, or those who plan to "evolve" it. The answer to this question goes to the heart of our cultural war.

One year after a boycott, in spite of all of the media attacks on their vote, and the insults of an activist court, Colorado voters are far from happy. They are, in fact, waking up. A recent poll revealed that not just 53.4%, but a full 58% support Amendment 2 today[10] . . . and this in a generally liberal state! The issue of judicial activism is likely to make or break a few candidates in Colorado's upcoming elections. In the long run, *The People v. The Colorado Courts* will be decided by the people, not by judges.

With all this unfolding drama, the Colorado experience looms even larger for informing the rest of the nation as to what lies ahead, and what is at stake in opposing gay politics. How, for example, did Amendment 2 overcome the opposition of the state's governor, Civil Rights bureaucrats, left-leaning religious leaders, and the educational establishment to win this election? The odds seemed unbeatable. How did it outsmart an army of lawyers, the

Colorado Bar Association itself, the clout of big business, chambers of commerce, city councils, mayors and the press? How did it defy the current trend of political correctness and the unpardonable sin of so-called "discrimination?" How did CFV convince non-religious people to take a stand for their besieged issue? What part did the religious "right" and "left" play in the battle? And what does the homosexual lobby really want? What will it cost the American taxpayer if they get everything on their wish list? What will it cost families? In short, what does the Colorado story offer a nation facing "the gay '90s?"

I moved to Colorado Springs from Texas one year before the '92 election. The petition drive had begun and media coverage ran strongly against the proposed amendment. I found the debate intimidating and somewhat confusing. News stories portrayed those who supported the initiative as bigoted and hateful. I had known people who felt same-sex attractions and wanted to be careful not to attack the human beings involved. I believed, then and now, that people who practice homosexuality are entitled to the same human rights and dignity as anyone else. This meant that I couldn't support any movement or any law which intended to single them out, rob them of those rights, persecute them, or deprive them of employment and housing. Because of press coverage, I at first assumed that Amendment 2 did all of these things. How misinformed I was!

Then Colorado for Family Values (CFV), the group sponsoring Amendment 2, asked me to sit on their media advisory panel. (Two of four CFV prime movers had been writing colleagues of mine for several years.) This request caused me to look closely at the proposed amendment and the organization behind it. For the first time I heard CFV's civil rights position clearly. In the process, I took it upon myself to hear the arguments of the homosexual activists and their defenders, too. I read anti-amendment literature and attended lectures and debates.

After examining the evidence for myself, I found that Amendment 2 made much better sense for Colorado than the special homosexual laws it would prevent and overturn in Denver, Boulder, and Aspen. These so-called gay rights laws had actually imposed homosexual values on many unsuspecting citizens. Rather than removing rights, as the media claimed the amendment would do,[11] it actually restored freedom of speech and association to business, education, families, churches, government, and individuals. Furthermore, the amendment would stop the rich homosexual lobby from grabbing the legal protections given only to the most powerless racial minorities among us. As such, it would restore fairness to the civil rights arena. The arguments that Amendment 2 discriminated unfairly against homosexuals simply wouldn't stand scrutiny. Amazingly, under Amendment 2 none of this liberation came at the expense of homosexual behavior. Which refuted the opposition's favorite charge—that Amendment 2 was simply a narrow religious law, singling out homosexuals for persecution.

All of this answered my personal objections, clearing the way for me to serve as a media advisor for Colorado for Family Values during the Amendment 2 battle. This ringside seat offered me an insider's perspective on CFV's historic campaign. That is the perspective I bring to the writing of this book.

What is the advantage of this perspective? First of all, this is the only full account of Amendment 2 told from the inside. A dozen major news scoops are included here—completely ignored or missed by the news media. Also, during the campaign, under a constant and disconcerting barrage of negative reporting, I sometimes wondered if Amendment 2 had inculcated hateful motives I had overlooked. Ofttimes I would grow unfocused over important concepts such as discrimination and protected class status. I would confuse the amendment's political position with Judeo-Christian morality (a common mistake). Each time I got off track, I turned to an examination of the amendment again and took advantage of CFV lawyers and political experts. This exercise helped clarify my thinking and filter out the poison of popular assumptions pushed by a press that has been rightly called "politically correct." Through each cycle of doubt and discovery, I grew more certain of Amendment 2's soundness, more committed to its healthy principles.

This, I believe, is the main advantage of an inside perspective. In that regard, the Table of Contents has been designed to serve readers who might likewise become confused on various issues and need to refresh their memory.

The untold Amendment 2 success story, beyond its ability to entertain and educate, reveals its share of human frailty, pettiness, some brilliance, blunders, botched strategies, counter-strategies, turning points, in-fighting, death threats, a politically manipulated suicide, betrayals, intimidation, eleventh-hour desertions, pressure groups, and private territorial bickering. The weaknesses of Colorado for Family Values are sometimes exposed in the telling. By contrast, the uncanny and compelling strengths of Amendment 2 become even clearer. Finally, it emerges that Amendment 2 articulated an issue that transcended any, and all, of its proponents.

I'm a novelist, a story teller who happened to get involved with an irresistible true story called Amendment 2. In the process I learned enough to be called an advanced student of homosexual politics. I have learned enough to become alarmed at the way this movement threatens to change the character of our courts, and thus, our nation. There are experts to be found with information to exceed mine in technical detail. Some of their contributions can be found in the appendixes and endnotes of this book. My pledge to the reader is to tell the Amendment 2 story so as not to bore, and to make its complex lessons accessible and understandable.

2

Colorado Springs

There is a momentum here that may not be able to be stopped; just as blacks dominated the '60s, women the '70s, and abortion the '80s, gays and lesbians and their fight for equal rights seem likely to dominate the '90s.
(*THE GAY '90S: SEX, POWER AND INFLUENCE*, NBC TV, Jan. 26, 1993)

In early '91 the homosexual lobby was on a roll. Opponents were painted as Biblical fundamentalists, cousins to the Ayatollah, soulmates of Hitler. Politicians, fearing any association with the so-called "religious right," embraced the politically correct gay agenda automatically. To gay activists political correctness seemed the perfect vehicle to favorable legislation.

Cultural leaders had no reason to believe Colorado would act differently from the rest of the nation in this regard. The cities of Aspen, Boulder, and Denver had granted gays protected class status in citywide ordinances. Specifically, Denver's city council had voted 2-to-1 in favor of a gay rights law in October of 1990. A repeal effort had been easily beaten back in the spring of '91. Essentially the state's *Who's Who* had endorsed homosexual politics—the governor, media leaders, influential businessmen, mayors, city councilmen, lawyers, educators, the civil rights establishment, to name a few. In Colorado, gay activists expected nothing more than a speed-bump on the road to national affirmation.

But then (perhaps drunk with success) a group of the state's cultural leaders miscalculated badly. They wrote and proposed H.B. 1059, a sweeping gay rights law disguised under the nice sounding title, "The Ethnic Harassment Bill." (Appendix B publishes the full text of this proposed statewide law.) H.B. 1059 sought to expand the powers of Colorado's Civil Rights Division in the following manner:

First it added "sexual orientation" to the list of protected classes. Colorado's law had heretofore limited itself to race, color, ancestry, religion, and national origin. In order to slip sexual orientation onto the list unnoticed, the writers buried it in a list which included, sex, age, handicap, or disability. (Using disadvantaged groups as camouflage is true of all gay rights laws.)

Next, H.B. 1059 claimed these disadvantaged people had the "right" *not* to experience fear, intimidation, or harassment. (To declare such a right, *extraordinary* powers would have to be given to the government in order to guarantee it. Which was the full intention of H.B. 1059.)

To add real teeth to the new classifications, H.B. 1059 declared that "the penalty for crimes motivated by bigotry and bias should be more severe than the penalty for the underlying crime." (This violated the founding father's principle that government should address actions only, not opinions or bias. Policing inner thoughts is Jefferson's definition of tyranny.) Nevertheless, the proposed law furthermore specified that any "class 1 misdemeanor" motivated by "bigotry" would "be reclassified to a class 6 felony."

In order to carry out the ambitions of H.B. 1059, the law elevated the powers of Civil Rights Division Director, Jack Lang y Marquez to that of a *civil rights Czar*. The sponsors of this law proposed to give him power above that of every state police agency and courtroom. He could subpoena witnesses, compel testimony, demand the production of evidence, and dispel information from his inquiries to any and all government agencies. In other words, he could ruin anyone's reputation whom he felt was harassing a member of a protected class.

Finally, Marquez and his successors in the directorship of the Colorado Civil Rights Division would be given wide latitude in deciding what would be "harassment" under the Ethnic Harassment Bill. Such definition in the workplace, for example, would not have to be proven by any "tangible or economic job consequences." The title *civil rights Czar* certainly fits such an unprecedented range of powers bestowed on this unelected civil servant.

Suddenly, under this gay rights law the values and freedoms of

BARBARA SHELDON of Denver warned that gay politics was about to impose itself on Colorado through H.B. 1059.

the entire state were at risk. Until now, such laws had only affected the unsuspecting citizens of Denver, Boulder, and Aspen. With H.B. 1059 on the state's doorstep, a fresh group of opponents came to defend Colorado's freedoms. Specifically, a group from Colorado Springs got involved, which proved to be the undoing of gay politics as usual, both for Colorado and the nation.

The critical link between Denver and Colorado Springs concerning H.B. 1059 came in a simple phone call between two housewives—Patricia Long of Colorado Springs, who called Barbara Sheldon. Sheldon had recently been named to head a Denver chapter of The Traditional Values Coalition (TVC). She had previously volunteered heavily in the failed attempt to repeal her city's gay rights law, and was well known as a "religious righter." Nevertheless, in her new capacity with TVC, she had learned the disturbing details of the pending Ethnic Harassment Bill.

Patricia "Pat" Long had an interesting reason for making her call. She had retired early from Digital Equipment Corporation in Colorado Springs because of the company's aggressive homosexual policies. Her bad experience in the workplace had alarmed her so much, that she now opposed the gay agenda in the public sector as well.

At Digital, under the guise of what seemed to be a harmless program called "Valuing Differences," homosexuals had become "the" power group. Pat and many other employees felt offended at being *forced* to affirm their lifestyle. The company had instituted a number of mandatory meetings in which homosexuality was specifically "valued" as a "difference." Managers were told that "participation becomes part of the employee's job plan with related performance measurements."[12] In other words, raises and promotions would now be affected by an employee's attitude toward lesbians and gays. Homosexual social calendars and celebrations began to proliferate in all company correspondence after this program began. The company went so far as to fund a secret organization of gay and lesbian workers called DECplus, which stood for "Digital Equipment Corporation People Like Us."[13] (See Appendix A for full text.) The purpose of this confidential group was to "socialize," "support," and "network" invisibly within the company for the purpose of advancing those "people like us" who claimed same-sex attractions. Like many other large, high-tech firms, Digital had gone hook-line-and-sinker for the gay agenda.

Pat considered the Valuing Differences seminars counter-productive and absurd, but her official objection, sent in a memo to upper management, had added the moral dimension, ". . . We should be valuing PEOPLE, not their sins," she said. This is a costly stand to take publicly these days. She argued that her faith gave her no option but to call homosexuality a sin. "I'm sure Digital policies would never require a Jew to eat pork or celebrate Christmas, please show some sensitivity toward the Christian values . . . Digital needs to either get the homosexual material out of the general distribution or permit the Christians their equal opportunity to respond and widely spread their Good News."[14]

Pat had then received an unwanted phone call from a high level manager. "I'm concerned about your forming a hate group," the manager said. "People can get fired around here for not following policies."[15] As it turned out, moral objections to homosexuality were simply not on the list of "differences" to be "valued" at Digital anymore. Diversity had found its limits.

The threat to Pat's career had come in spite of her record as a manager, in which she had consistently earned "Exceeds Job Requirements" ratings for 11 years.[16] Specifically, her Digital mission had been to salvage problem workers for the thirty-five-hundred employee production plant in Colorado Springs. Pat had loved this redemptive aspect of her career. Like the values of her Christian faith, she had found her role at Digital to touch the deeper needs of hurting people. She could imagine nothing more fulfilling, and she had been highly honored for her success—until now. Confronted by the demands of the gay lobby, her fine record didn't matter anymore. As she put it to her supervisors, it appeared to be "an overlay of conflicting values. . . . It appears to me, the Christian values take second place."[17]

After twelve months of resisting this trend, Pat had felt overwhelmed. At the time, she faced her fourth year of ovarian cancer. She had been told by doctors that this would probably be her last year to live. Not wanting to spend her final days holding out against Digital's pro-homosexual pressure groups, she negotiated a severance package and retired early. But she had made it known to her closest friends that she had left the job with a feeling of unfinished business. Somehow, she had let hundreds of Digital employees down. They had supported her and had looked to her to give them a voice against gay rights. She had a drawer full of their notes, cards and letters.

With a nagging sense of guilt she continued to privately look for opportunities to complete her mission against the tyranny of the homosexual social agenda. Meanwhile she had become a survival

PATRICIA "PAT" LONG of Digital in Colorado Springs battled the gay agenda in the private sector.

statistic, passing her terminal year of ovarian cancer in surprising good health. Hearing that Barbara Sheldon had been involved in opposing Denver's gay rights law, she had called to find out what she could do to help.

In Denver, Barbara had first encountered gay rights by chance, through the Jefferson County Schools. A homosexual man and woman had been invited by local educators to share their lifestyles with eighth-grade children. When parents learned of it they had strenuously objected, Barbara among them. Meeting with school officials in an attempt to air their concerns, they were forced to listen as the homosexual man in question took the occasion to tell them that he hoped to become a role model for their children. Those with traditional family values in the group nearly came unglued. Several religious leaders at the meeting stood and scolded the objecting parents for their narrow-mindedness. These church authorities declared homosexuality to be "a beautiful gift from God."

With this shocking introduction to the threat of gay politics, Barbara awakened. She next learned that the city of Denver had already passed its gay rights ordinance. Now she understood why the Jefferson County schools had put forward something so out of line with the values of parents; no doubt Denver's gay rights law had encouraged them. Something must be done, she thought. The city law, in her view, had legislated immorality. She involved herself vigorously with a local citizens group attempting to repeal the ordinance.

Why would anyone but a moralist like Barbara oppose a gay rights law? As it turns out, there are many good reasons: First, gay rights laws forbid discrimination based on a person's sexual orientation. Sounds harmless, but not so. Freedom of association is at risk here. Whether or not one agrees with the right *not* to associate with homosexuals, it remains an important freedom, an important choice in a free society. To remove this freedom is a serious step toward tyranny. Such a freedom should only be infringed in the most extreme cases, like the historic, immoral discrimination against black Americans. Or in the case of criminal action. This, in fact, is the one overwhelming reason anti-discrimination laws were created in the first place. Do homosexuals deserve the same level of special protection as black Americans? No.

A national homosexual organization called the Log Cabin Club agrees with this conclusion. They oppose gay rights laws as a solution to any homosexual problem. They actually say, "freedom of association take[s] precedence over gay rights."[18]

Or how about freedom of association based on family values? If a parent doesn't want their child exposed to homosexuality as a valid lifestyle in public school—they have no choice under gay rights ordinances. School boards rejecting the *Children of the Rainbow* curriculum, which normalizes *Heather's Two Mommies*, *Daddy's Roommate*, and *Gloria's trip to Gay Pride*, may face nasty anti-discrimination lawsuits.

Landlords and employers risk lawsuit for dismissing homosexuals. Or for failing to rent to or hire a homosexual. Quota hearings become a real threat. The burden of legal proof comes to rest in the wrong places: on businesses, religious organizations, authorities, and individuals who object to homosexuality.

Gay rights laws are opposed largely because they try to make the courts the public solution to private problems. Private sexual values—except those which are criminal or where public health issues are concerned—should be sorted out in the private sector. That's where they belong. Who wants lawyers in their bedrooms? Who wants more litigation? Who needs more manipulation of the courts? Who wants to give judges power over their private lives?

As seen here, there are many good reasons to oppose gay laws. But in recent years, those with moral objections to homosexuality have been first to see the danger. People like Barbara Sheldon and Pat Long have become "Paul Revere's" on the subject.

So it was in Denver, Barbara Sheldon and the others who opposed the city's gay rights law had principally moral reasons for doing so. They had every right to make their moral case. However, Denver didn't like it at the time. Their public testimony backfired before the television cameras and news writers. Separation of church and state has been pounded into the public consciousness. Most now accept this idea as part of the Constitution, though it is not. Coloradans, like most Americans, believe that religion and moral conviction are inappropriate in public life. The people of Denver did not vote to back up this repeal effort.

That, in all likelihood, is where the entire opposition to gay rights in Colorado would have ended—but for Colorado Springs.

In their historic telephone conversation on February 6, 1991, Barbara told Pat Long that good spokesmen were needed in Denver the following morning to testify against H.B. 1059, or the Ethnic Harassment Bill. She said that a Judicial Committee hearing at the capitol was in full swing. Buried in the law's legal jargon, Barbara explained, was the idea of giving homosexuality equal status to racial minorities statewide. Even worse, the harassment part of the bill would make verbal criticism against them a felony offense! She figured that under this law, Biblical and moral criticism (such as the moral objections Pat had voiced at Digital) could be construed as a form of harassment and criminally prosecuted. Valuing homosexual differences would become much more than "company policy"; it would become the law of the land.

(In this outrageous example it can be seen that most so-called gay rights laws are not about prohibiting violence against homosexuals, as they so sympathetically advertise. They are instead about prohibiting or limiting the freedoms of those who disagree with them. Not only would freedom of association have been infringed by H.B. 1059, but the fundamental freedom of speech as well.)

As Barbara explained it to Pat, the Ethnic Harassment Bill would go beyond tolerance, giving homosexuality the legal power to force the rest of the state to affirm their lifestyle. (Later, this strategy would be labeled by the Colorado Springs opponents as "forced affirmation" of the homosexual lifestyle.)

Her anxiety at this prospect was magnified by the fact that the bill had been quietly sponsored by members of Denver's cultural elite. The Mayor's wife, Wilma Webb, who was also a black state Representative, had become its champion. An esteemed Jewish Rabbi of the Reformed Tradition, Steven Foster also promoted it. Foster chaired both the state Civil Rights Commission and the state's leading gay rights advocacy group. What a power combination. Not only that, Jack Lang y Marquez, Director of the Colorado Civil Rights Division, had climbed on the band wagon. Very impressive.

Who could effectively stand up for family values against a black mayor's wife, a Jewish rabbi, and a civil rights authority with a Hispanic name? Between them they had every political base covered.

Pat still felt the nagging sense of that "unfinished business" at Digital. Regardless of the odds, she suggested to Barbara that she could pull together some people from Colorado Springs competent enough to testify at the hearing—herself among them. She then got on the phone and recruited a brave housewife named Linda Munson and a friend from her church named Tony Marco. Out of this group, Marco, a freelance writer and former Marxist-Leninist radical, emerged as a providential spokesman and the architect of Colorado's eventual winning approach to gay rights.

Pat called Tony explaining the Denver hearing as Barbara had explained it to her. Tony, with some pioneering civil rights experience under his belt, seemed to understand the implications of the law even more than Barbara and Pat did. The thing that rang his alarm was the fact that the Ethnic Harassment Bill was a statewide law. He knew that such a law could change the character of the entire State of Colorado. The values of Denver's cultural elite were about to be forced on all of Colorado without a proper debate. Once enacted, H.B. 1059 would prove exceedingly difficult to repeal, he predicted. Until Pat's call, he had no idea that the gay rights agenda was positioned for such a knockout blow. Pat Long's spark became a focused flame with Tony.

He thumbed through his Rolodex and called around town for help. Dr. David Noebel, a conservative author and educator, happened to have written a book about the aggression of homosexual rights laws. He had a personal library of other resources too, and readily made them available. This began an all-night cram course on gay rights for Tony. By morning he had pored through *The Homosexual Revolution* by Noebel, *Shadow in the Land* by Congressman William Dannemeyer, *Gays, AIDS and You* by Enrique Rueda and Michael Schwartz, and *Are Gay Rights Right?* by Roger Magnuson. When he left for the hearing, he had a 17-page position paper against the Ethnic Harassment Bill under his arm.

As Tony recalled it, one idea had leaped out of Magnuson's book that put all of the other arguments into perspective. It was the idea that homosexual behavior should not be considered equal to race or ethnicity. "I sensed instinctively that this was the basic weakness in all homosexual rights laws," he said, "and that it would provide the winning argument against them." He felt that too much time and energy had been wasted debating the morality of the issue in the public square. Those with moral convictions did not need to be addressed about it. Those without moral opposition to homosexuality would not have their minds changed by a political argument.

Still, Tony had no idea just how powerful this idea would prove to be. As he continued to read his resource books, he found himself sidetracked by the more bizarre behavioral aspects of homosexuality. Like most people who begin to study the issue, he suddenly became appalled to learn of the unhealthy and compulsive sexuality that much of the community seems addicted to. The sheer bulk of the medical and behavioral evidence began to overwhelm him. Call it the "bathhouse revelation," if you will. These shocking sexual statistics tend to turn normal citizens into raving opponents of the homosexual agenda—or, else, into ostriches that hide from reality. Tony found himself tilting toward attacking homosexual behavior. He had not learned enough yet about his basic civil rights arguments to rely on them alone.

This is a common tendency for those opposing gay politics. The homosexual lobby counts on it. They have learned to turn attacks on their behavior into charges of bigotry and homophobia. "God made us this way," they say. "How can you criticize behavior that we can't control?" Incredibly, many Americans are eager to sympathize with this reasoning—perhaps in order not to face up to it—even though it contains no more logic than the arguments of criminals who say they can't help themselves.

This naïve public sympathy has encouraged gay pride paraders to go to extremes in provocative behavior. Their outrageous public displays seem to say to those who are offended, "See? We have a license to offend you!" Furthermore, homosexual marchers often abuse patriotic and sacred symbols in sexually degrading ways in their parades and protest marches. A group of men called the Sisters of Perpetual Indulgence insists on dressing as nuns and publicly displaying artificial genitalia in blasphemous and lewd poses. Why? If they can make their opponents display the slightest anger—even when the anger is manifestly justified—in the current climate of political correctness they win the PR battle. This happens because many Americans no longer know the difference between anger and hatred, criticism and harassment, moral condemnation and gay bashing. They've become convinced that it's all intolerance. Consequently, bringing the facts of homosexual behavior into the gay rights debate runs a great risk of alienating the American public.

In the beginning, Tony succumbed to the behavior-argument temptation. He recalls, "I compiled all the statistics and facts about homosexual behavior I could find but I used them to pose rhetorical questions about sexual behavior and the Ethnic Harassment Bill. My purpose was to make the legislators think through the crazy possibilities this kind of bill would unleash on the population."

At the Denver hearing Tony and the Colorado Springs group met Denver area psychiatrist Richard Heckmann. This man had headed the Denver group's unsuccessful attempt to repeal the city's gay rights ordinance. Taking charge, Heckmann announced that he would pick those from the group who would testify. Without hesitation, Marco informed him that he had not crammed all night and driven to Denver to be told he would not testify. Heckmann backed off, deciding, perhaps wisely, not to disagree with Marco.

At Tony's turn he walked quietly to the podium in coat and tie. As he began to read his statement, it became immediately obvious that he had taken off his politically correct gloves. At his sharply chosen words the room filled with palpable tension. This dark haired intellectual refused to soft soap the delicate issue of homosexuality. Furthermore, he dared to use behavioral statistics in his arguments.

A committee Democrat interrupted, demanding that he stop reading and speak spontaneously (perhaps hoping to dilute the power of the testimony). Tony didn't wilt. Instead he demanded, in the name of fairness, to be granted the same courtesy as those who had read their statements for the other side. Permission reluctantly granted, he went on. This exchange unmasked the irrationality accompanying this debate. Especially among cultural leaders charged with handling the threats of the homosexual lobby. An assertive mind like Tony's seemed essential under the circumstances.

Perhaps the February 8, 1991 edition of *The Rocky Mountain News* best signaled the change in momentum for gay rights in Colorado: "'VERBAL FIST' KILLS GAY RIGHTS BILL," it announced.[19] The image of gay bashing had been launched by the press in this headline. Beyond the deliberately violent portrayal of the pro-family testimony, the article went on to say:

> Opponents of a state gay-rights bill unleashed a firestorm of verbal abuse against homosexuals yesterday, charging that they are a danger to children and transmit disease. Tony Marco, of Colorado Springs asked the House Judiciary Committee whether a proposed law barring violence against people because of their sexual orientation would mean that child molesters would be allowed into day care centers and farmers would be required to give people who practice bestiality access to animals? Should we let the necrophiliacs also demand open admission to our funeral parlors to exercise their sexual preference?

Tony admits that these were, in fact, the ridiculous behavioral questions he had posed to the committee. "The questions illustrate that racial laws applied to sexual orientations become ridiculous," he said.

It is important to point out that the *Rocky Mountain News*' description of the Ethnic Harassment Bill as a law "barring violence" against homosexuality was a typical media misrepresentation. Laws barring violence are standard fare across the civilized world—assault, battery, murder, rape. A crime of violence is a crime of violence whether the victim is sexually straight or not. The news reporter apparently chose this description to create the impression that Tony's remarks were designed to unleash violence against homosexuals. (Media imbalance raised its ugly head in this very first go-round.) The thinking of the news writer might well have been framed by the homosexual lobbyists themselves: Anyone who opposes the homosexual agenda is automatically a gay-basher, advocating violence against them.

Tony's so-called raw remarks made enough good sense, however, to split the vote along party lines. The seven Republicans on the committee voted against the bill. Five Democrats voted for it. His so-called verbal fist had indeed killed the Ethnic Harassment Bill.

TONY MARCO, architect of the winning civil rights arguments, and the "verbal fist" who killed H.B. 1059.

Following the hearing, Denver Mayor's wife, Wilma Webb, said that her "opponent's comments were an example of the bigotry she opposes."

"That's chilling," Tony observed, "because what she was saying is that, if H.B. 1059 had passed, she could have sent me to jail for saying these things. That's what the harassment bill was all about . . . to send you to jail for saying what you believe is wrong with homosexuality. I would have been charged with a *felony*. I'm telling you, gay rights laws are dangerous to freedom."

Asked if the rhetorical questions he chose deliberately demeaned homosexuality, Tony replied: "I cited a ton of researched facts and statistics about homosexual behavior they didn't quote. Facts don't lie; statistics don't hate; they just are. And from those medical and behavioral facts I posed the ridiculous questions that they raised with the harassment law. This is an aggressive tactic but I went in there to win. Hey, don't forget we were up against some very big guns."

Marco now claims that he has enough confidence in the basic argument that he would not raise the behavioral questions in public debate if he had it to do over again. He would rely on the basic civil rights argument, namely, "homosexuality does not equal ethnic status under the law."

Other leaders opposing the homosexual agenda disagree with Tony. They believe the behavioral questions cannot be divorced from the public legal arguments. "Homosexuality *is* behavior," they say, "it is not personhood. The idea of orientation is meaningless before the law. It can only be proven by behavior, therefore behavior is totally relevant to the debate. Without it, anyone can claim to have a homosexual orientation."

It remains a matter of disagreement, then, among gay rights opponents as to when and where the behavioral arguments are best suited. Marco favors confining them to leadership discussions. Others favor careful public and private presentations of these matters.

One other important trend seen in the extended version of the *Rocky Mountain News* report was the identification of those opposed to H.B. 1059 as religiously oriented. This had always worked for gay rights issues before: identifying the opposition as the religious right. Beginning with Tony's testimony, the news media and the homosexual lobby began to completely underestimate the depth of their opposition in this regard. In fact, civil rights arguments went far beyond the objections of the religious right.

Following the defeat of the statewide gay harassment law, a media feeding frenzy resulted. Tony became the lightning rod for the controversy. He made several public appearances to explain his position.

In the days and weeks to come he and his wife, Joyce, attended open forums. In one instance they chose to reveal that one of their adult children lived in a homosexual partnership involving a child conceived through artificial insemination. They did this to assure people that telling the truth about the unhealthy consequences of homosexuality did not imply hatred toward homosexuality. It implied the opposite—real concern. He explained that opposing gay rights did not eliminate normal parental love. In fact, an expression of real love required warnings about the consequences of destructive behavior, homosexual or otherwise. Their family example pointed out that having a homosexual loved one did not make support of the homosexual agenda reasonable nor automatic.

This received scant mention in the press. The opposition and the news media simply would not depict a sensible adversary to gay rights. Their stereotype was the raving homophobe, the religious gay basher—period.

Other Colorado people who had rallied around the issue began to perceive the unfair, inconsistent rules of media engagement. While anyone on the homosexual side of the argument could do no wrong as far as the news media were concerned, spokesmen against gay rights would have to carefully guard each word, each phrase. Even then, they could count on their words being deliberately twisted by news writers and editors.

The media intimidated. People of good reputation felt that they would be publicly dirtied if they dared oppose the homosexual agenda. Yet, for some reason the debate produced several leaders willing to put their reputations on the line in Colorado.

In Colorado Springs an astute businessman, Chuck Chaney, stepped forward as an early supporter. A man named Chuck Gosnell proved to be an energetic grassroots organizer. Volunteer Cliff Shakelton became an all around helping hand. Dr. David Noebel, author of *The Homosexual Revolution* and the huge volume, *Understanding the Times*, lent his considerable presence to early deliberations. These men were often joined in their activities by a young Noebel associate named Kevin Tebedo. He later became prominent in the Colorado issue.

These Colorado Springs citizens began to meet with concerned people from Denver. They shared information and learned just how far the homosexual agenda had advanced through the efforts of Colorado's sympathetic leaders. Many learned for the first time that:

1. Denver had already passed a gay rights bill, as had the cities of Aspen and Boulder;
2. Governor Roy Romer had issued an executive order protecting homosexual orientation in state hiring and employment;
3. In their own back yard the Colorado Springs Human Relations Commission was currently poised to propose a gay rights bill for the city called the Human Rights Ordinance;
4. Rabbi Foster's state Civil Rights Commission was holding hearings in Denver and Colorado Springs about creating statewide gay rights legislation;
5. State colleges and universities were under pressure to accept homosexual activists into all campus clubs . . . no exceptions;
6. Many other homosexual rights laws and resolutions had been planned and were waiting in the wings at chambers of commerce, big businesses like Digital, colleges, universities, and governmental bodies.

At this juncture, the Colorado Springs citizens group realized that their own city had been targeted for a gay rights ordinance without their knowledge. Unless someone stopped it, their city would join Denver, Boulder, and Aspen on the list of cities granting special protection to anyone claiming homosexuality. The group sharpened its arguments and decided to target the so-called Human Rights Ordinance. Dr. Noebel prepared a well-documented 15-page summary of background materials and facts. Tony organized the people who had already stepped forward. He began to educate them about how to testify effectively from various angles against the proposed law. The mistakes of making loud moral arguments in public were thus minimized.

As the city hearings neared, the Colorado Springs *Gazette Telegraph* described Tony as spokesman for this "ad hoc committee of church members and business leaders." They quoted a repeat of his illustration from the Denver hearings: ". . . what reason do we have to deny the same status to pedophiles, bestialists, necrophiliacs?"[20] Not the most flattering presentation of the argument, nevertheless it awakened a significant outcry from the local community. People began to sense the legal dangers lurking behind innocent-sounding gay rights legislation.

The same news story favorably introduced a coauthor of the Colorado Springs Human Rights Ordinance, Robin Miller, a homosexual lawyer with Shepard's/McGraw-Hill, a legal publishing firm located in Colorado Springs. She replied to Tony, "A person's adult sexuality has nothing to do with criminal sexual behavior."[21] (But adult sexuality *does* have something to do with criminal behavior. A sexual attraction to children predisposes one to criminal pedophilia. Still, Miller's statement was printed without challenge.) Miller further asserted that the city's top 16 private employers had anti-discrimination policies that included protections for homosexual employees. Among these were Digital Equipment, Schlage Lock Company, U.S. West, Safeway, and Shepard's/McGraw-Hill.

In spite of this intimidating pro-gay list, Dr. Noebel, Chuck Gosnell, Kevin Tebedo, and other members of the ad hoc committee asked for the backing of city residents. They had no idea if enough men and women would step forward to oppose the high powered homosexual agenda. But, surprisingly, over a thousand supporters showed up at the first City Council hearing. The meeting was forced out of council chambers to an auditorium to accommodate the interested crowd.

As the series of hearings went on through the spring of '91, Tony suggested that their arguments against the proposed Human Rights Ordinance needed a boost from national constitutional attorneys. A copy of the ordinance was sent to the National Legal Foundation in Virginia Beach, a conservative think tank. Within a month the committee received an analysis back.

Meanwhile, the Human Rights Commission (HRC) and gay lobby began urging the Colorado Springs Chamber of Commerce to endorse the ordinance. The HRC knew that City Council would not pass a law opposed by local small businesses—the heart and soul of the economy. The results could be disastrous come election day.

So the Chamber's support became a strategic goal for the gay rights lobby.

The ad hoc committee decided to present the National Legal Foundation's document to the Chamber, which seemed poised on the brink of endorsing the homosexual law. With the analysis in hand, Chamber members received their first well-reasoned argument against the Human Rights Ordinance. The analysis included the following conclusion:

> The sweeping powers given to the [Human Relations Commission] by the ordinance would create a body of officials with an ever-expanding ability to tread upon the fundamental constitutional rights of the majority in the name of equality. There is no need for such a body, not in Colorado Springs and not in this nation.[22]

The Chamber committee apparently agreed with the findings of the National Legal Foundation. They voted unanimously to reject the ordinance in spite of the positions of local giants like Schlage, Digital, US West, Safeway, Shepard's/McGraw-Hill, and the rest of the "big 16". The little ad hoc committee was off to a good start.

Next, volunteer Chuck Gosnell turned up the heat with more than 3,500 letters and postcards from citizens sent to City Council against the ordinance. (In an area of a quarter million residents, this kind of public interest makes local politicians salute.) The committee members also organized a stay-home boycott of a locally advertised Gay Pride Parade, so that the homosexual activists marched to empty streets. All of which contributed to the 8-to-1 defeat of the so-called Human Rights Ordinance in Colorado Springs' city council. Victory number two.

Next, the committee members looked over the list of remaining gay rights brush fires around the state. They soon realized they would be worn out fighting each and every battle one by one. The collected minds of those opposing gay rights laws began to look for a statewide solution. Dr. David Noebel called on his friend, Kevin Tebedo, the son of state Senator Maryanne Tebedo, to inquire concerning the process of a statewide initiative that might stop the homosexual agenda with one action. This would be a grassroots answer to the elite legislation the homosexuals were pushing in high places.

KEVIN TEBEDO, left, confers with DR. DAVID NOEBEL concerning a statewide "high frontier" defense against gay politics.

Unaware of Noebel's action, Tony posed to Chuck Chaney a statewide petition process at the same time. Chaney liked the idea. Being a well-organized businessman he told Tony to put his idea into an executive proposal which he could use to begin raising a war chest. Tony drafted a document and faxed it to Chuck the next day. Among three pages of outline the statement set forth his rationale as follows:

> Homosexual/lesbian/bisexual activists and liberal supporters have recently launched a human rights assault on the State of Colorado. Their goal? *To secure for their sexual orientations the same (plus additional) rights, protections, and privileges under law* as those now enjoyed by racial, ethnic, and religious groups . . . '

> . . . Two of these initiatives, one at the state level, the other directed at the city of Colorado Springs, have recently been defeated . . .
> . . . we can *take the offensive by mounting a statewide referendum drive to let the people decide the issue . . .*[23]

Looking back with humor, Tony confesses that he didn't even know the difference between an initiative and a referendum at this time. As he later learned, a referendum is an action to remove something from the constitution, an initiative is an action to add something to it. What he really meant was an initiative. Nevertheless, Chuck Chaney was simply glad that Tony had targeted victory: ". . . A referendum on this issue can win here," Tony wrote, "because homosexual behavior does not enjoy public support across Colorado."

A winning prediction was necessary to a businessman like Chuck. He didn't want his resources wasted in a futile struggle. But Tony admits that the prediction was merely a gut feeling at the time, not arising from any scientific numbers on the subject. The winning prediction had grown from his feel for the heart of the argument, "sexual behavior does not equal race or ethnicity." This argument made so much sense that it just seemed winnable in the public square. The feeling had been further reinforced by the number of local people who had turned out to support them at the recent hearings.

Based on this small beginning, the members of the loosely organized committee began to talk up the statewide approach in earnest. Such an approach would take away the forced affirmation the homosexual lobbyists were slipping into the system everywhere, they said. It would be a high-frontier defense. It would cover the entire state with a legal umbrella the way the homosexual lobby's own Ethnic Harassment Bill had meant to do. An important difference, in this case, would be that the new law would not go through the legislature but directly to the people. And it would not be a law to restrict freedoms, as the Ethnic Harassment Bill would have been. Rather, it would restore freedoms of association and speech to the citizens of Denver, Boulder, and Aspen where gay rights laws had removed them . . . in the name of equality.

By July 31, 1991 when this "referendum" had become a legal "initiative" carried by a volunteer army of petition signers all around the state, three key people necessary to its success had stepped forward. These three were not opinion leaders nor political experts, but a remarkable combination of talents all the same. Each made essential contributions to winning the fight.

First, Kevin Tebedo, a thirtysomething husband and father, handsome hometown boy. He had earned a degree in Human Resource Management from Colorado Christian University. With minimal political experience—nothing of the magnitude of a constitutional amendment—he nevertheless gained his place of prominence doing much of the legal spade work for the formation of the 501(c)(4) organization. He started the initiative language process—with an expert Denver lawyer—and developed a business plan and budget. Most of all, Kevin went on to organize an army of petition carriers to obtain the 49,000 plus signatures the law required for gaining the November '92 ballot. He also spearheaded unsuccessful attempts to win the allegiance of churches (read RELIGIOUS RIGHT, RELIGIOUS LEFT p. 129). Shortly after meeting Tony Marco, Kevin agreed to share the title of co-chairmen of the organization.

The second key person was Mark Olsen, an advertising copywriter with Shepard's/McGraw-Hill. (This was the same legal publishing firm employing the homosexual lawyer, Robin Miller.) Mark volunteered his after hours services in the area of written communications. He appeared an unlikely cohort to Tony and Kevin's straight-laced demeanor. Long brown hair pulled into a pony tail, wearing denim shirts, unstructured jackets, and loafers. He fulfilled the visual stereotype of the campus radical.

In the beginning, Mark worked closely with Tony to polish public statements and sound bites. He matched words that would satisfy CFV's philosophy, strategy, constituency, and goals at the same time. But Mark was much more than a good PR person. He read widely and came to understand the core issues deeply. These insights were reflected in his written communications. For the gay rights opponent who needed more than a sound bite to know how to vote on the issue, Mark Olsen came through.

MARK OLSEN, author of the "No Room For Hatred" campaign.

Last, but most essential to Amendment 2's success—Will Perkins. This respected Colorado Springs Chrysler dealer and lifelong Presbyterian was recruited into the amendment's ranks by fellow businessman Chuck Chaney after the initial ethnic harassment skirmish had super-heated the issue in the public mind. A mature man in his 60s, with some media savvy, Will stood five foot ten, trim, and healthy. He projected calm and sincere confidence beneath his full head of well-groomed, steel-grey hair. He didn't command respect so much as he earned it, and he had earned it the old-fashioned way: by personal integrity. After the election, *Conservative Review* hailed him as "a modern day Paul Revere"[24] on the dangers of so-called gay rights laws. Perpetually wearing a modest suit, or sport coat and tie, the amiable car dealer remained slow to speak, slow to anger, easy to approach, and always self-deprecating: "What can the opposition possibly say to tarnish the image of a used car salesman?" was his standard reply when asked why he had emerged as the leading spokesman for the amendment fight.

He became famous for his witty parables and easy sense of

humor under fire. "I got a letter from a Mrs. Rizzo in New Jersey," he said during the heat of the Colorado boycott. "She wrote: 'Mr. Perkins, you've ruined our vacation. We've been planning to come to Colorado for four years but now that you've passed Amendment 2, I'll probably never see the Grand Canyon.' I wrote her back: 'Dear Mrs. Rizzo, I've got good news. Your vacation plans are safe. We've made arrangements to move the Grand Canyon to Arizona.'"

Financially secure, with no political ambitions, Will stepped quietly forward to offer his services to the amendment on principle. "I'm doing this for my grandkids," he was often heard to say. "I don't want them to grow up in a world worse off than it is now." His clearly expressed motives captured the best of CFV's intentions and made them somehow understandable to the public, even with the malicious opposition of the press.

In the early weeks of the start-up, his personal donations kept the fledgling political effort alive as it struggled under Tony and Kevin's leadership to find its first viable donor base. Through crisis after crisis thereafter, Will's quiet confidence and wisdom placed him more and more in the eye of the Amendment 2 storm. His personal reputation attracted key help from former Senator Bill Armstrong and Colorado University's '90-91 national championship football coach, Bill McCartney, not to mention a host of other influential helpers behind the scenes. Under the constant strain of defending against media attacks, there could be no mistaking Will's voice—calm, firm, and ever reasonable.

In the final days before the election all the polls ran against the amendment. Political experts expected its doom. Even the original fire plug, Tony Marco, said, "Frankly, it will take a major miracle for Amendment 2 to be voted a part of Colorado's Constitution."[25] Still, Will Perkins kept on. "I'm doing this for my grandkids," he repeated doggedly. In so doing, he pulled off the kind of brinkmanship of which political legends are made. Following the election Will addressed the American Cause conference in Washington, D.C., where he was introduced as an esteemed "grassroots leader who fought and won."[26]

Among the many who were instrumental to the hard-fought

election victory, Colorado Springs residents Will Perkins, Kevin Tebedo, Tony Marco, and Mark Olsen remain standout performers. This unlikely group followed their instincts and convictions—battled their opposition and occasionally each other—until they had created and sold an amendment that benefited the whole State of Colorado. Out-funded and out spent 2-to-1 by the homosexual lobby, they toiled blindly at times, unable to pay for the sophisticated polling on

"I'm doing this for my grandkids," said WILL PERKINS, the man who sold Amendment 2 to Colorado.

which campaigns rely these days. New kids on the political block, they learned as they went, defied pundits, stumbled, flip-flopped, and made mistakes. They were occasionally brilliant beyond their abilities, shot themselves repeatedly in the foot, were blessed beyond their means, and, in the words of *The Washington Times*, accidentally emerged "as perhaps the brightest light in an otherwise disastrous election year for conservatives."[27]

So stunning was the upset victory, Colorado's political left has attempted to create a "CFV mythology" to explain its own ineptitude. The '93 summer issue of *Aspen Magazine* featured a cover story claiming "Amendment 2 was a brilliant piece of political work by the religious right and, in particular, by the umbrella organization Colorado for Family Values, the Colorado Springs-based group that sold it to voters."[28] (Reading this, CFV insiders blushed. "We were brilliant? Oh yeah! We *were* brilliant . . . weren't we?")

The *Aspen* article further quoted Denver pollster Floyd Ciruli, famous for wrongly projecting the amendment's defeat, lauding CFV as highly secretive, subtle, and sophisticated. To explain how his expensive political service could fail to read the true opinions of Colorado voters ahead of time, he said, "[CFV] supporters and campaign workers were advised . . . to lie to pollsters regarding their position on the measure to avoid alerting the opposition to their strength."[29]

Such shameless invention. Who could believe that a CFV directive would be so pervasive as to effect Ciruli's random sample? Besides, the thing he accused CFV of doing simply could not be done in America. (Perhaps in the old Soviet Union? Maybe not even there.)

According to CFV's political minds, the explanation for the false pre-election polls (offered here for free) is not that the state lied in obedience to secret orders from Colorado Springs, but that social pressure skewed the polling results. People were—and are—so intimidated by political correctness that they were afraid to speak their true opinions before the election. But they felt free to vote their conscience in the secrecy of a voting booth on November 3rd.

The real story of Amendment 2's success is more simple than *Aspen Magazine* conceived. And more profound. It is about people like Patricia Long, Barbara Sheldon, Linda Munson, and a long list of supporters, volunteers, and area leaders around the state who rallied to a good cause. It is the story (as we shall learn in the next chapter) of a well-worded amendment so profound in its meaning and implications that it overwhelmed an entire state in spite of the leading powers that opposed it. It is the story of family people who wanted to protect their values against the tyranny of gay rights laws.

Above all, the democratic process proved worthy in the Amendment 2 success story. CFV managed to build a list of only 7,000 core supporters during the campaign, but won 813,966 votes on the November ballot. Each supporter yielded 116 votes for the amendment. One-hundred-sixteen-to-one—what an incredible return on investment! These contrasting numbers are testimony to the wisdom of our founding fathers to make government ultimately subject to the will of the people. One-hundred-sixteen-to-one is also testimony to the strength of the truth about Amendment 2 . . . a truth that literally cleared a path through a jungle of media and militant homosexual lies.

Before plunging into the details of how it was done, it seems good to pause and pay homage to grassroots America. All of CFV's unlikely heros should encourage any concerned citizen to go ahead and try to change this country for the better. Vote, object, speak up, demonstrate, write letters, send faxes, circulate petitions, volunteer, call friends, work, pray. Regardless of which side of the issue one holds to, our constitutional republic is the best of all possible worlds in which to advance a good cause.

Of course, brave leaders must step forward. No matter the threats, a right cause is worth risking a reputation to win. But the Amendment 2 story shows that it can be done with everyday people working together. Imperfect people. No superstars. No political geniuses. No expensive pollsters. The process begins with the concern of one citizen, one housewife, one father, one teacher, one businessman.

It is still true in America that no one can predict, prevent, or completely control the fire that grows from the spark of an individual's concern.

3

The amendment

On March 7, 1991 Tony Marco convened a preliminary organizational meeting of the ad hoc committee in Colorado Springs. The meeting was not held in a civic hall, nor in a hotel facility, but in a church. (Religiously moral people seemed to be the only ones who cared enough to organize opposition at this early stage.) The heart of the meeting concerned what Tony had labeled a "Statewide Referendum Initiative" against gay rights laws. Thus began the process of finding the language of an initiative that would eventually become Amendment 2.

The attendance sheet listed Dr. David Noebel and Charles (Chuck) Chaney as co-chairs of the "Colorado Coalition for Family Values." This was the working title given to the group by Marco at this time. First to sign his name on the attendance sheet was Kevin Tebedo, followed by Linda Munson, Chuck Chaney, Jay Butler, Sharon Bath, Bob Linden, Rob Hughes, Dave Noebel, Ken Gray, David Yocum, Barbara Sheldon, Ruth Tuttle, Ron May, and Bill Perrett.

One local politician charged later that Amendment 2 had been hatched "by a small cabal of zealots" in Colorado Springs,[30] implying that the law was tainted by their religious motivation. This accusation backfired because the language these citizens created contained not one trace of the much ballyhooed religious bias.

Dr. David Noebel opened this meeting with prayer. The invocation became a CFV tradition in every meeting thereafter. As chairman Will Perkins later reflected, "If it was good enough for Ben Franklin, we didn't want to proceed without it." (He was speaking of Franklin's celebrated call to prayer of the Continental Congress, an action that would now be considered politically incorrect.)

Following the invocation, Tony gave an opening statement. Then Noebel briefed the group on the current homosexual rights laws across the state. A discussion of the petition drive and initiative process followed. Tony urged the group, "Do it right, according to the law so it won't be thrown out by some judge." On this occasion attorney Ken Gray set Tony straight about the difference between a referendum and an initiative. Then the discussion turned to insuring that all petitions were properly signed, in anticipation of the legal challenges that would surely come from the opposition. Sharon Bath, an active Republican, warned the group not to count on party support. Many Republicans favored homosexual rights laws. "Even George Bush has known homosexuals working in the White House," she said. "You are going to have to run this petition drive on your own." This sobered several members of the group who had naïvely assumed Republican support.

A fund raising discussion followed. Since the ad hoc committee consisted of mostly unknowns, the group realized that its greatest need was to find an established spokesperson to write a letter soliciting donations. Recently retired Colorado Senator Bill Armstrong's name was mentioned as a prime candidate in this regard.

As the initial meeting adjourned, Tony suggested follow-up assignments for those in attendance. Barbara Sheldon had submitted the name of a prominent Denver attorney with experience to research the initiative language. He had requested anonymity to protect his business and family. Kevin independently confirmed the attorney's reputation through consultations with his mother, Senator Maryanne Tebedo. He volunteered to contact the lawyer on behalf of the coalition and to pay a fee to begin the process. Tony assigned himself to contact Bill Armstrong regarding the fund raising letter.

Over the next two months, the Colorado Coalition for Family Values continued to meet regularly. In every subsequent meeting, initiative supporters fell into two camps:

1. those who wanted to write moral laws condemning homosexuality as sin, waging what amounted to a Biblical *jihad*, and,

2. those who believed the election could be won on civil rights grounds.

Tony became the primary champion of this second approach. In the beginning Kevin Tebedo tended the other way. This split in philosophy escalated into a personal tension between the two men.

When Will Perkins came aboard in April, he lent his wise counsel to the civil rights approach. "Politics," he repeated often, "is not about what you *should* do. It's about what you *can* do." Religion and morality, he said (for better or worse), were a "no-can-do" approach in current American politics.

Perkins had the personal stature to attract Bill Armstrong to some of these early meetings. The *New York Times* described Armstrong as "a man whose restless intellect is admired by his foes as well as his friends." The *Pueblo Chieftain* said he was a ". . . rare breed . . . a statesman . . . always attempting to shape and guide policies he believes best for the nation." After much soul searching, the retired senator put his sterling reputation on the line for the Colorado Springs citizens group.

Armstrong had learned of the volatility of the homosexual issue during his final years in Washington, D.C.. While serving in the Senate, he had led a controversial fight to stop the nation's Capitol from using its Human Rights Ordinance (essentially a gay rights law) to curb religious freedom. The city had forced Catholic run Georgetown University to admit a homosexual social club—against the school's strict religious code. Armstrong could not believe that America would stand by and let such a freedom be damaged for the sake of a gay social agenda. He then drafted and passed an amendment that exempted religious organizations from the gay rights law.

The homosexual lobby immediately challenged the exemption in court. The court, predictably, reversed Armstrong's amendment based on an obscure technicality. "The court changed the rules," he reflected. "If they had applied the same logic to the rest of the bill, all of it would have been overturned." Only Armstrong's religious exemption had been challenged in court, therefore only his exemption received the court's extreme scrutiny. (This is a reality the ACLU uses to advance a courtroom agenda, sometimes against the will of the people. They and other activists are involved in evolving laws away from their original meanings. It is a legal reality, however, which can work both ways. More conservatives should challenge such bad laws in court to counteract this militancy.) So Armstrong drafted a new exemption to work around the new rules and passed it. "That's the same pattern I believe you will find with the issue in Colorado," he predicted. "Whatever you do, be prepared for a court fight."

Based on those lessons, he stressed the need to draft a *narrow* Colorado amendment rather than a sweeping law. He instructed the ad hoc group to address the dangers of homosexual rights in Denver, Boulder, and Aspen—not to invent some speculative language that addressed fears for the future. This approach, he said, would cool the inflamed passions that were bound to attend the debate. He also thought it would give the amendment the best chance of surviving the inevitable court challenge from the ACLU and the gay lobby.

Kevin Tebedo, who greatly admired Senator Armstrong, now became convinced that the civil rights approach was indeed the only approach. He abandoned his personal antagonism with Tony and supported the civil rights approach thereafter.

In a May 3, '91 meeting at the Denver Marriott, attended by Bill Armstrong, Dr. Noebel briefed the group about a related election issue shaping up in the State of Oregon. Something known there as Measure 9. It called for government to label homosexuality "abnormal, wrong, unnatural, and perverse." This meant that, if Colorado stayed the course with a solid attack on the civil rights front, November would provide the nation two distinct models for opposing special homosexual laws: Measure 9 and Amendment 2. The vote would test the morality approach side-by-side with the civil rights approach. This possibility further convinced the Colorado group to stick with a civil rights approach in order to provide this alternative.

Tony seemed to find new evidence to support the civil rights arguments every day. His discoveries grew around the shared conviction that giving the wealthy homosexual lobby the benefit of racial and minority civil rights status would be a gross injustice. It would amount to granting special rights for all those who claimed same-gender attractions—an idea he believed America would reject as unfair. As his position paper grew, the confidence of the Colorado group grew proportionately. No one else had ever attacked the homosexual agenda solely on this ground.

In light of this, the Colorado Coalition decided to appeal to principled liberals and conservative Coloradans. Their unifying argument would be to protect freedoms of speech and association against the tyranny of political correctness now enforcing special homosexual laws over the land. The initiative language would be neither Republican, Democrat, Libertarian, nor Independent. The issue would be framed as inclusive, pluralistic—appealing to fairness in the law, crossing all political and religious lines.

Beneath this principled legal umbrella, these early thinkers saw that they could also protect the integrity of their own religious faith. Among the protected freedoms under Amendment 2, traditional, Judeo-Christian, and other natural and traditional objections to homosexuality would remain safe and unregulated by the government. A public debate on this basis, rather than strictly on a moral or religious basis, seemed winnable. The amendment itself would render no moral judgements. This fresh political direction now further distinguished Colorado from Oregon. (Though, before, during, and after the election, the news media refused to publicly appreciate the difference between the two.)

But good ideas must go on to survive many tests. Between May and June of '91 the (anonymous) Denver attorney prepared five drafts of the initiative language and presented them to eight nationally-recognized Constitutional lawyers for legal review. He took every precaution to insure that the wording would stand the scrutiny of the highest courts.

A June 13, 1991 letter from counsel Brian M. McCormick of The National Legal Foundation complimented the work as follows: "Let me begin by extending my congratulations to you and the Coalition for a job well done." McCormick went on to explain his admiration for the proposed language: "the initiative is not seeking to criminalize homosexual acts, merely to prevent them from becoming the basis for civil rights."[31]

Later that month, Colorado Springs talk-radio host Chuck Baker commented that the name Colorado Coalition for Family Values sounded as if Marco had married his old Marxist thinking to hometown America—a bad mix. To fix the problem he suggested dropping the word coalition. The idea took hold with the rest of the group.

On July 31, 1991, Colorado for Family Values (minus the "coalition") selected a final version of the proposed amendment. They called a press conference and filed the legal language at the state capitol in Denver. At this time Tony, Kevin, and Will announced the initiative's purpose:

> It is our conviction that our civil rights laws were not intended to give protected status to sexual orientation, including homosexuality, bisexuality, and lesbianism. It is the goal of Colorado for Family Values to gather the necessary 49,279 signatures to put the initiative on the November 1992 General Election Ballot as a proposed constitutional amendment, specifically as Article 2, Section 30.

No doubt the savvy political operatives behind the homosexual agenda knew immediately that they were in deep trouble. The axe had found the root of their surreptitious plans to hijack minority protection through civil rights laws. Now the battle would grow serious.

First to engage, of course, was the news media. They refused to present the issue in terms of protected class status and what it meant to the citizens of Colorado and the nation if homosexuals were given this advantage. Rather, they began to build a case against the motives of Colorado for Family Values. They quoted unofficial statements from CFV supporters, labeling them the religious right. They slanted descriptions of Colorado Springs to make it appear as an intellectual backwater full of Victorian moralists. The effect of their coverage was to suggest that anyone supporting such a measure intended to discriminate unfairly against innocent gays.

In August, CFV set about the business of building its 501(c)(4) organization for the difficult road ahead. The momentum of events had already escalated beyond the founders' predictions. Tony, Kevin, and Will, named in CFV's Articles of Incorporation, began to feel an increasingly uncomfortable level of pressure. A well qualified board seemed the next paramount need.

On August 10, 1991 the election of a Board of Directors included the following: Will Perkins, Sharon Bath, Barbara Sheldon, Nazarene Pastor Woodie Stevens, and businessman Chuck Chaney (who later found it impossible to attend meetings and was replaced by local lawyer Marty Kuhn). The board ruled at this time that Tony and Kevin would not be board members. The two of them agreed to serve as co-chairmen of the organization in *ex-officio* capacity until the legal ramifications of their dual roles became clear.

Will explained the small size of the board this way: "The traditional concept of a Board of Directors is to have 15-20 members, with committees and a wide range of influences represented. At the outset, that was our plan, but when we got down to it, we were so busy, and many of the people we would like to have had serve with us were already up to their ears in other activities. So we ended up seeking their counsel at an advisory level rather than asking them to serve formally on the Board."

This was precisely the case with Bill Armstrong. He had grown impressed with Tony's growing body of civil rights research and with Will's mature and steady leadership. The language of the proposed amendment had satisfied his concerns for a narrowly drafted law. He subsequently wanted to serve on the CFV board but couldn't find the time to do the assignment justice, so he agreed to accept the advisory position. He also agreed in principle to research and write the initial CFV fund raising letter. This gave a critical boost to the freshman group. Bill Armstrong was a favorite son of Colorado whose name would give the fund raising efforts a real chance of success.

Colorado University's prominent football coach, Bill McCartney, heavily involved in a pre-season schedule, similarly agreed to serve the advisory board at Will's request. Dr. David Noebel continued in the capacity of Educational Advisor. The other board members present nominated a long list of notables to fill out the rest of the advisory board.

By September the amendment's language had gone on to survive several more reviews and challenges by the state Legislative Council, the Secretary of State, and by Robin Miller, the busy homosexual lawyer from Shepard's/McGraw-Hill. These challenges did not succeed in changing one word of the following proposed constitutional amendment:

> NO PROTECTED STATUS BASED ON HOMOSEXUAL, LESBIAN OR BISEXUAL ORIENTATION. Neither the State of Colorado through any of its branches or departments, nor any of its agencies, political subdivisions, municipalities or school districts, shall enact, adopt or enforce any statute, regulation, ordinance or policy whereby homosexual, lesbian, or bisexual orientation, conduct, practices or relationships shall constitute or otherwise be the basis of, or entitle any person or class of persons to have or claim any minority status, quota preferences, protected status, or claim of discrimination. This section of the constitution shall be in all respects self-executing.

The proposal contained not one religious word. It expressed everything in precise legal language, prohibiting homosexuals, lesbians, and bisexuals from claiming "minority or protected status, quota preferences, or discrimination." These words would be fully understood by the court, by the homosexual lobby, and by the press. They would provide a legal umbrella beneath which freedoms would be preserved from the tyranny of politically correct thought police. Judgements about whether homosexuality was acceptable or not would be left to the individual. Freedom of choice, preserved.

However, as a public document, the amendment read like legal gobbledegook. The election campaign would offer time to explain all of that . . . or so CFV hoped. They counted on the public being able to comprehend the true meaning of the law, though the language might seem difficult at first.

Not waiting for the campaign, however, the opposition began its war of perception immediately. Those who wanted special gay laws enforced grabbed one word from the initiative language and screamed it over and over, as loudly, and in as many ways as possible: "*Discrimination!* Discrimination! DISCRIMINATION! This law discriminates against homosexuals!" (For a full discussion of these issues read, PROTECTED CLASS STATUS p. 101, and DISCRIMINATION p. 108.)

Looking back, it seems as if the homosexual lobby and its elite sponsors counted heavily on the voters' ignorance in this area of law. It is as if they assumed that the citizenry could not grasp the difference between racial discrimination against blacks, and the whining complaints of a rich, politically powerful, special interest group.

This superior attitude permeated the language of a letter to the Secretary of State written by gay lawyer Robin Miller. In it, she revealed perhaps a politically fatal arrogance: ". . . there is a strong likelihood that a voter of average intelligence will misinterpret . . ." she said, then a few lines later wrote, "It is impossible for a voter of average intelligence to know, upon reading this expression, what it means. The question 'protected from what?' will naturally arise in the mind of the voter of average intelligence. . . ."[32]

Perhaps Robin's repeated concern for the "voter of average intelligence" should have also included a *respect* for the voter of average intelligence? But then, this is often an elitist's mistake, considering anyone who disagrees with them to be of lesser intelligence.

The Colorado voters turned out to understand the issue far better than she could imagine. So did the Secretary of State, who flatly rejected Robin's attempt to demean the amendment's language.

The petition race was on.

4

The petition drive

A full public debate seemed premature following the filing of CFV's petition language. The election campaign had not begun. The challenge of finding at least 49,279 people in the state willing to sign the petition lay directly ahead. Getting so many signatures can be exhausting under ordinary circumstances but with the media trumpeting the idea that the petition represented bigotry against a persecuted minority, the task seemed nearly impossible. Nevertheless, failing to gain the necessary signatures before the March 12 deadline would kill the amendment before it saw the ballot. It had to be done.

On October 12, Colorado for Family Values officially launched the sign-up effort. By now CFV had finished incorporating. Since August it had operated out of a one-employee, one-volunteer office near Colorado College in Colorado Springs, with Kevin Tebedo supplying the day-in and day-out crunch work. The office had a few donated computers, one leased 386-machine, and donated database software. A first employee (other than Tony and Kevin), Jim Witmer, gave up a higher paying position to join CFV. He came on board in November to run the database—the nuts and bolts of fund raising mail—and to coordinate a growing list of office volunteers.

At this point Will began feeling the need for more wisdom than he could readily find. The impossibility of doing what Tony and Kevin had set out to do descended as a heavy weight on his shoulders. The financial obstacles came first. During these early days, CFV made many decisions limited by simply how much money they had in the bank. Not much, usually. Under the circumstances, the board decided to reduce Tony and Kevin's salaries significantly. They also decided to do fund raising and database collection in-house to save the fees normally paid to a professional company. They initiated Bill Armstrong's first fund raising letter to 30,000 Colorado homes. Foul-ups in timing and mailing contracts, plus database problems, made these efforts produce less income than they might have otherwise.

Tony Marco, a professional fund raising writer for major national clients, had access to the most sophisticated budgets and techniques available in the field. He had little patience for Kevin's occasional mishandling of this costly aspect of the operation, opening another source of tension between the two men. Will Perkins, feeling the pressure of accelerating events, continued to mediate the rift.

The personality conflict between co-chairmen became perhaps irreparable when Tony compared Kevin's work to that of a mechanic. Tebedo's recollection of the term is "ditch digger." (Such are the hazards of human ego.) Bill Woodley, a seasoned political leader from Denver, visited the CFV offices with a warning: "From my experience, these personality rifts can sink your ship. Someone must take the helm and eliminate the bickering."

No one exactly took the helm. In arbitrating the differences between Tony and Kevin, Will's influence grew beyond anything anticipated. His steady and mature personality became essential to the character of the amendment itself. He appreciated Tony's insistence that CFV pursue the civil rights attack on gay laws. This position had proven itself to him. On the other hand, Kevin's ability to roll up his sleeves and do the work remained indispensable.

Compounding the situation, a personal factor began to eat at Tony's ability to function with this fledgling organization. His own writing had suffered from a recession-based cut back in writing services. The reduced salary CFV could now afford to pay him, plus a heavy financial loss foisted on him by an unscrupulous relative, maximized his personal strain. He found it necessary to put nearly all of his energies back into making ends meet for his family.

Meanwhile Kevin, whose financial burdens were not nearly so critical, adjusted to his reduced salary. He busied himself organizing a grassroots network to carry out the goals of the petition process. His plan was to obtain an area leader in every town across the state. He never reached that goal, but he worked hard toward it. His recruiting successes came in the distant corners of Colorado where people seemed more willing to risk their reputations against the tide of gay rights. It seemed the high pressure of political correctness had not yet intimidated them.

The Denver metro area was another story. Few wanted to wear the Amendment 2 bull's eye in this cultural shooting gallery. Eventually, CFV operated through four key Denverites who happened to represent four conservative political groups. These were Barbara Sheldon of the Traditional Values Coalition, Jayne Schindler of Eagle Forum, Beatrice Nelson of Concerned Women for America, and Dave Nelson of the Christian Coalition. These four used their networking abilities in and around Denver on behalf of the amendment.

Surprisingly, in the process, these four drew little attention from the press. Perhaps they escaped the hard shots because their political activity involved existing memberships known to be sympathetic to the amendment. For whatever the reasons, CFV remained the high profile media-target throughout the campaign.

At this time I moved my family to Colorado Springs from Texas, spending several days in the home of Tony and Joyce Marco in the process. Marco had been a writing colleague of mine. In fact he had edited part of my first novel fifteen years earlier. Joyce ran a relocation service from their home in Colorado Springs. She helped me locate a suitable house and directed me to other needed local services.

Kevin visited the Marco home during my brief stay, prompting an explanation of Colorado for Family Values, the on-going initiative and petition process. Tony attempted to recruit my television production experience at this time. He thought I should produce commercials for the campaign if the petition drive succeeded. It all seemed well over my head at the time. I remained noncommittal. The most remarkable thing I learned was that CFV's communications director, Mark Olsen, was another former book editor of my mine. He had edited my current novel. This coincidence of two former colleagues working in the same political group seemed too uncanny to ignore. I promised to look into CFV when I settled.

I subscribed to the local *Gazette Telegraph* and the *Denver Post*. Between both papers and the local TV news I learned that Colorado for Family Values had stirred up the biggest media feeding frenzy since the Gulf War. The negative press surprised me. It caused me to be reluctant to follow through with my promise to look into CFV.

Meanwhile, Kevin carried the amendment petition responsibilities forward. Tony, focusing on his personal business, found it increasingly difficult to give time at the CFV office. Suddenly, on October 17, Marco resigned. His reasons were that financial problems had become too much to handle. Will and the Board took his resignation with regret. His pioneering thoughts on civil rights, his energetic pursuit of research, and his writing of the basic position paper had all been essential to the launch of CFV. Some even questioned whether victory could be achieved without him. Bill Armstrong seemed hit hard. But the realities of money and providing for his family had become overriding factors for Tony.

"I have nothing but the highest regard for the mission, intentions, and personnel of CFV and its Boards," Tony wrote. "My employment with CFV has been in every way gratifying, challenging, and rewarding. And I wish in the future to continue aiding CFV in the pursuit of its goals in every way feasible and possible."[33]

Tony continued to hover in CFV's wings after that, volunteering his advice and talent at whatever point he could. Will sought his counsel and CFV paid him retainer fees on a job-by-job basis. Kevin persisted in the spade work. But the CFV torch had been officially and irrevocably passed from Tony's hands . . . something he would later regret.

At this low point for CFV, Kevin's petition efforts sputtered and nearly failed. As he reported it, "We printed 3,100 sixty-name petitions in November with the hope of averaging 25 signatures each, for a total of 77,500 names. We knew we would need extra signatures and that some would be disqualified for technical reasons, so we chose this number because it sounded good. But winter is a terrible time to try to do anything so ambitious. Between

Thanksgiving and Christmas everybody with an ounce of family values is booked up. Sure enough, by January 1, we had distributed less than a thousand petitions and had seen, at most, 4,000 signatures returned."

About this time, Mark Olsen reported that Bill Armstrong, the most politically astute member of the CFV advisory circle, had seen the signature responses and declared: "The initiative is probably dead. With only 4,000 signatures at this date, you'll need a miracle to gather the rest of them by March."

Fresh from Texas, I learned what Armstrong meant. January, February, and March dump tremendous amounts of snow on the state. While the weather is great for powder skiing and tourism, it does little to motivate petition carriers.

Meanwhile, Kevin began holding seminars for amendment backers, using the network of recruited area leaders around the state to bring in the audiences. He motivated signature gatherers and exhorted volunteers to deepen their commitments. Aiding this effort, he assembled a notebook of information to help supporters understand the difficult points of the debate. He used it to point out the strong debate position the amendment's language afforded them in the public square. He encouraged them to use this information to convince fence sitters to sign up for the fight. He also encouraged them to use the information to compose letters to the editor.

This second piece of advice seemed to find fertile soil. The press had demeaned the amendment so viciously that supporters often found themselves reacting and defending the wrong aspects of it. Many letters to the editor fell into the trap of morally attacking homosexuality. This compromised the amendment's civil rights position and fulfilled the media's religious right stereotype of CFV. Not that moral considerations were unimportant; they simply would not be the reason most Coloradans would vote for or against the amendment. In each area where Kevin held seminars and made the information notebook available, CFV noticed a marked improvement in the quality of letters to the editor. By the time the petition process finished in March, he had held 13 seminars with an average of 100 supporters in each meeting.

After turning down a couple of invitations to attend CFV

committee meetings, I decided to take advantage of Tony and Kevin's written materials to educate myself on the amendment. The reading was fascinating. I learned enough to overcome my media-fed fears of involvement. So, when Mark Olsen next asked if I would sit-in on an evening meeting of the CFV media committee, I agreed to do so.

Tony showed up at this meeting. Kevin was on the road with his seminars. Mark ran the agenda with Tony advising heavily from the sidelines. This was when I first met Will Perkins. Seeing him in action helped me understand the principal players in the CFV story and how they compared to one another. When Will spoke, which was not often, his words carried weight, revealing a man of cautious humility. His hesitancy at times frustrated the others, but, in the main, it signaled his healthy appreciation for the fact that CFV was a human enterprise, with human strengths . . . and *very* human weaknesses.

By the end of this long evening, in which I had taken copious notes, I had learned enough to settle my remaining doubts. I volunteered to continue advising the media committee. The amendment's civil rights arguments had so impressed me that I imagined a high-road approach to the public mind during the upcoming campaign. I felt that the basic message should be that "Amendment 2 made good sense for everyone in Colorado." On this naïve assumption, I volunteered to write a series of good-sense television commercial scripts, totally underestimating the irrational aspects of the fight ahead.

With the petition drive still floundering, Kevin received important knowledge concerning the psychology of signature gathering. In a telephone conversation with Oregon's Measure 9 folks, he learned that they were doing much better than CFV by using shorter forms. The Oregon group had found that people seemed less intimidated to gather fewer names. Completing a shorter form, the carrier would feel a sense of accomplishment and commonly ask for another. "Good idea," Kevin thought. He checked with the Colorado authorities and found that CFV could authorize shorter twelve-name petitions. He ordered 7,500 new ones. Five thousand were shorter versions.

CFV had still not distributed its existing petitions. Only a few thousand names had trickled into the office. In light of this, Kevin's optimistic order of more forms seemed insupportable. There had been no new strategy, no accompanying decision to get them into the hands of new carriers. What was he thinking?

In fact, he doesn't really recall that he thought about it much. He ordered the petitions on blind faith. He also recalls feeling that the whole issue had come down to a do-or-die situation anyway. In retrospect, one thing seems clear, if CFV had not been sitting on Tebedo's pile of new petition forms, they would not have been ready to take advantage of the extraordinary events to follow.

A month before the petition deadline, Will asked me to meet with him and a radio promotions expert named Bob Dobbs. Will wanted us to crank out radio spots to induce petition carriers to step forward and accept Kevin's pile of dormant petitions at the CFV office. At the meeting we had no survey numbers, no guiding statistical evidence for our creative session. Each of us had been involved with a few direct response successes over the years, and even more failures. We simply put our heads together and flew by the seats of our pants. In about an hour we had hammered out a series of public service radio announcements designed to stimulate calls from would-be petition carriers. CFV's telephone number, prominently featured, of course.

To us, nothing seemed exceptional about these scripts. We thought they were good, but not really outstanding. We felt sure that they would pull a few calls and therefore were worth the effort. No one suggested that these simple messages might mean the difference between success and failure. Dobbs produced the spots immediately and distributed them to Christian radio stations statewide . . . the only ones who *might* care enough to offer public service time.

Even if the spots had been great, it seemed unlikely to us that the stations would air them. Even religious stations. The controversy against the amendment had grown so hot, no one imagined station managers would be willing to take the heat. Especially for a few unpaid, public service spots. They cared, but *that* much? As it turned out, they did. They began to air the spots immediately.

In a few days, Dr. James Dobson, head of Focus on the Family, decided that he would air a national radio program about the amendment. This family issues program, newly headquartered in Colorado Springs from Pomona, California, had the largest daily pro-family radio audience in the world. This particular one-hour format featured a discussion between Will Perkins, Senator Bill Armstrong, and Ignacio Rodriguez, a sympathetic Colorado civil rights leader. The specific impact of the event remains impossible to measure scientifically, but suddenly CFV's public service radio spots began to have marvelous results.

Kevin recalls, "Our phones began ringing off the wall. We had volunteers suddenly begging to carry petitions."

No doubt Bill Armstrong's presence on the Focus radio show had something to do with the responses. His name had gone out on letters across the state for months. The letter had specifically asked for petition carriers and donations. The synergistic effect of the Armstrong letter, the radio spots, and hearing Bill's voice on this special Focus on the Family radio program, no doubt, activated a good number of these calls.

By mid-February CFV's exhausted office volunteers had sent out all 9,700 petitions and the phones were still ringing. This situation seemed like the end of the rainbow, especially to those of us new at the business of political action. But when Bill Armstrong heard the particulars, like the veteran politician that he is, he asked questions.

"Do you know who these people are? Did you keep an accurate list?"

"No." In fact, the donated computer database had died. CFV had not been able to keep track of who had received the petitions.

Armstrong was not optimistic. A campaign must keep on top of its volunteers, he said. Leadership must motivate them with follow up calls, cards, and letters. At this stage, CFV had 9,700 petitions out in the hinterlands and no one knew for sure if these people were even legitimately on CFV's side of the issue.

The facts were that CFV had been under heavy telephone harassment for months. With each new media broadside the office answering machine would fill-up with threats and accusations in the vilest form. No one doubted that this kind of caller would be capable of dirty tricks. "You may have given your petitions to an army of gay activist callers out there who are keeping your petitions off the street," Armstrong suggested. "They may be using them to start a celebration bonfire in Aspen."

Kevin was speechless. The image too frightening. If the worst had truly happened and the opposition had intercepted the petitions through a concerted telephone campaign, his under funded, under manned, under equipped, and overly enthusiastic office volunteers must *not* be told. Morale would plummet. Hearts would break.

He cautiously asked the volunteers about the petition carriers who had responded by phone. They could only supply a few names, even fewer addresses, and practically no telephone numbers. He worried until his worrier broke. Then he simply returned to the blind faith mode. "They must be our people," he mumbled to himself, as he went through the motions of being in charge.

I, for one, thought this might be the end of the Amendment 2 petition story. Far too few of those enthusiastic volunteers would gather their share of signatures, I believed, even though they had responded to the radio ads. "Even if these petition carriers are your true supporters," I suggested, "a radio spot can't do much more than create momentary enthusiasm. Going door-to-door with a petition requires much more than that. The petitions will likely be dropped into a utility drawer and eventually tossed out with the spring cleaning."

But two unexpected factors lit a fire under the Amendment 2 petition carriers, charging them with an entirely new burst of energy. We came to call it the "Colorado miracle." Central to this marvel were Bill McCartney and Bill Armstrong.

Of course, the miracle probably wouldn't have been possible if, during the '90-91 college season, McCartney hadn't taken his CU Buffalos to the NCAA National Title in the Orange Bowl. Before the eyes of the nation they had upset Notre Dame and brought the trophy home to Boulder. This had afforded McCartney something close to living legend status among the state's sports writers and fans. (During the struggles of his '93 season, however, the press adulation has proven quite fickle.) Neither would the miracle have been possible without the fine reputation of Bill Armstrong on the line. And even more strangely, the petition miracle would not have been possible without the total, and seemingly mindless, antagonism of the news media.

The convergence of these providential sources began one fine February morning as McCartney sat in his Boulder office reading his *Denver Post*, *Rocky Mountain News*, and *Boulder Camera*. McCartney had been publicly criticized for allowing his name to appear on CFV's letterhead as an advisor. The University had been miffed seeing their name linked to CFV through McCartney's title on the document. With all of the piling-on in the press, the entire confab seemed suddenly like a moral call to battle for the coach. Like Pat Long at Digital, he had Biblical convictions about homosexuality and was tired of everyone calling them by other names, like "discrimination," "homophobia," and "hate." Enough was enough. He called his secretary and told her to arrange a news conference in fifteen minutes—he had something to say.

The words that McCartney spoke to the assembled press on February 10, 1992 became the shot heard 'round the state. He spoke for himself, not for the University, and not exactly for CFV and Amendment 2. He spoke as a Christian, a man, a coach, a husband, and father. Referring to a particular passage in the Bible, he said, "It is very clear to me, as I read the Scripture, that homosexuality is an abomination."[34] He further made clear that as a Bible believing Christian, the Scripture left him no choice but to take a stand against it. "It's a responsibility," he said. "It's inherent in the Christian faith."[35]

Here lies perhaps the greatest irony of the Amendment 2 campaign. After working so diligently to avoid putting a moral statement into the language of the amendment, McCartney's moral statement became the perfect example of what Amendment 2 was about—not morality, but freedom of speech.

McCartney's words amounted to ground zero in a politically incorrect explosion in every newsroom of the state. Religious, political, educational, and media leaders leaped eagerly forward to blast the coach for his religious bigotry. The surge of criticism made the former controversy seem like a teapot tempest. But strangely, Amendment 2 lost nothing. It leaped forward in popularity.

Such sequences cannot be arranged by the world's best political minds. McCartney's loose-cannon comments, and the criticism storm that followed, awakened every household in Colorado. A surge of signed petitions began arriving at the Colorado for Family Values offices in Colorado Springs. Calls came in from the corners of the state requesting even more signature forms. Petition carriers were besieged by citizens all across the state, saying, "If McCartney's not afraid to stand up for his convictions, then, by golly, here I am." Door to door responses became highly productive.

For the next several days McCartney continued to be relentlessly persecuted. The petition rate increased. The University threatened firing and censure because the coach had worn his University colors during the press conference. A school logo had been visible. More petitions. McCartney apologized for using the school facilities. He made a clarification to the press that he had been speaking for himself, not for the University in any way. More signatures. Privately, McCartney asked that his University coaching title be removed from CFV's letterhead to help ease the tension. CFV quickly obliged.

Pat Schroeder, the state's congresswoman, accused McCartney of hate-mongering and dubbed him a "self-appointed ayatollah." Another surge of petitions arrived in Colorado Springs.

McCartney reflected later, "As far as the congresslady, I didn't put a lot of stock in that. But I had no idea the media was so saturated with this liberal thinking. I thought there were still more people on both sides of the issue."[36]

Apparently much of the state felt the same way. And when asked to choose between McCartney's freedom to speak his moral convictions, and Schroeder's demand that he shut his "ayatollah" mouth—most Coloradans within reach of an Amendment 2 petition promptly registered a vote for the coach.

The drama was not over. After a couple weeks of McCartney bashing, suddenly and bewilderingly, the newspapers began to attack the state's respected former senator, Bill Armstrong. The focus of the attack was the CFV letter Armstrong had written months before. Three mailings totaling 90,000 letters had been sent to potential donors over the course of the campaign. Nothing had been said by the press during all of that time. Of course, CFV had not sent the letters to just anyone. They had been selective, sending it only to voters likely to support the work of the struggling little political group from Colorado Springs. (Will Perkins had not yet emerged as a personality strong enough to pull support from across the state, therefore Armstrong's name seemed necessary to the effort. Perkins insists that without Armstrong's letter CFV would have died in its cradle.) Suddenly, in the midst of the McCartney affair, the news establishment decided that Armstrong's letter had become a serious item.

ARMSTRONG LETTER CALLED 'TRAGIC, HURTFUL, PAINFUL,' "'Such views may provoke backlash against gays,' activist says";[37] ARMSTRONG SHOWS PREJUDICE TOWARD GAYS, ". . . a prime example of the discrimination and hatred gays face daily;"[38] NOTE TO BILL ARMSTRONG: HATE IS NOT A FAMILY VALUE, ". . . he must be held accountable for the hatred his far-right rhetoric may inflame";[39] ARMSTRONG'S GAY 'THREAT,' "We need protection from the likes of Bill Armstrong."[40]

Perhaps the sentiments of the offended media elite were best expressed by the *Denver Post's* Ken Hamblin: MENTAL DINOSAURS SPEWING BIGOTRY AND HATE. ". . . Armstrong and McCartney have a right to be homophobic and bigoted," he wrote, "but that entitlement must stop when they begin contributing to an environment that motivates hate, fear, and even death against gays and lesbians. When shallow people like Armstrong and McCartney are permitted to float like scum on top of a sea of knowledge, they take us back to the 14th century."[41]

Nothing in the Armstrong letter came close to the virulence of this attack on his reputation. (See the full text of the Armstrong letter in Appendix C.) Furthermore, some news stories pulled statements from context, marrying them to ideas found elsewhere in the letter. This allowed them to fake the legitimacy of their assault on his character.[42] Armstrong said that he had never suffered such malicious words in 30 years of public service. He was shaken and taken by surprise at the personal level of the onslaught.

The media offensive also inspired the most bizarre level of phone obscenity of the campaign. News descriptions of Armstrong and McCartney seemed to give moral impetus to those who had long claimed that CFV was a hatred-motivated group. CFV, Armstrong, and McCartney's offices were inundated. Many threats were specific and violent. In these calls, CFV supporters were often accused of advocating the murder of homosexuals. In this, the weird irrationality of the homosexual issue had finally exposed itself plainly.

News stories continued to accuse McCartney of calling homosexuals an "abomination." Not true, he protested, *homosexuality* was the abomination, not homosexuals. The Bible makes a distinction between sinful behavior and personhood, he said. He tried to explain the classical Christian argument that God loves sinners while hating their sins. News reporters either could not, or would not, grasp this important subtlety. Irrationality escalated.

CFV remained pretty quiet about now. Unbeknownst to the rest of the state, they had the best seat in the house when it came to understanding how all of this was playing across Colorado. The more the news media turned up the heat, the more the demand grew for Amendment 2 petitions. The most interesting signatures began to come from people who told petition carriers that they did not oppose homosexuality on moral grounds. Their signatures were offered because they figured this country would be better off as long as men like Armstrong and McCartney were around. "Too many of these wishy-washy types around anyway," they said, publicly recording their names and addresses on Amendment 2 petitions. They were Democrats, Republicans, Libertarians, Independents, liberals, and conservatives. Heady days at CFV.

As the signed petitions streamed into Colorado Springs, Will declared them to be among the most important documents in America. He and the CFV board asked themselves what might happen if these incredibly fragile, yet historic pieces of paper, were somehow destroyed? Taking no chances, they rented a bank vault for safekeeping.

The filing deadline grew near. Will called various armored car services to see if they would escort the petitions on the day of their delivery to Denver. Interestingly, they all declined, fearing the homosexual backlash they would suffer for providing the service. Finally, one company mustered the courage to reverse its original decision and accept the contract.

By the March petition deadline, Will, Kevin, and Tony followed a loaded armored car from Colorado Springs to the state capitol. They walked into the Secretary of State's office with 84,445 signatures. A few more than the 49,279 required—just in case any proved contestable. It was the highest number of signatures ever gathered in Colorado by an army of volunteers.

The news media and homosexual lobby were stunned. They might have seen this as the first indication that their attacks on CFV had misfired. But no. Rather than rethink their strategy, they arrogantly increased their aggressive tactics.

Instead of heralding the petition success the next day, the front page of the *Denver Post* leveled another attack on Bill Armstrong: ARMSTRONG: GAYS A "GRAVE THREAT," blared the banner headline. The story was old news, more about the Armstrong/CFV letter. Not only did the headline obscure the petition victory, it was a lie. Armstrong had labeled the militant homosexual agenda "a grave threat," not homosexuals. Like most Biblically moral people, he worked hard to preserve the healthy separation between a behavior of choice, and personhood. Never mind truth, using the accusation as a pretext, the *Denver Post* news editors had found their way to bury the CFV petition success story on the last page of the section.

On the same day, Colorado Springs' *Gazette Telegraph* played their own version of poor loser. The story on the petition success contained a prominent inset announcing where to find other news items related to the signatures: GROUP SAYS ANTI-GAY VIOLENCE UP IN '91/A6; CU REGENT SEEKS TO BROADEN ANTI-BIAS POLICY/B7. Obviously these related articles cast aspersions on the motives of 84,445 Colorado citizens.

How could one be sure this was the *Gazette Telegraph* news editors' intent in this issue? They were not subtle. The second page of the petition article contained a picture of Will Perkins announcing the signature success, but the caption read: "The group opposes laws protecting gays from bias." Add to this the enlarged quote from homosexual lawyer Robin Miller, "WE SEE IT AS AN ISSUE OF PREJUDICE AND DISCRIMINATION"—and it could be fairly assumed that the *Gazette* news team had stacked the headlines to make their point.

No matter how the press minimized and subverted the truth, the unthinkable had still happened. Anyone present at the press conference saw for themselves a pile of signatures the likes of which the homosexual lobby, and even CFV, had not imagined.

Kevin Tebedo looked back on the sequence that had produced the victory and felt humbled. "By all normal means, we shouldn't have made the ballot," he admits. "You can do everything right in politics and lose under these circumstances. We did so many things *wrong*. For this kind of response to come in? You figure it out."

5

Confronting queer politics

Sunday, March 17, 1991 proved a rude awakening for the worshipers at Boulder's First Presbyterian Church. Three months earlier, it seems they had made the mistake of removing Carolyn Val-Schmidt as singles choirmaster because of her lesbianism. Though she had served voluntarily, the church barred her from any role of leadership after her sexual preference had become known. Church officials had encouraged her to remain a part of the congregation and she had attended that very morning, even hugging one of the church officials who had ousted her.

"I feel strongly that we can love people but not always approve of everything they do," commented a Boulder woman who had attended First Presbyterian for 15 years.[43]

Suddenly a fire alarm interrupted the worship routine. Smoke poured from a fifth grade Sunday school room on the second floor. Children screamed and ran. Church members quickly snuffed out the blaze with fire extinguishers and evacuated 500 worshipers into the street. City fire fighters were summoned. But as the congregation waited, the strangest coincidence of all took place: they were accosted by a group of homosexuals—including several men dressed in drag—carrying signs reading "Ladies in Support of Prejudiced Presbyterians." The paraders said they were there to protest Val-Schmidt's removal.

Fire inspector Cliff Harvey arrived and examined the torched Sunday school room. He suspected arson but tried to calm fears: "We believe from the way the fire was started that it was intended to disrupt rather than do any major damage," he soothed. Both the door to the classroom and an exit that opened onto the roof and down to the street had been found unlocked.

The church's pastor hid himself from the curious press, refusing to answer questions. It was reported that the church office had received a flood of very threatening phone calls after Val-Schmidt had been disciplined. "It's scary, that's what it is," said a parishioner who asked to remain anonymous for fear of a gay reprisal.

"What are you going to do if your children are gay," shouted an angry cross-dresser in the street?

"It's a tough way to get attention," mumbled a church member, requesting anonymity from the reporter taking notes.

Another parishioner sympathized, "I'm saddened that there are a lot of people who are hurting."

"They all claim they love us," retorted a lesbian protester, "but they still see us as a behavior and a lifestyle. We're not a lifestyle! We're a cultural minority!" she raged.

Welcome to the gay '90s.

Anyone old enough to remember when gay meant happy can remember a time when homosexuality was considered immoral. Not so very long ago. Unleashed from the closet of history by the sexual revolution, in a few short years the topic has raced to the top of the national priority list. Many Americans have begun to ask, "Does it *really* belong there?"

After the successful petition drive, suddenly everyone with CFV had to look much closer at homosexuality than they wanted to. Stories like the Boulder church fire came uncomfortably to mind. What was the fuss really about? What were the underlying dilemmas? The election campaign would demand a much deeper understanding than had the petition drive. Each CFV volunteer and staff member had been awakened reluctantly from a political sleep. None preferred to spend the next year away from home, family, or career, fighting something in the public square that shouldn't have been there in the first place.

The whole mess lent itself to a call for homosexuality to go quietly back into the closet . . . to let morality reign once again in America's legal system. After all, it is immoral *behavior* that moral people find offensive, not necessarily the human beings involved. People of morals are not bigots, so take these gay rights laws out of America's face. Thank you.

(What a fantasy.)

As each CFV volunteer looked closer, weighing the legal position homosexuality had gained in recent years, they knew that the good old days of moral America were gone. The agenda of homosexuality had descended like an errant cloud around the nation. More gay rights laws were being introduced and passed every day, replacing deep rooted and historic traditions against sexual deviation.

"We're here whether you like it or not," sneered Larry Kramer, homosexual founder of Gay Men's Health Crisis, "so if we have to ram it down your throat, tough s___!"[44]

Wearily—at times almost regretting the petition drive's success—CFV insiders began to analyze their enemy. Before the campaign could begin in earnest, they would have to be schooled in the nasty politics of homosexuality.

FORCED AFFIRMATION

If nothing else, CFV strategists liked Larry Kramer's honesty. He expressed the underlying truth they found everywhere in homosexual politics, ". . . *ram it down your throat.*" CFV labeled this attitude in more palatable terms: forced affirmation.

As they listened to homosexual spokespersons, studied their literature, and read gay laws, CFV volunteers saw that the gay intention was to remove all choice about accepting their lifestyle. That is exactly what was meant by "*ram it down your throats.*" This had been seen in Colorado's proposed Ethnic Harassment Bill. Social activists were ready to charge anyone criticizing homosexuality with a felony. It had been seen at Digital Equipment Corporation, where Pat Long's morals had threatened her career under the Valuing Differences program.

"Celebrate Diversity," homosexual cheerleaders urged from the Colorado sidelines. But they didn't mean *diversity*. They had no intention of valuing *all* differences: only those which sprang from moral relativism. Diversity, when confronting traditional morality, becomes a misnomer. It exhibits a fierce intolerance. As Torie Osborn, then spokesperson for the National Gay and Lesbian Task Force, confessed, "Our agenda is extremely militant."[45] Her confession made no apology for the intolerance inherent in this statement. In fact, she seemed to celebrate it as if none of the journalists in her audience would call her to task. (She was right about that.)

Long before Torie confirmed it for the press, CFV had warned of the militant goals of gay politics a thousand times: "It's forced affirmation," they said, "not tolerance." CFV believed that if the "extremely militant" gay agenda could be made clear in Colorado, the voters would reject it. They would not remain the passive partner to this form of political rape.

In an early strategy meeting at Tony Marco's home, Barbara Sheldon had brought along a remarkable document called *The Overhauling of Straight America.* The article, published in a November 1987 issue of the homosexual *Guide Magazine*, had been an outline for waging political war against heterosexual values. It predicted how homosexuality would come to dominate American culture in the '90s.

As the Colorado campaign developed, Tony found that *Overhauling* seemed to summarize the day-by-day approach of the local homosexual alliance. "We have an advantage, here," he said, waving the article before our unbelieving eyes at a subsequent media meeting. "We can predict what our opposition will do." He began to read excerpts:

> . . . The way to benumb raw sensitivities about homosexuality is to have a lot of people talk a great deal about the subject in a neutral or supportive way.
>
> . . . So far, gay Hollywood has provided our best covert weapon in the battle to desensitize the mainstream.
>
> . . . First, we can use talk to muddy the moral waters. This means publicizing support for gays by more moderate churches, raising theological objections of our own about conservative interpretations of biblical teachings . . .
>
> . . . Second, we can undermine the moral authority of homophobic churches by portraying them as antiquated backwaters, badly out of step with the times . . .
>
> . . . Portray gays as victims, not as aggressive challengers.

> . . . Our campaign should not demand direct support for homosexual practices, but should instead take anti-discrimination as its theme.
>
> . . . Along these same lines, we shouldn't overlook the celebrity endorsement.
>
> . . . At a later stage of the media campaign for gay rights . . . it will be time to get tough with remaining opponents.
>
> . . . The public should be shown images of ranting homophobes . . . bigoted southern ministers drooling with hysterical hatred . . .
>
> . . . A campaign to vilify the victimizers is going to enrage our most fervid enemies, of course. But what else can we say? The shoe fits, and we should make them try it on for size, with all of America watching.
>
> . . . Solicit funds . . . because those gays not supporting families usually have more discretionary income than average, they could afford to contribute much more.
>
> . . . Daytime talk shows also remain a useful avenue for exposure.
>
> . . . The AIDS epidemic is sparking anger and fear in the heartland of straight America. As the virus leaks out of homosexual circles and into the rest of society, we need have no illusions about who is receiving the blame.

The Overhauling of Straight America indeed gave CFV an advantage of knowing what to expect. It also gave all who read it a shot of pure, sobering fear. The instructions revealed how far the homosexual agenda had already succeeded. Also, the extent to which they were aware of their true behavior and health issues—and their full intentions to lie about them.

In political terms what exactly did this mean? What was, and is, the militant homosexual agenda? During the campaign, CFV warned Colorado voters of the gay agenda's coercive intentions. At that time, the local homosexual lobby simply denied having an agenda. The press faithfully reported their claim without challenge. Thus encouraged, the homosexual lobby further stated that any so-called agenda had been invented by CFV to make gays seem sinister. The press quoted this line, too. Much later, after losing the election, the Gay and Lesbian Task Force suddenly switched tactics. Not only did Torie Osborn admit to an "extremely militant" agenda, at the May '93 march on Washington, D.C., the gay lobby spelled it out for America. Never mind that they had previously lied to Colorado. Here are the main points of the self-confessed gay agenda as seen on C-SPAN TV:

1. to win protected status under the Civil Rights Act of 1964,
2. to force an end to the ban on homosexuality in the military,
3. to repeal remaining state sodomy laws, and
4. to secure domestic partnership laws.

This published list vindicated CFV and its campaign claims, though the press ignored this fact. Everything the gays spelled out in Washington, D.C. amounts to the forced affirmation of homosexuality described by CFV during the amendment campaign.

The ambitions of such an agenda can only be enforced through the Civil Rights Act of 1964. No wonder their fight for its advantages took on such irrational tones in Colorado. CFV had warned that, if homosexuals were given access to that group of special laws and powers, they would literally be able to ram it down our throats.

Though they vigorously denied it, homosexual strategists were, and are, specifically lusting after the power of affirmative action lurking in the Civil Rights Act of 1964. This is the most coercive government tool of forced affirmation in existence today. Winning point #1 of the agenda would give them this tool. How? Because affirmative action is already in place for anyone listed as a protected class under the Civil Rights Act of 1964. Homosexual activists know this. Visit almost any business in any town and ask to see the personnel bulletin board. You will find the following posted there:

> Executive Order 11246, as amended, prohibits job discrimination on the basis of race, color, religion, sex or national origin, *and requires affirmative action* . . .[46] [emphasis added]

If you add homosexual orientation to the list of "race, color, religion, sex, or national origin," guess what you get by executive order? Affirmative action. This means employers would be forced to hire a quota of homosexuals or else be sued for discrimination. Anyone claiming same-sex attractions could take advantage of these affirmative action policies, whether they were really gay or not. The pro-gay ACLU, in their published guide for homosexuals, lists five American cities in which affirmative action clauses have already been attached to sexual orientation laws.[47] The ACLU is sharpening its skills even now for federally empowered affirmative action litigation on behalf of gay America. They see it as something desirable, inevitable, and certainly profitable for their member lawyers.

Incredibly, President Clinton has promised to support the homosexual bid to gain status under the Civil Rights Act. Only Congress stands in his way.

During the campaign, CFV addressed the fact that homosexuals had been added to the local list of protected classes in Denver, Boulder, and Aspen. Even though the laws were not being used for affirmative action yet, a real loss of freedoms had been mandated by government in these cities. Gays were not going to attempt total forced affirmation until they had a statewide law like the Ethnic Harassment Bill in place, or had the even more powerful Civil Rights Act of 1964.

For now the gay lobby is trying hard to prove that they do not want affirmative action. They know America won't buy it. Therefore, Denver, Boulder, and Aspen have only seen the "nose of the camel." Later, when they have the laws they want, gays can unleash the "unsightly derriere" of affirmative action and no one will be able to stop them.

Throughout the amendment campaign, CFV literature referred to protected class status as conferring special rights on anyone claiming same-sex attraction. Amendment 2 had been framed to reverse this unfair advantage statewide. Some people began to catch on right away. Others seemed irrationally pledged to the homosexual cause, whether good or bad for Colorado.

CFV held that most American citizens would reject protected

class status for homosexuals if they properly understood it. They believed that: traditional families would reject it because it undermined the very definition of the family; that conservatives would reject it based on two thousand years of Western Civilization (which had never condoned the lifestyle); that true minorities would reject it as an insult to their struggles; and that Americans with moral objections would reject protected class status for gays because to them it would amount to legislating immorality. Most of all, the idea of using government to force someone to affirm a behavior and lifestyle smacked of pure tyranny. Forced affirmation of homosexuality amounted to policing the thoughts of others. It went against the American ideals of freedom of conscience, speech, and association. If Americans understood this clearly, they would not act irrationally: they would reject the gay agenda.

As the campaign debate intensified, every encounter with the homosexual agenda revealed that it was, as Osborn had stated, "extremely militant." New York journalist Jonathan Van Meter put it this way: ". . . people *have* to put up with me as a gay editor . . . . The mission that I'm on is *to make people learn* that . . . gay people are just like everybody else . . . that they *have* to tolerate us"[48] [emphasis added]. Here we see the forcefulness and the eagerness to remove all choice. If one "has to tolerate" something, we are not talking about tolerance at all: we are talking about forced affirmation.

One thing became clear from all of this: to the homosexual lobby, there simply exists no valid objection to their lifestyle—morality included. This assumption fueled them with an inflated sense of rightness. They didn't hesitate to say that they intended to *force* others to see things their way.

In light of these evidences, CFV dared to address the future, though political experts had advised them not to do so. In public speeches and literature they began to articulate the following questions: "What if homosexual militants succeed? What if they have their way? What if laws are bent to their purpose? What if the laws of Denver, Aspen, and Boulder are enforced uniformly across the state? What kind of world will government-mandated homosexual affirmation create?" The answers:

□ Parents would fear the influence of public homosexual role models on their maturing and vulnerable children, but would have no voice in the matter. Day care operators could not deny employment to people practicing homosexuality. School teachers and administrators would be forced to hire gays. Children would be taught that homosexuality is both normal and attractive. Sensitivity training would be mandated for those who displayed so-called homophobia in public. In these sessions, the likes of Jonathan Van Meter could play out his power fantasy to: "make people learn that gay people are just like everybody else."

□ Employers, business owners, and the military services—already facing coercion in hiring practices—would have to manage another bureaucratic nightmare. Not only would they have to tiptoe around gay hiring laws, but they would also have to prove they felt no homophobia when they fired an individual. Every business in America would be forced to implement a Valuing Differences program like the one at Digital.

□ Under government-mandated homosexual affirmation, imagine the thought police who could parade their affections in any public place and watch for adverse reactions? ("Did I detect a trace of disgust there, sir, when I kissed my lover? I have no choice but to recommend sensitivity training for you.") Health care workers would be forbidden to ask if their patients were AIDS infected. This would constitute an unequal invasion of homosexual privacy. Banks, insurance companies, and the military would lose their ability to discriminate relative to any risks involved with medically underwriting homosexual behavior.

□ In the world of mandated homosexual rights, every government agency—falling beneath the strictest scrutiny of the law—would be subject to quota hiring, leading the way for the rest of the nation. Full marital benefits for domestic partners and full advocacy of the homosexual political agenda would be swallowed wholesale. The heavy costs for this action would no doubt come to the taxpayer in some cleverly disguised legislative package. In all branches of government, we would see the enforcement of homosexual advantage statutes and the public would have to bear the cost of court challenges.

□ Racial minorities, now protected by hard won civil rights laws, would see their place in line taken by lucrative homosexual court cases. Overburdened courts would dispense even less justice. Landlords would be forced to accept people who expressed same-sex affections publicly—say, at the swimming pool or clubhouse—and would have no recourse, even if traditional residents chose to move to other housing for reasons of their own revulsion.

□ Churches, pastors, para-church organizations, and religious schools would face two awful government-mandated options. Either (1) they would be forced to hire homosexual activists as any other employer, regardless of their religious beliefs, and would be threatened with criminal proceedings and a loss of tax exempt status for speaking against homosexual behavior (similar to the Georgetown University affair), or (2) they would be given a legal exemption from homosexual rights laws.

THE DANGER OF RELIGIOUS EXEMPTIONS

In fact, religious exemptions are attached to certain gay rights laws even now. Many religious people seem happy with this, wrongly assuming that the exemption is a generous allowance for their faith. Not so. If one projects ahead, an exemption guarantees that morality will one day be at odds with the court. How? An exemption from a law is a license of sorts. In effect, an exemption from a gay rights law is a license to discriminate. A religious exemption lowers Biblical morality to the level of discrimination in the eyes of the court. One must never think that these religious islands of discrimination will be left unmolested in politically correct America.

Warning! Flee any law that begins to swell up with exemptions. Exemptions are made to be changed later. They are seldom necessary to well written and legitimate laws. A religious exemption from a gay rights law leaves moral expression within one activist judge's ruling of being outlawed.

A second warning! Exemptions are a succession of death blows to freedom. Any citizen who supported Bill McCartney's right to speak his moral convictions in public, for example, must not be suckered into trading gay rights laws for religious exemptions. You might as well bury religious freedom when you do.

In Colorado, during the Amendment 2 campaign, certain people began to imagine this strange world of government-enforced affirmation. For those with foresight, it began to scare the bejabbers out of them. It did not look like equality at all, but superiority for a special interest group, a package of special rights and unfair advantages for anyone claiming same-sex attraction.

Amendment 2 offered the state a clear shot at stopping this nonsense. It gave citizens a chance to close the legal can of worms with one simple act.

THE LARGER THREAT TO FAMILIES

In New York the Montefiore Medical Center decided to give their homosexual workers official domestic partner recognition (item 4 on the homosexual agenda). This policy for the first time made health insurance available which would cover the employee's homosexual partner. A year later only a fraction of homosexual employees had signed up. When managers asked why, homosexuals complained that they remained at a disadvantage to married couples because gays could not legally marry.[49] Their insurance benefits would be taxed at the higher, "single" tax rate. For this, they had boycotted the policy.

Suddenly it appeared that granting domestic partnership opened a can of worms that threatened the status of traditional families. Beneath the simple sounding idea of honoring homosexual couples lurked an entirely new level of competing rights and discriminations that had never occurred to anyone. Only a gaggle of ACLU lawyers could sort it out—charging fees, of course, by the hour. The only losers in the process were the unsuspecting traditional families for whom marriage and tax laws existed in the first place.

Homosexual marriages threaten not only the financial advantages of traditional families, they threaten the very meaning of marriage and family itself. Many citizens behind CFV believed strongly that throwing society's arms open to homosexual marriage would send destructive signals to the nation. Among other things it would say that the glue of heterosexual matrimony no longer provided society's primary building material. In its absence, any old domestic partnership would do; if people merely claimed to care about each other, that would be enough to grant family status. Most thinking citizens sensed that granting this kind of legal status to homosexual marriages would do great damage to American families. They felt that the fabric of marriage had already endured too much under a reckless divorce rate and its many attendant evils.

As the campaign began in earnest, CFV addressed the fact that Aspen, Boulder, and Denver had passed homosexual rights ordinances in the '70s, '80s, and '90s respectively. CFV subsequently became aware that more than one hundred other cities and fourteen states[50] across the nation had done the same. CFV thinkers posed the question: What do these laws say to the nation? The politically correct crowd replied that it was a simple message of tolerance and diversity. If they had been right, CFV might as well have packed up and gone home—game, set, match.

However, the many concerned citizens backing CFV believed the politically correct thinkers were seriously shortsighted on this point. Gay rights laws were not harmless. Neither were any of the points of the homosexual agenda, especially not for families. For this very reason, CFV's name, Colorado for Family Values, continued to make sense even though the amendment addressed strictly the civil rights question.

Today, most people discuss the issue of gay rights unaware that on college and university campuses the debate has gone far beyond marriage and family. We are promised by the most elite professors in the land that gender liberation will be the next wave of homosexual activism.

To visualize how near it is, recall the cosmetic transformation of pop star Michael Jackson. Unless Americans had observed it slowly over the years, none could tell today if they were seeing or hearing a boy or a girl on stage. During his celebrated Oprah Winfrey interview it became clear to many viewers that he is an expensive vision of the gender attack on our culture. Gender liberation is serious business with what are now called Queer Theorists in American academia. They tell us that "the future will give birth to a new revolutionary people . . . no longer male and female, but queer."[51]

The latest official line of the homosexual lobby is that queer is good. Queers, they say, are what we will all become when the power of the government finally abolishes gender discrimination.[52] (Yes, they are saying this. And yes, they mean it.)

Of all people, children are the most vulnerable to the power of these radical suggestions. Remember Michael Jackson surrounded by all of the Los Angeles children at the '93 Super Bowl Half-time Show, singing "Heal the World?" Since then, one-half *billion* children around the world have watched his video *Black and White*. In it a person changes ethnicity from white to black and changes gender from male to female in rapid succession. This visual message is a serious one. Michael himself is an experiment in gender liberation. A rebellion against nature itself is brewing behind the gay rights agenda.

Children do not need this. Those who supported the idea of family values in Colorado agreed that children are sexually overexposed in our society. But politically correct parents and educators seem oblivious to this reality.

Children of Horizons is an esteemed scholarly book from Straus & Giroux, at $25. It has been authored by two University of Chicago professors, Gilbert Herdt and Andrew Boxer. The book asserts that teens can—and possibly should—decide for the rest of their lives that they are homosexual or heterosexual. *Teenagers*! These professors, who have counseled extensively at a Chicago homosexual center for troubled adolescents, are claiming that these children are "leading a new way out of the closet." Aside from serious doubt about who is leading whom, America has traditionally held that children should be sheltered from choosing something so profound as sexual preference. Childhood has been viewed as a natural time of experimentation. It has always been hoped that the experiments would be well guided and not dangerous to their well being. Now we have homosexual university professors bowing to the shrine of teenage sexual choice? The obvious personal advantage they may make of their scholarly authority cannot be ignored by any serious parent.

A healthy adult may make a wrong sexual choice in life and correct it, but . . . "as a twig is bent so grows the tree." A child is apt to be traumatized by a sexual experiment (or seduction) so that he or she loses a sense of identity for years to come. This is the very heart of normal revulsion toward pedophilia. If during that vulnerable time the child seeks the advice of a university educated counselor, imagine the help they might receive: "How can you be sure that you are not gay? How can you hope to become a whole person if you remain unwilling to explore and develop your normal, natural, healthy, homosexual potential? Could it be that all you lack is a good gay lover?"

Do these questions sound like CFV scare tactics? They are not. They were actually recommended in a publication titled *Gay and Lesbian Youth Tools for Educators*,[53] offered to teachers attending a Denver seminar. (These are the questions that enlightened authorities want to ask your children at school . . . should the little rascals ever grow confused over the moral values of your home. And what teen doesn't?) With leading questions such as these, more children will likely "lead a new way out of the closet" and wind up a statistic in Herdt and Boxer's sequel.

In effect, this so-called normalization of homosexuality threatens to legitimize what used to be called child molestation. It is the danger sensed by New York City parents in opposing the *Children of the Rainbow* curriculum. Perhaps this surprising revolt in "liberal city" is a signal that the tide of mindless tolerance is turning toward sensible limits again.

The most baffling allies of the militant homosexual agenda are politically correct *hetero*sexuals. They seem to completely embrace the idea that the traditional family has utterly failed and is no more worthy of society's esteem. They have bought every exceptional news story of divorce, spouse battering, family murder, incest, emotional abuse . . . and have declared the traditional family a loser. It is as if they cannot discern between a social tragedy and the value of the social institution itself.

No one denies that families are facing extreme pressures today. But most are thriving. We haven't seen the end of the American family by a long shot. But heterosexual activists seem bent on helping the homosexual lobby push the traditional family over a cultural cliff. In its stead they intend to give equal, normal, and moral status to domestic partners of every stripe. This is their version of a *moral* imperative.

It further seems appalling that heterosexual activists dismiss as harmless one of the more obvious facts about same sex partnership, the natural one: homosexual partners cannot reproduce. We are talking sperm-to-sperm or egg-to-egg match-ups. Homosexual defenders claim this has no bearing on the homosexual desire to educate children. Oh, really? Alyson Publications of Boston, publisher of the educational books *Daddy's Roommate* and *Heather has Two Mommies*, is also the publisher of the manual *Gay Sex* which advises pedophiles on how to avoid getting caught.[54] These two ideas are not related?

Our schools are filled with the most impressionable young hearts and minds among us. Where else could the confusion about sexual identity be more exploited? Where else could recruiting take place more effectively? But these possibilities are declared irrelevant by the cultural elite . . . unfair and off limits in a discussion of full approval of homosexuality.

The following are a few well-published facts assembled by CFV researchers during the Amendment 2 campaign: *(1)* 73% of homosexuals in one study had at some time had sex with boys 16 to 19 and younger,[55] (the researchers reporting this were themselves gay); *(2)* the mean age for same-sex first encounters is 15, and homosexuals are about 18 times more likely to engage in sex with minors than heterosexuals[56]; *(3)* homosexuals, who represent at the most 3% of the population, perpetrate more than 33% of all reported child molestations[57]; *(4)* more than 50% of adult homosexuals had been seduced by older homosexuals before the age of 14 in this study[58]; *(5)* Masters and Johnson wrote "In most cases, homophile interests developed in the early to mid-teens . . . . Recruitment usually was accomplished by an older male . . . the teenager was left with the concept that, whether or not he continued as an active homosexual, he would always be homophile-oriented"[59]; *(6) The Gay Book of Lists*, published by Alyson Publications, Inc. (now in its fourth printing), boldly lists 49 instances of child/adult sex—no apologies. The book lists them as a benign matter-of-gay-fact.

As the gays-in-the-military debate erupted during Clinton's first weeks in office, CFV obtained a copy of an official report citing the following record of homosexual offenses in the Army between 1989 and 1992:[60] First of all, homosexuals were cited as committing twice as many criminal acts as the rest of the Army put together. The rate of criminal incidents for homosexuals was 5.40/1000/year, whereas the rate for the rest of the Army was 2.45/1000/year. Eighteen percent of these incidents involved threats of physical violence or the use of weapons. Specifically, homosexual sex crimes were reported at seven times the rate for heterosexual soldiers: 3.52/1000/year compared to .47/1000/year. Five percent of the homosexuals involved were HIV positive. Sixty-two percent of the incidents where both partners were military personnel involved fraternization, i.e., the unlawful association of senior and subordinate personnel which is totally destructive of military discipline and morale. Eighty-four percent of homosexual sex crimes involved a non-consenting victim. Forty-seven percent of these involved children.

Normalizing this level of sexual instability seems unwise, not only for the military, but for families and society. In politically correct America, however, these scientific studies of homosexual behavior are routinely censored from the public debate. One prominent gay rights advocate testified before a Colorado judicial committee that stating medical or behavioral facts that cast homosexuality in a negative way are discriminatory even if true. The person suggested that they should become illegal.[61]

When gay rights opponents cite behavioral research during debate, the politically correct shout them down like a Donahue talk show crowd. They say that the facts and figures are extreme examples and cannot properly characterize the whole gay community.

Not so. The statistics listed here speak for themselves. One report does not stand alone. Each independent body of research reinforces the other. None are absolute; by no means exhaustive. However, all of them taken together are compelling. After all, the public discussion today is not about tolerating homosexuality in a closet, but about giving it full status with marriage and family. The potential consequences must be considered in a decision like this. The behavioral evidence cannot be ignored by anyone who cares about the welfare of children and families.

Besides, the statistics above are probably far too kind. The full intentions of the homosexual alliance to legalize sex with children are indicated by the following public comments: *(1)* ". . . the love between men and boys is at the foundation of homosexuality"[62]; *(2)* "What is a pedophile? A pedophile is not a rapist or a murderer or a devil, but a person who loves. . . ."[63]; *(3)* "NAMBLA [North American Man/Boy Love Association] calls on the Boy Scouts of America to cease its discrimination against openly gay and lesbian persons . . . . This will permit scouts to be exposed to a variety of lifestyles . . . ."[64]; *(4)* The Boy Scouts take the threat seriously. They have reported; ". . . 416 men have been arrested or banned from Scouting for molesting," at least 1,151 boys (over a 19-year period)[65]; *(5)* "Take the media and apply to become a scout leader," says this piece of advice from a *Queer Nation* internal memo[66]; *(6)* a 1983 editorial appearing in the Colorado Springs *Gazette Telegraph* quoted a gay activist as follows: "I think that pederasty should be given [society's] stamp of approval. I think it's true that boy-lovers are much better for their children than the parents are. . . ."[67]; *(7)* The 1972 *Gay Rights Platform* stated, (a) "Repeal all state laws prohibiting private sexual acts involving consenting persons" [adults not specified], (b) "Repeal of all laws governing the age of sexual consent"; *(8)* "Sex by eight or it's too late," is the motto of the Rene Guyon Society and many current NAMBLA associates. (And Will Perkins usually adds, "And when they say 'sex by eight' they're not talking about the time of day, folks.")

"Foul!" cry the social engineers. "These statements do not represent anything Americans would consider legislating."

Oh really? How about the State of New Jersey? Under intense

homosexual pressure it has already agreed to lower the age of sexual consent to 13. It has further proposed to make sex legal at an even younger age if the partners are separated by less than four years in age.[68]

We would never legalize pedophilia in an enlightened democracy, you say? In September of 1992, the University of Massachusetts at Amherst revised its anti-discrimination policy to offer protected status to those "whose sexual orientation involves minor children as the sex object." At the 31st Annual Conference of the Society for the Scientific Study of Sex, an expert on sex offenders and child sex abuse argued that pedophilia may be an orientation—not a perversion—and not even a deviation. She suggested pedophiles, too, may have sexual rights.[69]

When the so-called gay pride parade finally invaded Colorado Springs in June 1993, several marchers blatantly wore T-shirts and signs emblazoned with the words "We recruit." Can they make the threat to traditional families more graphic than this? Same-sexers are forced to recruit to perpetuate their values. This prejudices their case where children and families are concerned.

Politically correct heterosexuals argue blindly in favor of full legal status for homosexuality. They defend this feel-good position for the sake of those gays who are supposedly committed, monogamous domestic partners. But isn't that backwards? Shouldn't society err on the side of caution for the sake of children first?

As to the definition of family, the politically correct crowd would say that medical science has changed the rules of procreation, therefore homosexual marriage should be allowed. Females can have children through artificial insemination, they say; families defined by nature are no longer normal and valid.

In an attempt to discredit nature, a recent edition of the *Denver Post Magazine* glowingly featured scenes of domestic bliss in the home of the founder of Colorado's Lesbian Avengers. Focusing on the Avenger's seven year old daughter, a *Post* caption read, "The fact that her parents are lesbians makes no difference to her."[70] Wrong. Later in the piece the little girl set the reporter straight. Pointing to her mother she said, "She had me." Pointing to the other woman she said, "She didn't." At least one person in the room acknowledged the limits of nature.

The lesbian "father" went on to complain that she had no genetic bond to the child. What did she expect, to actually *be* a father? "My feeling," she said, "is probably not much different than a guy who's impotent or sterile." Wrong again. No matter how this woman meditated on it, she could never produce a sperm. Her situation and feelings are quite different from "a guy who is impotent or sterile."

The little girl in the story had a daddy, in fact. Her mother admitted that her daughter had been conceived through the cooperation of an ex-boyfriend. Imagine the scene in their home some day when the ex-boyfriend comes for a visit? The precocious little girl will probably point to him and say, "He's my father." Pointing to the other woman, "You're not." It remains impossible to deny nature (and most children.)

Insemination for infertile heterosexuals is not equal to insemination for homosexual women. On the one hand you have a natural union, on the other women must rip-off the opposite gender for a basic endowment of sperm. Society is justified in giving its blessing to only the natural situation.

Against this societal norm, the homosexual community suddenly promotes whatever is queer. They celebrate diversity, magnify dysfunctional families and bizarre sexuality, and publicize every non-traditional means of conception. Loathing the limits of nature, they seem driven to prefer the unnatural, the artificial, the queer. It follows that their political agenda would demand that artificial insemination be declared normal and equal to natural insemination.

"What about children of divorce who find themselves with Heather's two mommies, or Daddy and his roommate," someone might ask? "Shouldn't we allow adoption in these cases?"

Suddenly we are no longer speaking of family values but of divorce values. No matter how many divorces we suffer in our population, they are a blight on our national record. They should not become the standard, nor should they create a new family definition. (I write as one who has suffered this catastrophic failure. I feel great sympathy for those who go through divorce, yet. . . .)

A rampant divorce rate does not justify gay adoption. Society should not bend its norms to fit its deviations. Marriage remains the standard. A man and woman, a mother and father define a family. There are broken families, but only one ideal family.

Civilized Western society should *tolerate* children in same-sex arrangements when divorce has created this possibility. Kind tolerance is the *humane* response here. But taking the plunge into the abyss of calling these arrangements normal, and giving them society's stamp of approval, is social suicide. Homosexual adoption takes this destructive plunge. Discrimination of the highest order is required to preserve the wall of separation between a child in custody of a divorced homosexual parent and a child being adopted by a homosexual couple. It seems in the best interest of society to draw the line against homosexual adoption to preserve the very idea of marriage and family.

On the heels of the child custody issue, the politically correct crowd relentlessly unloads their demand for legal same-sex marriages. (Why shouldn't they? The questions are practically the same.) But historically heterosexual marriage, with its natural ability to procreate, receives the exclusive blessing of Western societies. To grant homosexual marriages, that high standard must first be cheapened, and perhaps discarded. With the media screaming about the failure of the traditional family, we seem perilously close to doing just that.

Not long before he lost his re-election bid, New York Mayor David Dinkins licensed same-sex domestic partnerships. His diverse city hardly needed more legal definitions of family . . . or non-family. (If everything is a family, nothing is a family.) Nor did the city of New York need weaker glue to the ties that bind its near-chaos together. In the age of AIDS, for example, homosexual sex clubs proliferated under Dinkin's nose. So much so, the city Health Department created a new job description, "Sex Monitor." Believe it or not, a force of New York City inspectors oversee gay orgies at 25 sex clubs under their jurisdiction. They are paid to keep an eye on things lest the lusty participants forget to use their condoms.[71]

Dinkins didn't seem to have a moral—or even an historical—

clue in handing out his cheap domestic partnerships. Before the dominant influence of Judeo-Christianity, homosexual arrangements were common in ancient cultures.[72] Western Civilization rejected these marriages for the good of the social order and so should New York City. No society is meant to carry every conceivable social burden just because it exists. The standards of marriage and family can help keep cultural overload from overwhelming a population. What the former mayor did to New York, for whatever political expediency, seems the societal equivalent of shooting his city up with a dirty needle. Perhaps his Republican successor will do better.

The compelling need for society to give away the bonds of matrimony to homosexual arrangements is simply not there. Desire for the status is not reason enough. A lot of people in our society want things they cannot, or should not, get.

There should be wise deliberation as we pause to consider changing the definition of marriage and family for the sake of the homosexual agenda.

HOW MUCH WILL IT COST?

The following story is digested from the *Wall Street Journal*, July 20, 1992.[73]

Anne Ready and Maureen Rowe of Madison, Wisconsin had put a notice in the classified ads for a third roommate. They didn't know about the city's gay rights ordinance. When a woman who claimed to be a lesbian answered the ad, Ann replied, "No thanks." The lesbian filed a discrimination complaint with the city. Ann and Maureen were summoned before Madison's Equal Opportunities Commission. They were interrogated for hours, assessed damages totalling $1,000, and ordered to write "an acceptable letter of apology" to the lesbian. In addition, they were to have their rental decisions monitored for the next two years. They were also assigned to attend a sensitivity training course conducted by the United, a local homosexual organization.

At this point Anne and Maureen obtained the services of a lawyer *pro bono*. He requested a formal hearing with the Equal

Opportunity Commission to review this case. It was finally held two years later. At that 1991 hearing things went from bad to worse. Anne and Maureen's moral objections to lesbianism were not considered valid. They were ordered to pay damages of $3,000 because they had caused the lesbian to suffer "humiliation, crying spells, and an inability to concentrate." They were also ordered to pay $300 to reimburse the lesbian for a deposit she had lost on a subsequent apartment due to her emotional distress. To add insult to injury, they were told to pay the lesbian's legal fees, which amounted to several thousands of dollars. They pleaded that the ruling would bankrupt them and were told "that's not our problem." The Equal Opportunity Commission ruled that Anne and Maureen had lost their constitutional right to privacy when they had entered the public marketplace with a classified ad.

In June of 1992, the city council of Madison was besieged with public outrage over this case and they belatedly realized their mistake. They ruled that they never intended to hold roommates to the same anti-discrimination standards they demanded of landlords. (Big favor to Wisconsin landlords!) This meant that Anne and Maureen would not have to pay the $3,000 in damages, the $300 deposit, nor the lesbian's legal fees.

When a semblance of justice finally prevailed in this case, the cost in time and wasted energies had been high. Anne and Maureen's lawyer added up his legal tab for reaching this decision, it totaled near $10,000. Among other things, this true story of gay laws gone amuck reveals how difficult it is to make reasonable changes in politically correct systems once they are in place.

Gay rights policies are already in place all across the United States, many of them instituted through businesses and local municipalities. The policies seem generous and enlightened on the surface. As someone said, "they seem like the nice thing to do." But it is unlikely that many administrators have looked far enough ahead to see what the nice policies will mean when push comes to shove.

CFV decided to dedicate at least a portion of its campaign efforts to education, especially for those in Colorado who felt that giving homosexuals their agenda would cost them nothing. "Quit picking on these poor people," many well-meaning voters said. "Let them have their way."

Instead of capitulating to the easy tide of political correctness, CFV began to catalog the new problems gay rights laws were creating across America. They began to publish case histories of precious freedoms that had already been lost:

. . . In 1991, a California Superior Court ordered Shell Oil to pay $5.3 million for the wrongful discharge of Jeffrey Collins, a homosexual manager. Collins was fired when his superiors discovered a memo he wrote on an office computer advertising an off-the-job safe sex party for homosexual men. The court ruled that Collin's memo was "political activity" protected under California's Supreme Court precedent.[74]

. . . In 1982, the *Christian Science Monitor* fired an alleged lesbian because of her sexual orientation. Though the Massachusetts Supreme Court ruled that the *Monitor* had grounds to terminate based on religious interests, they have allowed the alleged lesbian to pursue tort damages. The *Monitor* has decided not to reveal the amount of their escalating legal expenses for fear of encouraging a rash of malicious lawsuits.[75]

. . . In Laguna Beach, California, a city with a gay mayor and one of the nation's largest homosexual communities, a nine-year-old boy entered a little league baseball rest room. He saw three men engaged in group sex. He ran to his mother, crying and frightened. She attempted to file a complaint with the city but the city had enacted ordinances especially protecting gay people, and prosecuting homosexual activity had little priority in Laguna Beach.[76] No one went to jail.

. . . In Boulder, Colorado, with a gay rights ordinance on the books, the chief of police refused to open his department to a Boy Scout Explorer program. The program amounts to an internship for boys 14 to 21 years of age interested in a career in police work. Boulder's Chief Koby trashed the project, saying, "The Boy Scouts have a discrimination policy. They don't allow gays, so that's that."[77]

. . . Also in Boulder, residents report being told by the city that they will face legal action if they ask prospective roommates any questions about their sexual orientation. And Colorado University (located there) informed students that sexual orientation is not an appropriate reason to request switching dorm roommates.[78]

. . . In Minneapolis, the Big Brothers organization was prosecuted for telling a mother that a prospective Big Brother for her son was homosexual. Years of legal harassment followed. The Big Brothers caved-in. They adopted a national policy of "accepting gay men as prospective Big Brothers to fatherless youths."[79]

. . . In Minnesota, the Catholic Archdiocese was assessed a fine and damages of $35,000 for refusing to open Church facilities to a homosexual club.[80]

. . . Again in Minnesota, a Catholic priest was sued in a case that dragged on for years, for refusing to hire a homosexual to teach in a Catholic school.[81]

. . . In Hawaii, churches were warned that regardless of their beliefs, all staff positions save the pastorate would have to be made available to homosexuals. This absurd ruling was only altered after vigorous legal challenge.[82]

. . . In New Jersey, a gay rights law threatened to force churches to unite homosexuals in holy matrimony. After legal intervention, now they have been exempted from complying with the discrimination laws.[83] (This means that Scriptural Judeo-Christian morality has now been redefined by that court as discrimination, leaving the church's ability to express and practice morality completely in the hands of a judge.)

How much has been lost through aggressive homosexual court action? Under the combined efforts of the ACLU, the homosexual lobby, and politically correct judges and politicians, 25 states abolished sodomy laws between 1961 and 1983 (before AIDS began giving the country second thoughts on the matter). A growing list of 14 states have enacted hate or bias-crime laws that include sexual orientation. Many more are pending. To date, 16 states and more than 90 cities have created local rip-off laws incorrectly patterned after the federal Civil Rights Act of 1964[84]. Other states, like Colorado, fell to special executive orders from their governors to the same effect.

It is the opinion of the author that each of these laws can be removed if the local citizenry will take them to court. Many gay rights laws infringe the rights of people with moral convictions as well as those with natural or traditional objections to homosexuality. In most cases, local gay rights laws grant homosexuality protected class status even though sexual orientation does not qualify under federal guidelines. These laws should be challenged in the same way the homosexual lobby has challenged Amendment 2 in court.

Someone—somewhere and sometime—must begin to care enough to win back this legal ground. It will be expensive. Constitutional attorneys estimate that fighting one case to a Supreme Court decision (which is where Amendment 2 will go) will take perhaps five years. Each case will cost nearly $250,000. Does any group in America care enough to mount this kind of resistance?

Many undecided voters in the Amendment 2 campaign began to ask: How did the homosexual lobby become so powerful and pervasive? Through the ballot box? No. Because they are a large part of our population? No. The answer: "money" provides homosexuals their most influential numbers. Their own posh magazine, *Out*, boasts that its "readers have an average household income of $72,300 and 94 percent of them carry a major credit card according to a survey conducted by Beta Research."[85] This is one rich sexual lobby.

Investigative journalists have revealed all too often the appalling susceptibility of elected officials to the lure of cash and perks. These tempting trinkets are dangled before their eyes by wealthy special interest groups like the homosexual lobby. Homosexuals have more financial persuasion power *per capita* than just about any other influence group. They had enough to drop $3.5 million into Bill Clinton's presidential campaign. They have raised much more than that fighting Amendment 2 and other gay rights opponents. Their Washington, D.C. political budget has expanded rapidly in the first months of 1993 alone. This kind of money turns heads in high places:

. . . "Everybody is going after gay business," says Sean Strub, owner of the Strub Media Group. "This is happening in such a targeted way that no one else would recognize it."

. . . *Advertising Age*, the media insider's magazine, boasts the following space ad: TAP INTO THE $377 BILLION UNTAPPED GAY MALE MARKET.[86]

. . . Eric Miller, editor of *Research Alert* writes, "America's gay and lesbian community is emerging as one of the nation's most educated and affluent, and Madison Avenue is beginning to explore the potential for a market that may be worth hundreds of billions of dollars."[87]

. . . "Gay greenbacks are very powerful and the gay and lesbian community is a virtual motherlode of untapped sales," says Robert Bray of the National Gay and Lesbian Task Force in Washington, D.C.[88]

. . . Denver's Mayor Wellington Webb has a gay and lesbian advisory committee to monitor the interests of the same-sex community statewide. (Is this really necessary? Or is it simply one of the more profitable minorities to pay attention to these days?)

. . . According to *Time* magazine, "Because [homosexuals] are highly mobilized and tend to have more discretionary income, gays have an impact on elections that is disproportionate to their number." Citing Clinton's campaign donation from homosexuals, the article goes on to confirm the weakness of the ruling elite to be influenced by these funds: "This power has even greater effect on the congressional level," *Time* says.[89]

When asking city councils, mayors, governors, legislators, media executives, and other big government types to grant them favorable treatment, homosexual lobbyists cite their combined billions in annual incomes, their millions of discretionary political dollars, their expensive college degrees earned at three times the ratio of the general population,[90] their high levels of representation in Hollywood and other media power centers, and their high rates of professional and managerial positions.

In the presence of this politically eager group, elected officials can suddenly feel that they know what is best for their city and state (not to mention for themselves). In an effort to appear tolerant and enlightened, they may forget things like family values and moral restraint, accommodating the wishes of this wealthy sexual lobby.

During his campaign Bill Clinton could not refuse their millions, along with the Hollywood celebrity perks that went with it. Of course, pay back meant that our new president would allow gays-in-the-military to dominate the nation during his first weeks in national office. It also meant that the homosexual lobby would hold a $500,000 Democratic Party pledge hostage until the President followed through on his campaign promise to reverse the military ban. Nothing is free after all. Pay back also meant Clinton would support the homosexual lobby's efforts to gain special protection under the Civil Rights Act of 1964.

But the homosexual lobby cannot be blamed for this, strictly speaking. They are looking out for number one. They have gained their economic power and are using it to sweeten their own legislation. Unfortunately, their efforts to get ahead walk over families, even robbing the civil rights empowerment intended for historically disadvantaged racial minorities.

For this, then, the homosexual lobby *must* be held accountable, without pulling any punches. Their greed, selfishness, and hypocrisy are not to be excused simply because they seem driven to live life in excess. The laws and policies they demand for themselves are parasitical. The essence of this is seen in their insistence that we put *our* money where the consequence of *their* behavior is, despite their high level of per capita wealth.

"Foul!" cry the politically correct liberals, "AIDS is everybody's problem!"

A contradiction exists here big enough to swallow the Titanic. Why do homosexuals stage their AIDS victims at the head of their political parades? Why do they continue to make their huge quilts, commemorating homosexuals who have died of AIDS? Why do they display the quilts on national TV during AIDS fund raisers?

Why have they argued in court that Amendment 2 will spread the disease of AIDS? If AIDS is everybody's problem, why is it suddenly a homosexual problem in these cases?

The answer reveals why straight thinking Americans must oppose the gay agenda: AIDS is a homosexual problem when it gains sympathy for their lifestyle; it is everyone else's problem when the medical bills are due. This is completely self-serving. Ten percent of the National Institutes of Health budget goes for AIDS research, far outstripping the proportionate dole for cancer and heart disease, the real killers in America. And yet sexual lobbyists are screaming for more, more, *more!*

These are the kinds of excessive policies that America is being told to swallow wholesale, or else wear the scarlet label, "bigot." At the very least, it makes no sense to allow such social and political deals to be struck in high places between this rich sexual lobby and the ruling elite. Inevitably, the people not represented at the table will pay more than their share.

Which is another reason why Colorado's fight has become so important to America. Until Amendment 2 came along, gay rights laws were not fully debated and voted on by the general population. Most gay rights laws were passed, not by the people, but by enlightened elected officials. This backroom approach has provided the gay lobby their best route to forced affirmation. In Colorado, the first clear choice given to the people on the question of protected class status for gays, the cultural elite and homosexual lobby landed on their backsides.

6

Lessons from the campaign trail

Colorado for Family Values' nine-month campaign to sell Amendment 2 employed three chief strategies:

1. attack the major premise of the gay rights movement, disputing their claim to protected class status under civil rights law, and,
2. only if necessary, raise the behavioral and health statistics about homosexuality in order to motivate voters to think about the issues, and,
3. throughout the campaign, let the homosexual agenda and its threat to democratic freedom provide grist for the on-going debate.

The position-paper Tony had written had by this time grown from 17 to 60 pages of material addressing these areas of concern. Packed with more than enough argument to fuel the fight ahead, CFV committees pored over his research. The homosexual civil rights position seemed full of holes and CFV felt it could prove that they did not deserve protected class status. It was clear that for people claiming to be homosexual, this status amounted to special rights and advantages over the general population.

But from the petition process, CFV had learned that its greatest problem would be in learning to effectively deal with the press. All naïve notions of journalistic integrity had already been destroyed through the news reporting during the petition drive.

NEWS MEDIA IMBALANCE

As soon as the language of Amendment 2 had been made known

to the public, the news rooms of the state were faced with a major decision: How would they describe Amendment 2? And what would they say it ultimately meant to the people of Colorado? According to CFV Chairman, Will Perkins, "Language doesn't shape the campaign—it *is* the campaign." At the very least, the news media could give a distinct advantage to one side or the other in the coming election. Or they could surprise everyone and choose to present both sides fairly.

Unfortunately, homosexual watchdog groups had a long score card of successes in getting the media to swallow their lexicon of self-interested definitions. For example, when it served the homosexual agenda to refer to themselves as "gay" rather than homosexual, they got the media to go along. When it served their agenda to use the term "sexual preference," they got it. When sexual preference backfired, sounding as if they had chosen the behavior, the pliable news rooms switched to "sexual orientation," sounding like something that can't be helped.

When homosexuals began dying of AIDS in disproportionate numbers, they got news editors to eliminate the term "innocent AIDS victim," which distinguished those who were infected through sexual behavior from those infected through blood transfusions or the indiscretions of a spouse. Why? Because Congress had used the term "innocent AIDS victims" to justify the blocking of public funds for groups that promote high risk homosexual activity. Homosexuals were determined not to be left out of Uncle Sam's dole so they worked to erase "innocent victim" from America's news rooms. They were successful. In the words of Robert Bray, spokesman for the National Gay and Lesbian Task Force, "When we were able to educate the press not to use 'innocent victims,' we saw Congress back off."[91] Unlike other diseases with risk factors, AIDS funding now flows freely, regardless of the behavior contributing to the infection.

With a powerful track record like this behind the homosexual lobby, Colorado for Family Values had no illusions that their own efforts with the press would prove effective. Still, they had to try. Tony Marco possessed perhaps the most news media savvy in this regard. He knew how to cultivate media relationships in spite of the antagonistic environment. Unfortunately, much of his effectiveness had been neutralized by his financial crisis and resignation from CFV. Still, he advised the procedures used by CFV, and sometimes accompanied delegations to news organizations in the state.

The first CFV objective was to win a truthful—or at least a *sane* definition—of Amendment 2: "Amendment 2 denies protected class status to homosexuality, thereby prohibiting government from dictating sexual values in the private sector." This description told the truth about both the negative and positive effect the amendment would have on the state.

News outlets flatly rejected such balanced definitions. Instead they focused myopically on the fact that gay rights ordinances in Denver, Boulder, and Aspen would be nullified by the new law: "Amendment 2 bans laws protecting gays and lesbians from discrimination based on their sexual orientation," they said. While this description could be called technically half-true, the half of the truth they left out concerned the amendment's effect on heterosexual Colorado, roughly 99% of the state. Amendment 2 removed the government's hand from imposing homosexual values over them, and restored and insured for them freedom of speech and association. To describe Amendment 2 in purely negative terms was a half-truth that simply amounted to a lie.

One militantly narrow news description read: "bans laws protecting gays from discrimination in housing and employment." They were essentially saying: "big bad Amendment 2 strips helpless gays of their rights." This assertion however, was *proven totally false* in July of '93, seven months after the election. A court action in Denver under an existing state law upheld a wrongful discharge suit brought by a homosexual man. He had been fired because he was gay, but his court action was not taken under a gay rights law. He filed as any wrongfully fired employee might file—he had recourse against wrongful discharge. Makes perfect sense.

CFV had said all along that homosexuals were adequately protected under existing laws. That they didn't need gay rights laws to get justice in America. Here was a case in point. Not only did this gay man win his case, he took home a whopping $91,000 damage award![92]

During the campaign CFV spokesmen had been labeled "bigoted" and "hateful" for claiming that this kind of court action was possible for any homosexual. But following this large cash award, Colorado experienced a sudden media silence on the subject. No apologies to Amendment 2 supporters for the former defamation of character. No credit given to the clear foresight of CFV . . . where credit was due.

Throughout the Amendment 2 campaign, television news coverage tended to follow newspaper policy rather than provide fresh angles on the Amendment 2 story. Ed Sardella, Channel 9 TV news anchor in Denver, went so far as to quote the *Denver Post's* legal experts on Amendment 2, calling the amendment the law "that would legalize discrimination against homosexuals." His claim was applauded by the *Denver Post's* TV-Radio editor the next day, writing that, indeed, Sardella had described the very heart of Amendment 2.[93]

Sardella did not describe the heart of Amendment 2. He described the heart of a cabal of news associates who wanted to kill Amendment 2.

"People need to understand," Will Perkins often repeated, "there is no blanket protection from discrimination in America. People have learned to abhor the word because of our experience with racial discrimination, but the fact remains that no one can claim they are discriminated against unless they are part of a special protected class. The law is not out there to put everyone in this special class. If it did, what would be special about it? That's why we say, 'to get to claim discrimination in this country is a special right, not an equal right.'"

The press seemed incapable of grasping this. After the election, Colorado Springs' CBS affiliate, Channel 11, continued to describe the law as: "Amendment 2 prohibits laws which protect homosexuals from discrimination"—period. This description left out the all-important qualifying phrase, "based on their sexual orientation." The effect of this irresponsible description was to throw gasoline on the hatred-fire already burning in Colorado. Channel 11 News committed an act of societal arson. As the state fights to regain its fine reputation nationwide, many such newsrooms owe Colorado an apology.

The truth is, under Amendment 2 a homosexual may claim discrimination *based on* the same criteria as any other American: race, religion, gender, handicap. To claim discrimination *based on* a sexual orientation, however, is another matter. (For a full explanation see, PROTECTED CLASS STATUS p. 101)

One more point about discrimination *based on* sexual orientation: a sexual orientation may include anything that arouses a person. (Make your own list here.) Adultery, for example, is a sexual orientation for some men and women. It is an orientation that suffers discrimination, too. (Ask former presidential candidate Gary Hart.) Why should a homosexual receive special protection *based on* having a same gender orientation? Saying no to this unreasonable use of the law is what Amendment 2 was about. It was not about depriving homosexuals of their ability to claim discrimination, as was repeated every day in the press.

Colorado news headlines were sometimes perniciously skewed to damage Amendment 2. Two weeks before the election a headline writer for the *Rocky Mountain News* perverted perhaps the best legal analysis of Amendment 2 published during the entire campaign. A clear description had been written by a respected attorney, Shawn Mitchell, President of the Colorado Federalist Society. Mitchell's legal analysis, among other things, confirmed CFV's description of the amendment, saying: "Amendment 2 is the only way to keep government out of the values business and truly 'leave family values to families'."

Instead of displaying his article with a pro-amendment sub-head, the *Rocky Mountain News*' editor warned potential readers: AMENDMENT 2 COULD FORCE ONE-SIDED AGREEMENTS.[94] This statement reversed the actual meaning of the article. A proper rendering would have read: *GAY RIGHTS' LAWS FORCE ONE-SIDED AGREEMENTS*. Big difference. Apparently the *Rocky Mountain News*' headline writer felt no qualms in misleading the reader about the contents of this rare pro-amendment article.

The national press took its lead from Colorado newspapers and largely followed their descriptions of Amendment 2. However, after the election, the *Washington Times* independently described the law as, "Amendment 2, the landmark state constitutional amendment that prohibits granting homosexuality protected class status under civil rights laws."[95] This description reveals that the news media *is* capable of approximating fairness when it decides to do so. In Colorado they simply decided not to do so.

Analyzing the news media's consistent description of Amendment 2, three distortions emerge:

First, in the phrase "Amendment 2 bans laws protecting gays," Colorado newsmen chose to characterize the amendment by its effect on a sexual minority, ignoring its benefit to the majority. That approach blindly pledged allegiance to a self-proclaimed minority.

Second, they deliberately characterized Amendment 2 negatively, ignoring its positive effects. They said it banned something good, "protection from discrimination," instead of something bad, "government coercion."

The need for gay protection from discrimination is a disputed idea in America and Colorado. The federal government has consistently ruled for more than fifteen years that homosexuals do not suffer the level of deprivation that makes protected class status necessary. Since that is true, it must be said that not only Amendment 2, but Congress itself, has denied to homosexuals what Colorado newsmen called "protection from discrimination." The language of Amendment 2 was—and is—in harmony with the federal government standards in this regard.

Therefore, the entire idea that homosexuals needed protection from discrimination remained *a disputed idea* between Denver, Boulder, and Aspen, and the federal government. However, government coercion was a sure thing in these Colorado cities. Their gay rights laws made it so. The major description of Amendment 2 for the State of Colorado was that it repealed these bastions of government coercion. The unproven claim to protection from discrimination was the lesser issue. It could not be truthfully used to describe Amendment 2 and its meaning for the state.

Third, newsmen cast Amendment 2 as the aggressor against a helpless group of victims. They said it "banned laws protecting gays and lesbians . . ." ignoring the fact that gay rights laws in Denver, Boulder, and Aspen had aggressed against freedoms of association, speech, and moral expression for the heterosexual population. But no aggression was ever acknowledged in these laws. Not even the proposed Ethnic Harassment Bill, which tried to make criticism of homosexuality a felony, was labelled aggressive. Always, this description was given to Amendment 2.

A post-election analysis of 571 Colorado newspaper articles sponsored by Focus on the Family's *Citizen Magazine* revealed some irrefutable numbers. These numbers properly indicate the level of press antagonism against Amendment 2:

> Quotes supporting the amendment were printed only half as often as quotes against it. Supporters making statements in favor of the amendment were outnumbered by those against, six-to-one. Not one religious authority was cited supporting Amendment 2 in the 571 articles. Nine religious authorities were cited opposing it. Forty-eight government authorities were cited opposing Amendment 2, including the governor, most mayors, city council members, and civil rights bureaucrats; only eleven government officials were quoted as having anything positive to say about the amendment whatsoever, and these were not all sterling endorsements.[96]

Anyone who opposes the homosexual agenda should not expect to win the war of words with the news media. It is already lost. Headline writers and editors are pledged to publish anything that advances the official homosexual line. This has become so obvious that Maria Shriver, in NBC's homosexual showcase, *The Gay '90s: Sex, Power and Influence,* dared to ask a New York magazine editor: "We often hear about how liberal the media is. Is it also gay?" To which the young man replied, "I think so."

In Colorado, we can only agree.

The same appears to be true nationwide. In February '93, a Joseph Sobran column appeared concerning the pro-homosexual campaigning in a single issue of the *New York Times*. "The old journalists had a sense of duty," he wrote, "the new ones have a sense of mission. There's a big difference."

Then he described the issue of the *New York Times* in question: "First there was the front-page headline 'Pentagon Aides to Study

Option of Segregation for Gay Soldiers.' I get it, Segregation, him bad! Then there were the accompanying stories 'Open Hostility to Homosexuals Outside Navy Base.' Hostility! Open! When you read the story, it turned out that the 'hostility' meant only discomfort at the prospect of being cooped up with homosexuals in the tight quarters of a ship. Turning the page, one found 'Death of a Gay Sailor: A Brutal Killing in Japan Brings Questions and Fears.' The murder of the sailor, Allen Schindler, occurred months ago, and isn't news either. It's being hyped now to support the gay agenda. This illustrates why so much of what now passes for journalism is really propaganda . . . *the point of propaganda is to soften the public mind to the point where it accepts contradictions without question.*" [emphasis added.]

If nothing else, understanding how committed news teams are to homosexual rights begins to give a clue as to how their laws made so much progress before anyone figured out how to stop them. Or even that they needed to be stopped. Imagine having the news media's help to soften all the nightmare stories about forced affirmation of homosexuality? David Koresh might have become governor of Texas with that kind of help.

EDITORIALS, COLUMNS, & CARTOONS

Under the circumstances, Colorado for Family Values wisely decided not to try to influence the press to their advantage. Instead, they decided to tell the truth as best they could and let the chips fall where they may.

As the campaign progressed, a hopeful sign emerged. The opinion pages of Colorado newspapers began to reveal that CFV's message was getting through to the people in spite of the media slant. Letters to the editor began to take the news media to task for their reporting on the amendment. More and more people seemed to confirm a Joseph Sobran conclusion: ". . . the public is wising up to propaganda techniques."[97]

The other area of support came from newspaper editorial departments and columnists. While the front page of the Colorado Springs *Gazette Telegraph* remained politically correct, the editorial department put on their thinking caps and presented Amendment 2 according to its clear legal analysis. *Gazette Telegraph* editorial chief Dan Griswald and his staff are to be commended for analyzing the amendment and its effect on Colorado with courage and accuracy. Homosexual demonstrators marched against the newspaper because of their clear editorial position.

The *Gazette* opinion pages also boast one of the most effective political cartoonists in America today, Chuck Asay. Also, one of the most conservative. His simple pictures proved to be worth a thousand words in favor of Amendment 2 on any given day.

Thankfully, CFV also found its cause presented well by nationally syndicated columnists like George Will, Don Feder, William F. Buckley, Jr., Suzanne Fields, Mona Charen, Joseph Sobran, and Cal Thomas.

The *Denver Post* and the *Rocky Mountain News* published pro-amendment local columnists as well, most remarkably, Al Knight at the *Denver Post*. While these remained far fewer in number to the anti-amendment news page diatribes, their work seemed to have a more than equal effect on the public mind.

Still, it must be noted that in the world of journalism, nothing published on an opinion page is considered news. As far as fairness dictates, both sides of an argument should be presented on the front pages equally. In Colorado, front page policy and news headline selection consistently fell in favor of gay rights, and against Amendment 2. In Colorado, without the opinion pages, columnists, and cartoonists, CFV simply would not have had its side presented in the Amendment 2 debate.

CIVIL RIGHTS

The U.S. Constitution guarantees civil rights to all citizens. Amendment 2 in no way compromises that.

— Ignacio Rodriguez, Chairman, Colorado Civil Rights Commission, 1992

One false assumption made early in the campaign was that the entire civil rights establishment was one monolithic obstacle to Amendment 2. No one entertained the idea that CFV might actually win the favor of civil rights professionals. After all, Rabbi Steven

Foster, the recent Chairman of the state Civil Rights Commission, doubled as both a commission member, while heading the anti-amendment organization, EPOC (Equal Protection of Colorado). The seven sitting Civil Rights Commission board members had voted 6-to-1 to publicly oppose Amendment 2. The lone dissenting vote had come from incoming Chairman, Ignacio Rodriguez. Not only that, Jack Lang y Marquez, Director of the Colorado Civil Rights Division, had thrown his official weight in favor of gay rights laws and against Amendment 2. Who could blame CFV for not expecting any help here?

CFV hoped that the actions of the Civil Rights Commission could be exploited during the campaign as self-serving, knowing that increasing the number of protected classes would enlarge their bureaucratic power over the private sector. The conservative principle of less government might work for the amendment here, but probably none of the civil rights luminaries themselves would come CFV's way.

Tony Marco, the former '60s civil rights radical, did a doubletake when in the spring of the campaign he received unsolicited support from six of Colorado's top former and present Civil Rights leaders: Ignacio Rodriguez, the new sitting Chairman of the state Civil Rights Commission; Tom Duran, a civil rights professional over four regions of state jurisdiction; attorney John Franklin, past Chairman of the Colorado Civil Rights Commission; and Robert Wintersmith, Director of Research and Education for the state Civil Rights Division. Furthermore, leading members of the black civil rights movement stepped forward: Rev. Joseph L. Morrison, a pioneering civil rights giant; Rev. Milton Proby, a former Colorado Civil Rights Commission Chairman who had served under four Colorado Governors; and inner city youth gang ministers from Denver, Rev. Leon and Priscilla Kelly, who amounted to local living legends in humanitarian circles.

If these six state civil rights authorities spoke-out publicly in favor of Amendment 2, CFV knew that it would split the civil rights establishment right down the middle. It would also bring in a portion of the inner city and minority vote, a part of the electorate Amendment 2 seemed bound to lose. In other words, these endorsements amounted to CFV's first major break in the campaign.

These civil rights leaders were liberals who clearly understood the damage that would result from adding homosexuality to the list of protected classes. It would undo the entire progress of legitimate minorities through civil rights. For one thing, civil rights insiders had seen a 19% reduction in staff in recent years, concurrent with a 30% increase in case loads. Adding another class of people who didn't even qualify to this overburdened administration, would further erode ethnic gains. On the strength of this understanding, these principled civil rights leaders stood ready to publicly refute the politically correct agendas of Rabbi Steven Foster and Jack Lang y Marquez.

On June 11, Colorado for Family Values called a press conference to announce their incredible civil rights coup. Tom Duran, John Franklin, and Ignacio Rodriguez were present before the cameras to endorse Amendment 2 and to field questions from the press.

Franklin said, and underscored in a signed statement: "homosexuality, bisexuality, and lesbianism does not lend itself to what is known among civil rights authorities as special class protection." He went on to conclude that homosexuals already have the protection they need under normal civil litigation. They can fight against harassment, defamation, or verbal abuse. They can protect their property and persons through normal criminal laws. Why seek special protection under extra civil rights laws unless they are seeking more than equality?

Ignacio Rodriguez confirmed CFV's contention that including homosexuals as a new *minority* class would "seriously damage the legitimate civil rights protections that had been gained by ethnic and racial minorities." He also added his professional opinion to that of CFV, that homosexuals were using state civil rights laws to ultimately go after protected class status under the Civil Rights Act of 1964 at the federal level. (This was long before the gay lobby admitted it themselves at their '93 march in Washington, D.C.)

Tom Duran bluntly challenged, "I don't see gay ghettos, I don't see the gays homeless, I don't see the gays being disadvantaged politically or economically. I don't think they are in a class with the traditional minority groups, Hispanics, blacks or Indians, women. I think they have tremendous economic control—all elements not present with the other [minority] groups."

To conclude the press conference, Tony Marco quoted an old black preacher from the deep south: "The freedom bus that went to Selma was never meant to go on to Sodom."

Ignacio surprised everyone during questioning, revealing that he had received death threats after breaking solidarity with the state Civil Rights Commission on this issue.

News? Hardly. Following the conference, CFV looked in vain for the coverage of this significant story. At last a few meager quotes from Rodriguez and Franklin were found buried in the second page of a *Gazette Telegraph* article about the income levels of the homosexual community.[98] Incomes of homosexuals? How did this rate top billing over a story of a major breach of civil rights solidarity concerning Amendment 2?

Rodriguez, Duran, and Franklin's opinions counted *bigtime* in this debate, yet not even a picture of these civil rights stalwarts warranted the paper's attention. Instead, the paper featured a picture of two homosexual lovers. Why? Because these two men claimed that their neighbor had expressed a hateful and discriminatory remark to one of them: "Listen, sweetheart," the bigoted neighbor had allegedly said. This was news?

The buried second page quotes from Rodriguez, Franklin, and Duran were further countered with the disclaimer, "Rodriguez and Franklin don't represent a consensus in the civil rights field." (Oh, thank you for pointing that out, *Gazette*. This sums it all up. It isn't that these men demonstrated courage in breaking rank with the rest of the civil rights board. It has nothing to do with one of them receiving a death threat for doing so.)

Ten days later, in a telling column on the *Denver Post* perspective pages, Al Knight showed his boldness by reporting on the news blackout of the historic news conference with Rodriguez, Franklin, and Duran:

> . . . [the news conference] received no coverage by major Denver media which had been duly reminded of the event.

IGNACIO RODRIGUEZ, 1992 Chairman of the Colorado Civil Rights Commission, stood against his collegues in support of Amendment 2.

> One might suppose that when a current and former chairman of the Civil Rights Commission and one of the highest ranking Civil Rights Commission staffers stick their necks out and endorse a controversial amendment that it might have received more notice.[99]

Among other things, the news conference with these civil rights experts demonstrated effectively that Amendment 2's motives and language had been well founded—not on hatred, not on bigotry, not on religious moral standards—but on solid civil rights thinking: good policy for political liberals as well as conservatives.

In the days to follow, Tom Duran was pressured by his civil rights superiors to change his position. He resisted. They began to harass him until a threatened lawsuit backed them off.

In all of this drama the press found nothing worthy to report to the people of Colorado.

PROTECTED CLASS STATUS

The Amendment 2 campaign claimed that through gay civil rights ordinances, homosexuals were trying to take for themselves the privileges and special advantages given to racial minorities. The Colorado attorney general backed CFV's claim, stating:

> Properly analyzed, the guiding intent behind Amendment 2 was not to deprive homosexuals or bisexuals of any constitutionally guaranteed rights, but to remove any state-based grounds for putting such individuals in a more favorable position vis-a-vis other citizens than would be required under federal law.[100]

A favored position for homosexuals under the law seemed completely unfair and uncalled for to the supporters of Amendment 2. To remove that favored position, the CFV campaign went forward under the slogan "Equal rights, not special rights. Stop special class status for homosexuality."

The arguments backing up this slogan arose from the evidence of homosexual rights laws already on the books, like those in

Denver, Boulder, and Aspen. These ordinances had been worded according to a predictable pattern. Each had added "sexual orientation" to the list of protected class statuses. As Denver's human rights director had put it, "Without the [gay rights] ordinance . . . civil lawsuits are possible, but illegal behavior is tough to prove when 'you're a member of an unprotected class.'"[101] What he meant to say here in plain English is that gay rights ordinances make it easier for homosexuals to convict people of discrimination against them.

Politically correct liberals say homosexuals need protected class status because of the harassment they suffer for their orientation. While most civilized people understand and accept that no one should be verbally or physically abused, they also believe the solution to the normal level of harassment is not the federal Civil Rights Act of 1964. That seems far too drastic under all but the rarest of situations.

The federal courts and Congress have consistently agreed that such protected class inclusion for homosexuals would be overkill. The real solution to normal claims of discrimination is to use laws already on the books against violence and sexual harassment. CFV supporters believed that homosexuals simply needed the courage to bring these charges to court, prosecute them, and stop asking for special consideration. The Denver gay who won a $91,000 wrongful discharge suit would likely agree.

But to homosexuals, laws against wrongful firing, violence, and harassment have never been enough. These laws merely make them equal, giving them no special advantage to force society to affirm their lifestyle. Forced affirmation requires going beyond policing actions. It requires the power to punish people for their thoughts, motives, attitudes, prejudices, hatreds, private biases—even their moral convictions.

Several states, and hundreds of local city governments, are falling under the spell of gay rights laws, and their thought police cousins, hate, and bias-crime laws. All of these fall into a new kind of tyrannical category. They are attempts to police the minds of people, not just their actions. This was the line our government is never supposed to cross.

If cities and states continue to give to homosexuality what the federal government denies them, the homosexual lobby will eventually win inclusion under the Civil Rights Act of 1964. They will do this by pointing to the growing list of gay rights ordinances around the states, saying "If the states are broadening the definition of protected class status, why not the federal government?" The government's resistance to this argument will grow weaker with each new gay rights ordinance. This ACLU empowered strategy is promoting an end-run around civil rights standards.

In Colorado, this explains why the support of the state civil rights establishment remained all important in making the homosexual case against Amendment 2. And perhaps explains why the media ignored Ignacio Rodriguez, Tom Duran, and John Franklin's testimony on behalf of Amendment 2. Their testimony was truly devastating to their strategy.

On nearly all public occasions, when campaigning against Amendment 2, the most visible spokesperson for the homosexual opposition was not the head of the Gay and Lesbian Task Force, but Rabbi Steven Foster. He, of course, gave them triple-PR-power whenever he spoke: a man of the race Hitler had persecuted, a religious leader of the same, and the immediate past chairman of the state Civil Rights Commission. More than politically correct, this spokesman was politically perfect. Through Foster the homosexuals could *Overhaul Straight America* by muddying the legal and moral waters while, "portraying themselves as among history's greatest victims" and attacking the federal civil rights guidelines as inadequate, all at the same time. Not to mention, the news media ate-it-up like an eager lap dog.

Nevertheless, under the federal civil rights guidelines, CFV found the homosexual claim to protected class status completely bogus. The story of how this discovery was made turned out to be another of the benevolent accidents of the CFV campaign. Kevin Tebedo had been in Denver browsing a Traditional Values Coalition tabloid. He ran across the federal criteria for attaining protected class status under the federal Civil Rights Act of 1964. The article stated that the homosexual community did not qualify, but offered little detail in this regard. Kevin telephoned Tony and read the main points of the article to him. Bells and whistles went off in Tony's head. He immediately recognized that explaining these criteria would supply most of CFV's civil rights argument from then on. The behavioral arguments could become secondary. No one, not even Tony, the old civil rights rabble rouser, had known about these federal standards.

Kevin faxed the article to Tony and thus began the most devastating evidence-gathering mission against the homosexual agenda in its history. It proved to be its undoing. This information not only laid waste their civil rights position, but if Amendment 2 succeeded, it would likely insure that they never were able to mount the same strategy again. (This being true, is it any wonder they have subsequently gone to court against the amendment? Only in court can a sharp, highly paid lawyer help a judge declare black to be white.)

The federal government's three main tests, or criteria, to decide who will be added to the list of specially protected classes are these:

> (1) evidence of a lack of ability to obtain average economic mean income, adequate education or cultural opportunity . . .
>
> (2) exhibit obvious, innate or immutable, non-behavioral, distinguishing characteristics, like race, color, gender, handicap, or national origin . . .
>
> (3) clearly demonstrate political powerlessness.

In these three criteria, Amendment 2's original language began to seem truly historic—of significance to the entire nation.

Here in these three criteria, then, are the compiled arguments that can defeat gay rights laws anywhere in the land.

In the case of test #1 — economic, educational, and cultural deprivation—as a group homosexuals claim an annual household income of between $50,000 and $60,000 while disadvantaged African-American households average only $12,166.[102] An even greater disparity exists in comparisons of *per capita* income. When the household size factor is figured in the studies, one finds gays supporting households of only 1.5 persons with their income, while disadvantaged black households support an average of 4 persons. By this factor, gays end up making $36,800 each,[103] while blacks fall to $3,041.[104] This means gays, who are trying to claim the same protected status as blacks, make 12 times the average individual income level.

After learning that this information had damaged their cause, a homosexual polling firm did another study lowering homosexual male households to $42,689 and female homosexual households to $36,072.[105] No matter how they manipulated the numbers gays do not qualify as a suffering minority under criterion #1.

As Tony expressed it, "If you let the rich folks into the poor folks line, then pretty soon the poor folks will be at the back of the bus again." This captured the essence of CFV's fairness and justice arguments concerning who should or should not be given protected class status.

On the educational scale homosexuals boasted graduating from college at more than three times the national average.[106] More than three times as many homosexuals have achieved managerial positions as the average American and more than four times as many homosexuals travel overseas.[107]

As to suffering cultural deprivation, one need only cite the list of Hollywood celebrity endorsements for gay rights and AIDS causes. Count the blood-red AIDS sympathy ribbons at the Academy Awards, MTV Awards, Emmys, or the number of homosexuals claiming positions in the media and journalism fields; or check the subsidies for homoerotic art given-out by the National Endowment for the Arts. This group is far from culturally deprived. Criterion #1 is a washout.

Criterion #2 — "must exhibit obvious, innate or immutable, non-behavioral, distinguishing characteristics."

On the federal list of protected classes under the Civil Rights Act of 1964, all but one of the classes (i.e., race, religion, handicap, gender) shows clearly identifiable physical characteristics. Religion is the only non-physical category here. Gay activists argue that if an exception is made for religion, homosexuality should also be given the power of these laws. It's another version of the kid brother argument: "If Johnny gets to stay out past midnight, why can't I?"

First of all, the idea that protected class status for religion would open the door for homosexuality is an insult to religion. Human spirituality is fundamental. Sexuality (never mind homosexuality) is secondary. Our original pledge to the flag, for example, recognized the sovereign place of human spirituality when it invoked the phrase "one nation under God." It would not likewise recognize human sexuality: "One nation under various sexual orientations?" Ridiculous. Putting these two ideas on the same level requires shallow thinking. Religious freedom is a First Amendment right. Sodomy remains illegal in half of the United States.

Beyond that, some would argue that religion does not need to be on the list of protected classes in the first place. In fact it should be removed. Freedom of religion is the very first American civil right. It is guaranteed even before freedom of speech in the Bill of Rights: "Congress shall make no law respecting an establishment of religion, or prohibiting the free exercise thereof; or abridging the freedom of speech. . . ." What better protection can religion have than the First Amendment? The idea that it also needs inclusion under the Civil Rights Act of 1964 trivializes religion's role in American life and culture. The purpose of the '64 act was to help poor black Americans who had no specific protection built into the Bill of Rights for them.

For the record, the Civil Rights Act of 1964 was proposed by President Kennedy one year before his death. It was the strongest civil rights bill in U.S. history, and the most controversial. Its purpose was to remedy segregation and other forms of discrimination in the South. In order to correct these wrongs, America had to sacrifice a piece of its own diversity, outlawing certain liberties held sacred by all states. It is not the kind of law America passes for just any group. For this reason the '64 debate became one of the longest and most divisive in Senate history, including a 75-day filibuster.

The '64 Act eventually won majority support because black Americans were being denied the vote, equal access to restaurants, hotels, drinking fountains, public restrooms, housing, education, and employment. They needed this exceptional law if they ever hoped for equality. But no similar record of abuses exits against religion in this country, much less homosexuality. It is quite possible that religion could be removed from the list of protected classes without losing an ounce of its precious freedom in this land. On the other hand, under the growth of special civil rights categories—especially giving gay rights a free ride on the Civil Rights Act of 1964—religion stands to lose the strength of its Bill of Rights status! And black America stands to have the true meaning of its historic struggle frittered away.

Therefore, religion—the single exception to *physical characteristics* on the protected class list—does not become a valid precedent for adding any other non-physical category. Especially not homosexuality.

What about the immutable part of criterion #2? Science and homosexuality refute it: one Kinsey study found that 85% of homosexuals changed orientation at least once in their lives, 32% twice, 13% five times or more. Meanwhile, homosexual researchers have worked overtime to gain sympathy for their orientation by claiming genetic links to homosexual behavior. No matter how many studies claiming genetic patterns related to homosexuality are cited, however, the researchers themselves quickly admit that sexual behavior is not genetically *compelled*. It may be genetically *influenced*, but nothing more.[108]

On the other hand, evidence for homosexual behavior as a choice proliferates. The *Wall Street Journal* recently cited a New York bisexual activist asking to be called "omnisexual" because "sexuality is fluid, with some people being variously heterosexual, homosexual, and bisexual at different periods in their lives."[109]

What a self-defeating confession. It shoots holes in the very idea of a protected class. How can a class be protected if it is one thing one day, another thing the next day? What's to protect? At any rate, in this admission, sexuality is showing itself to definitely be a changeable behavior, "fluid" as the omnisexual said. Orientation seems to be driven by the lust of the moment. Some are predisposed to one attraction or the other, but, in the end, the sex object is chosen. Hardly innate. Hardly immutable. Will we give people protected class status simply for having no self-restraint?

Criterion #3 — "politically powerless?"

How about a 3.5 million dollar contribution to a presidential campaign for powerlessness? How about out-spending Colorado for

Family Values 2-to-1 during the Amendment 2 campaign? How about having the favor of the Hollywood elite? (In Colorado, receiving a $20,000 check from David Geffen? A cool million from computer mogul Tim Gill?) How about demonstrating the ability to mount a nationwide boycott to punish an entire state? How about the PR power to relabel Colorado, "The State of Hate?" How about getting the news media to publish a lexicon of self-promoting terminology? Politically powerless? Enough said.

Amendment 2 correctly argued that protected class status should not be granted on a state or local level to this advantaged homosexual lobby. Furthermore, it could now be seen that protection from discrimination should be granted only under the strict federal guidelines. As Ignacio Rodriguez said, "Civil Rights is not, and never has been, a 'home rule' issue." This means, roughly speaking, that the federal government invented the special class of civil rights laws; the federal government's interpretation is a higher authority than that of local city governments like Denver, Boulder, or Aspen. Amendment 2 stood its ground in good company.

Long after the Colorado election, homosexual journalist Jonathan Rauch woke up to CFV's irrefutable logic concerning civil rights. He warned his fellow activists: "As more and more homosexuals come out of hiding, the reality of gay economic and political and educational achievement becomes more evident. And as that happens, gay people who insist they are oppressed will increasingly, and not always unfairly, come off as yuppie whiners, 'victims' with large incomes and vacations in Europe."[110]

The hypocrisy of so-called homosexual oppression is thus exposed. The possibility exists, as revealed by Amendment 2, that every state and city gay rights ordinance now listed in the ACLU's guide for homosexuals[111] is vulnerable under the federal civil rights guidelines. These laws should be challenged in court. It would behoove American citizens to begin using the courts aggressively in this cultural battle to do just that.

DISCRIMINATION

Based on the federal guidelines then, Amendment 2 continued

to challenge the notion that homosexuals deserved protected class status. Of course, the other side disagreed. They pointed to the local gay rights laws in Denver, Boulder, and Aspen, which thumbed their noses at the federal guidelines. Clearly these cities had given homosexuality protected class status.

In their favor, the homosexual lobby could also cite Governor Roy Romer's executive order prohibiting job discrimination for state employees based on sexual orientation. Or the state colleges with special gay anti-discrimination policies. They also had a Colorado statute on the books through the state General Assembly prohibiting insurance companies from determining insurability based on one's sexual orientation—AIDS dangers notwithstanding. Essentially all of these local laws freely gave homosexuality the protected class status that the federal courts, Congress, and Amendment 2 denied them.

Anti-amendment forces took the position that the local Colorado gay rights laws represented the future for America. They asserted that the federal government would eventually evolve its standards to follow the lead of Denver, Boulder, and Aspen. They believed the cities would lead the states, and the states would lead the federal government into the new world of the gay '90s.

At this point it should be said that this argument is the pure essence of reasoned debate over Amendment 2 and all similar laws. The critical question is this: "*Does homosexuality deserve protected class status or not?*" CFV and Amendment 2 said "no." The gay rights ordinances of Denver, Boulder, Aspen said "yes." Anyone can honestly disagree on this question. (Though one argument seems definitely better for America.)

But this is where all reasoned debate ended in Colorado. Why? Because the anti-amendment forces could not win this basic argument. They could not prove to the satisfaction of voters that homosexuals suffered the kinds of discrimination for which protected class status was created under historic civil rights precedent.

Perhaps nothing in Mark Olsen's CFV Tabloid did as much damage to the homosexual claims to discrimination as his chart comparing the black experience with the homosexual experience.[112] It posed the following questions: Have homosexuals ever been denied the right to vote? Have they ever faced legal segregation? Have they ever been denied access by law to public drinking fountains, restrooms? Have they ever been denied access by law to businesses, restaurants, barber shops? Do we find evidence of systematic discrimination in housing and jobs in Colorado today? Do we see the homosexual community in a ghetto, or suffering economic hardship as a class because of discrimination? The answer, "no," on all counts.

Homosexuals do not compare to the experience of black Americans. General Colin Powell, Chairman of the Joint Chiefs of Staff, wrote, "Skin color is a benign, non-behavioral characteristic. Comparison of the two, racial and sexual discrimination, is a convenient but invalid argument."[113]

Yet this invalid argument was all the homosexual lobby had going for it in the Colorado election. Civil Rights champions Rabbi Foster and Jack Lang y Marquez, along with the homosexual/-politically correct/media coalition, continued to insist that homosexuals suffered oppression and persecution from heterosexual society, with nothing for proof.

The news media tried their best to invent the necessary proof. They uncritically printed the Gay and Lesbian Task Force's own assembled hate-crime statistics, ignoring or ridiculing the official police numbers. For example, state news rooms announced many stories such as the following during the debate over the meaning of the Colorado vote: HOMOSEXUAL RIGHTS GROUP SAYS ANTI-GAY VIOLENCE SURGED IN '91: TASK FORCE CITES A 'MESSAGE OF HATRED.'[114] After touting this story with full sympathy for the homosexual side, the article ended with the small disclaimer (for those tenacious enough to read it), "While the group reported increases in incidents in Boston and New York, police in those two cities reported decreases in anti-gay crimes last year of 21 percent and 14 percent, respectively."

Likewise, police in Colorado reported no such increase in harassment against homosexuals during the period specified, even though Gay and Lesbian Task Forcers claimed gay bashing was going through the roof because of CFV and Amendment 2.

How did Colorado newsmen treat the issue? Predictably. The

same post-election media study mentioned earlier by Focus on the Family's *Citizen* Magazine revealed 84 paragraphs by Colorado's three leading newspapers citing unofficial hate crime and harassment claims. Journalists only challenged 20% of these statements, justifying 14% of them in the process. At the same time official police sources, cited in only 62 paragraphs, were challenged 43% of the time, and justified only 10% of the time.[115] This study indicated clearly that the Colorado news media chose to automatically trust the Gay and Lesbian Task Force, and mistrust the police. How could the voting public be properly served by this news bias?

Add to the Colorado scenario the official national picture of homosexual suffering and harassment. In '93 the first official FBI hate crime report under the Hate Crime Statistics Act of 1990 came out. It listed nationwide, 63.7% of hate crimes targeted against race or ethnicity, 19.3% against religion, *and only 8.9% against sexual orientation.*[116] Where's the homosexual lobby's justification for protected class status in these figures?

At this FBI revelation, the Gay and Lesbian Task Force with their news media faithful in Colorado, screamed, "Foul!" As soon as the report hit the newsstands they claimed that the police were to blame for the low level of reporting of homosexual crimes. In Colorado Springs the local homosexual militants took up the cause: Ground Zero leaders urged homosexuals "to contact the CSPD [Colorado Springs Police Department] with ALL complaints, *no matter how trivial you think it might be.*"[117] [emphasis added]

Two months later, the Colorado Springs police report of 1992 crimes motivated by bigotry for all of El Paso County (which included Colorado Springs) listed the following results: Against blacks, 23; Whites, 8; Hispanic, 3; Korean, 1; Arab, 1; Japanese, 1; Gay/lesbian, 2; Christian, 1; Other, 1.[118] An investigation of the two gay/lesbian crimes revealed that both were name calling incidents, not crimes of violence.

How does any of this justify the inclusion of sexual orientation under the Civil Rights Act of 1964? "If it ain't broke, don't fix it," CFV proponents said. These figures clearly revealed the low level of homosexual hatred in Colorado and in the nation as a whole. Gay rights should not have become a national priority. But would the press quit its campaign against Amendment 2 after these figures came out? No. More than ever they ran uncritical stories claiming that Amendment 2 discriminated terribly against homosexuals.

This news media agenda pressured Colorado for Family Values to defend its motives unnecessarily. "No, Amendment 2 is not out to 'bash' gays," CFV said. "We simply do not believe homosexuals need special laws and protections that rob the rest of us of freedom of speech, association, and religion."

This defensive posture against the media accusation of discrimination absorbed a lot of campaign time and energy. However, Kevin Tebedo and others came to believe that the discrimination debate began to eventually strengthen their cause. "Without the word 'discrimination' in the amendment's language for the media to attack," Kevin said, "we would not have had the opportunity to continue to explain what protected class status meant. We also had better discrimination arguments than they had. So it seemed like an advantage all the way round."

Tony Marco disagreed. He believed discussing discrimination in public actually gave the impression that "Amendment 2 created discrimination." He suggested sticking to the public argument that Amendment 2 preserved a vital distinction between legitimate claims to protected class status and the illegitimate claims of gay militants. "Unless this distinction is preserved," Tony urged, "the entire meaning and structure of minority rights as we know them will disintegrate."

Basically, Tony's argument appealed well to principled liberals, minorities, and civil rights officials. An important constituency, but Amendment 2 would probably not have won an election with this coalition alone.

The undeniable fact remained that, under CFV's approach to the Amendment 2 debate, the broad public received an education about discrimination and protected class status that eventually brought a majority of the state's voters into the Amendment 2 camp.

The arguments CFV most often made to counter the charges that homosexuals suffer discrimination were two-fold:

1. Everyone suffers discrimination to some degree. They don't automatically qualify for protected class status.

2. Certain kinds of discrimination are good; other kinds are necessary for survival. It makes no sense to try to oppose all discrimination as if it is an evil in need of government regulation.

CFV's first discrimination argument cited examples of other groups that suffer a level of disapproval similar to the reasonable levels suffered by homosexuals. These groups would compare in a society that tolerates, but does not fully accept and affirm their behavior, lifestyle or disability:

> Homosexuals not more than left-handed people, bald men, fat people, homely people, the mentally deficient, those with too little formal education, those who are overqualified for jobs, those who are right-brained, those who are left-brained, professional athletes who are not born with the cross-brain coordination advantage, people lacking etiquette or other social skills, stutterers, aliens, the physically weak, non-English speaking people.

These people must all endure a level of discrimination. If one so desired, it is a safe bet they could dig up hate-crime statistics for several of these categories, too—providing they formed a task force for that purpose. CFV held that claiming legal protection from discrimination for every wrong suffered is simply absurd.

Consider the discrimination today's executive must endure who does not play golf, or won't go into debt for a power wardrobe, or for a status automobile. Or the businessman who puts his family first. They suffer discrimination.

A recent study of finicky hiring practices reveals a company that insists on managers with a golf handicap of 10 or less.[119] Now that seems like unfair discrimination. Another company only considers candidates who can finish a marathon run. One company demanded that its executives sprout hair, another walk dogs, another shed weight.[120] Is it exactly fair to demand these standards? No, it's discriminatory. Grow up.

How about the homophobe who is denied the bartender's job at a homosexual nightclub? That's discrimination. Should a white supremacist be allowed to administer affirmative action policies in racial cases? That's discrimination. How about a homosexual military man who wants to be free to take showers with lots of people of the same sex? Or sleep with them in close quarters? Or how about the gay man who desires to be a Boy Scout leader? Or a Big Brother? Discrimination anyone?

These types of discrimination reflect common sense and, in some cases, real wisdom. Simple prudence and courage are all that is required to deal with them. Nothing more . . . certainly nothing like government protection.

In a public debate with a homosexual lawyer, Will Perkins was challenged by the claim that Amendment 2 would remove government protections from homosexuals in housing, employment, and public accommodations. (This is the classic line that has worked wonders in advancing the cause of homosexual rights among bureaucrats and soft-headed voters.) Will didn't flinch. He stood and asked the live audience how many of them had ever gone to a convention, or on a ski outing or a church retreat and had stayed in a hotel room with a person of the same sex? Nearly all raised their hands. Then he asked how many had been asked by the hotel desk clerk if they were homosexual? No hands raised. "OK," Will asked, "where is the discrimination? How would anyone deny a homosexual couple a room unless they announced they were homosexual?"

He then asked a similar show of hands over employment. "How many have ever been interviewed for a civilian job and have been asked if they are attracted to people of the same sex?" No hands. "How many of you, when you were in college, or otherwise single, shared rent with a member of the same sex?" Many hands. "How many were asked about sexual preference by your landlord?" No hands. "Well," he asked, "how do you get discrimination to happen in housing, employment, and public accommodations? You can only *make* it happen by announcing your sexuality. You can force the issue. But is this really discrimination?"

At this point the homosexual lawyer interrupted, "OK, OK, so it hardly ever happens, but when it does happen there should be a law against it."

Most people understand that laws are not here to solve every human problem. Especially not homosexual discrimination (when and if it occurs). But this lawyer assumed that all discrimination should be solved by the law. That is exactly what's wrong with our courts today. This approach to the law creates an impossible load of litigation. Politically correct lawyers and politicians seeking to extend their profession often play on this idea. But if government is allowed to continue to regulate private lives, especially concerning sexuality, we'll no longer be a government *by the people*. We'll be a nation of bureaucrats and lawyers.

Which leads to the second major argument: discrimination isn't all bad. For example, look at the dictionary definition:

> **dis/crim/i/na/tion**, n. 1. the act of making or recognizing differences and distinctions: *Do not buy clothes without discrimination. Discrimination between fact and theory is sometimes difficult to make.*[121]

CFV's media director, Mark Olsen, put it this way: "To discriminate is to choose. We are talking about freedom of choice here. Some choices are good, some bad, some better than others, some turn out to be the best of all. But in all cases, choice requires discrimination. When we make laws against discrimination we lose our power to make choices. We should make these kinds of laws only in the rarest of exceptions, as in the case of correcting the problems of historic black slavery."

The only people making a bad word out of discrimination are those who wish to distort the meaning of the Civil Rights Act of 1964. Racial discrimination is an exceptionally bad choice, we accept that. But somehow in our popular culture we have broadened this racial distinction to include things like sexuality. This goes way too far. It will ruin civil rights.

At a party recently, I was castigated for my stand on Amendment 2 by a pretty young woman who boldly declared that she didn't care what kind of government intrusion it took, all discrimination must be wiped out. I asked her, "All discrimination?"

"All," she replied haughtily.

This is a sign that propaganda has had its effect in our culture. This young woman had bought into an idea like "all discrimination is bad" and could endure the idea's inherent contradictions without a second thought.

But the subtleties of discrimination and civil rights law seemed lost even to the most enlightened members of the politically correct crowd. Just two days before the '92 election, a group of nearly 300 Jewish and Christian community stalwarts went on record against Amendment 2 with a half page newspaper ad. It featured the following doctrinaire quote: "*No* citizen of the State of Colorado should be excluded from making a *claim of discrimination*."[122]

As Will Perkins would often say, "If everyone is a protected class, then no one is a protected class. If everyone gets special rights, then what's so special about them? These laws only apply to special groups that qualify. We are saying homosexuality doesn't qualify. Period."

The clear thinking here continued to fall on deaf ears among the cultural elite. The battle was truly not a rational one. Perhaps the most disturbing appearance of this opposition to *all* discrimination appeared in response to the voter passage of Amendment 2. Since the election, a group calling itself Equality Colorado: Colorado Anti-Discrimination Coalition has set forth a high pressure campaign against Colorado businesses (already gun shy from a six-month boycott). The statement of purpose of this newly funded homosexual lobby is to "lead a fight against discrimination in all forms."[123] One can only hope that business leaders will have the good sense to realize that eliminating discrimination *in all forms* would be very bad business. It makes as much sense as eliminating all informed advice from a major business decision. Discriminating businesses are efficient businesses and, in many cases, profitable ones.

Beyond politics and business, in sexual matters, discrimination is required for survival and good health. For example, it takes discrimination not to engage in high risk activities even when the passion of the moment might urge one to throw caution to the wind.

Knowing that condoms fail 14% of the time in vaginal intercourse,[124] it takes discrimination to accept that there is no such thing as safe sex even when it is advertised as such. (This is ancient knowledge. To quote a woman of the seventeenth century, condoms are a mere "spider web against danger.")[125]

If morality, chastity, self-control, and abstinence are no longer valid considerations for this society, then it still takes discrimination to understand that condoms that fail through vaginal intercourse will certainly not withstand the pressure of the average anal sphincter. More than that, the HIV virus is a hundred times smaller than the microscopic holes that occur naturally in synthetic rubber. It takes discernment to remember that what you can't see can kill you. Or that even a lubricated condom will not prevent leaking bowel syndrome, after repeated insults to the anus.

Finally, it takes discrimination to recognize the time tested safety net built into the morality of matrimony and fidelity. That, like Adam and Eve, one man and one woman before God make a family, the basic unit of civilization. All other associations are merely domestic, and vastly inferior.

Discrimination mostly turns out to be a matter of wisdom. In times of uncertainty, like these complex times, wise and good discrimination grows more valuable than gold. Instead of making laws to ban all discrimination, why not recognize that there are only a very few forms of it that should be prohibited by law? The fewer the better. Historically, these few have been kept in place by the standards of Western morality. But if it is truly too late for morality, if society is determined to discard that old Western standard, it would seem all the more essential not to discard wisdom along with it. It is the cultural baby in the bathwater. By all means America, discriminate.

After making all of these good arguments, one irony remained for CFV: discrimination as it appeared in the precise legal language of Amendment 2 had still not been addressed. The word in the amendment did not apply to general discussions of inequity in everyday life, it applied only to those specific "claims" of discrimination made by people who had attained protected class status. Amendment 2 claimed that this status had been granted unfairly in Denver, Boulder, Aspen, and everywhere else gay rights laws had been enacted.

As Tony Marco continued to stress, discussing discrimination in any other context, no matter how strong the arguments were, ran the risk of confusing the true meaning of the legal term in the minds of the public. Debates about discrimination remained purely philosophical, while the amendment usage of the term remained strictly legal.

Any discussion of discrimination became a trap to the amendment. A trap almost impossible to avoid during the campaign. It is now apparent that the media and pro-homosexual opposition used this inflammatory word to divert CFV from debating the true issue of protected class status. A better approach for CFV advocates might have been to constantly put the discrimination shoe on the other foot and press for proof from the homosexual lobby, never discussing discrimination philosophically.

This approach happened, more or less by accident, in a public debate at Calvary United Methodist Church in Colorado Springs. My wife and I attended, and from an audience microphone, I stood to press Jack Lang y Marquez of the state Civil Rights Division to prove that the homosexuals needed protected class status.

The Methodist sanctuary was full of proud homosexuals with their lovers. I drew attention to their diversity, bizarre clothing, hairstyles, weird earrings, nose rings, and tattoos. Others were impossible to distinguish from heterosexuals. I then pointed to the fact that many had been loud and boisterous during the evening. At times they had dared to be rude, interrupting the panel with comments and laughter.

"These people do not live in fear," I suggested. "They seem—excuse me—*pampered*. Help me out," I asked. "Tell me why Colorado should give this group the added protection of special civil rights laws? Where is the evidence that they are suffering from anything more than their own behavior?"

Mr. Marquez swallowed. Then he pointed to a bulky file claiming that the evidence within it was "anecdotal but overwhelming." I took this to mean that it was a bunch of stories told by homosexuals who wanted the protection of his laws, similar to the

Gay and Lesbian Task Force's own hate crime statistics. By social science standards these figures could hardly be deemed a compelling body of evidence. Yet, incredibly, Marquez had decided to believe the overwhelming stories and commit the state Civil Rights Division to their aid. He had made a *feel good* decision. Such decisions seldom serve the public's best interest.

I then challenged Mr. Marquez to at least categorize the specific types of homosexual oppression and persecution in his "anecdotal" file. Could he give me numbers or percentages to attach to each category of complaint? Incredibly, he replied that he could *not* do any of that. I should just take his word for it as an expert in these matters. To me, that evasive reply meant that there must have been as many varieties in his files as their were homosexuals. The whole body of evidence began to sound like a collective whine against heterosexual society.

To the rational mind, the implications of Mr. Marquez's confession were that the state Civil Rights Commission could not categorize homosexual persecution in any sensible numbers. If so, what sort of confusion would reign in the courtroom when they unloaded this anecdotal file of complaints there? (The arguments of Tom Duran, Ignacio Rodriguez, and John Franklin, *illustrated.*) Blacks and Hispanics had no difficulty counting incidents of specific discrimination against them, I suggested. "The whole comparison is apples to oranges. Homosexuals do not prove that they need the special protections of racial minorities."

Of course in the Methodist Church, which had endorsed the homosexual rights agenda, my opinion was quickly shouted down by the politically correct crowd.

Months later I ran across a profile of the probable contents of Mr. Marquez's bulky file. This chart opened my eyes wide. The study was a national survey of specific discrimination complaints lodged by homosexual men and women during 1991.[126] It applied the very categories and percentages I had asked Marquez to produce at the Methodist Church. Among other things, the study revealed the incredible differences between racial discrimination and the kinds of discrimination on the homosexual's complaint list (see below). In spite of the repeated public claims that homosexuals suffer discrimination in housing, employment, and public accommodations, the actual claims of discrimination lodged by homosexuals themselves ran as follows:

#1	Employment benefits	20%
#2	Taxes	17%
#3	Insurance	17%
#4	Membership in clubs	11%
#5	Credit/banking	5%
#6	**EMPLOYMENT**	**5%**
#7	**HOUSING**	**5%**
#8	**HOTELS**	**4%**
#9	**HOSPITAL VISITATION**	**3%**
#10	Adoption	2%
#11	No discrimination indicated	11%

The self-interest of the rich homosexual lobby was definitively seen in this list. How cynical for Jack Lang y Marquez, newsmen, educators, lawyers, religionists, and the ACLU to suggest that homosexuals suffered discrimination in housing, employment, and public accommodations! At most, these complaints comprised 17% of their official, uncoached complaints in 1991. Furthermore, what does this homosexual lobby chart suggest about the fairness of giving them the legal status of racial minorities? There's no comparison.

It makes one wonder all the more about Jack Lang y Marquez and Rabbi Steven Foster. No doubt these ambitious bureaucrats would have enjoyed using the power of civil rights law to assist the agenda of the richest sexual lobby in the state. And if they had benefited from a few of the perks involved, they would not have been the first public servants to do so. At least it can be clearly seen now that chasing a court full of homosexual discrimination claims would hardly compare to the thankless litigation of racial injustice, for which the Civil Rights Act of 1964 was created. (Someone please applaud the federal government for keeping the homosexual lobby's hand out of the protected class cookie jar for the past 15 years.)

Amendment 2 had a built-in genius: When enacted, this law told the homosexual community to put-up or shut-up where claims of discrimination were concerned. With the Colorado state law in place, they would have had to go straight to the federal government and qualify for protected class status under the three criteria or drop their bid to gain civil rights law advantages. (How can it be construed as hateful to suggest that they do this? The suggestion makes too much good sense.)

If the homosexual lobby qualified legitimately at the federal level, Amendment 2 and all laws like it would be overturned in one clean sweep. Problem is, the homosexual lobby knew it couldn't qualify. So did Colorado for Family Values. Amendment 2 slammed the back door to special protected class status.

Knowing this, is it any wonder the homosexual lobby resorted to name calling? "Bigots! Homophobes! Discriminators! Religious righters!"

After the amendment won the election, a sobered homosexual journalist wrote, "The standard political model sees homosexuals as an oppressed minority who must fight for their liberation through political action. But that model's usefulness is drawing to a close . . . oppression politics fails because it denies reality."[127] He went on in this incredibly candid account to detail why homosexuals should not qualify for protected class status. It almost appeared that he had found CFV's campaign material and resourced it for his article.

The best news was that he honestly conceded the entire first point of the homosexual agenda, inclusion under the Civil Rights Act of 1964. If a homosexual writer could come up with these arguments, it seemed the more absurd that the Colorado homosexual lobby would call CFV "homophobic" for articulating the same position during the campaign. Thankfully, at least 53.4% of the people of Colorado had the good sense to see through it all.

BEHAVIOR AND HEALTH

After examining the whole of the civil rights issue, few CFV insiders had confidence that winning the legal arguments would mean enough to the state's voters to put the amendment over the top on November 3rd. Polls continued to run against the law. The true irrationality of the issue began to seem insurmountable. CFV insiders sensed their need for another appeal, something more fundamental, something that related to every community regardless of race or creed. That common ground had already been established, it was something called the homosexual threat to marriage and the traditional family.

Deep down, it seemed people really wanted to protect their families against homosexual behavior, not to mention from the high statistical disease rates among those who practiced the lifestyle. Not only AIDS, but reports had begun to emerge that females practicing homosexuality suffered triple the risk for breast cancer.[128]

To galvanize the pro-family support, everyone sensed that they would have to bring out the number two issue—homosexual behavior. Still, this behavioral thrust of the campaign remained the most reluctant, divisive, and controversial issue for CFV thinkers.

Some argued that America had become so compromised by the sexual revolution that addressing behavior (or misbehavior) would backfire. No one would want to cast a stone at homosexual excesses for fear of hitting their own heterosexual infidelities.

Others replied that infidelity was not a family value anymore than homosexuality. Those family men and women who carried the responsibility of raising children, whether married, divorced, faithful, or unfaithful, recognized the value of monogamous marriage even if they didn't practice it. It remained a goal, an ideal, if nothing else. Family oriented people would likely be motivated to vote for Amendment 2 after learning of dangerous homosexual practices.

Still others suggested that addressing homosexual behavior would backfire because the public believed homosexuals were sexually addicted, or even genetically determined. Some thought they functioned according to the popular romantic notion, "*I can't help myself, I'm in love . . .*" The counter to this argument came from science. No serious studies backed up the popular claims that this behavior could not be helped or changed.

Besides, the same kinds of studies linking genetics to sexual behavior could be used to excuse the behavior of murderers and rapists. In fact, genes have been located that seem to make some people more prone to violence. Do we thus excuse their behavior? No. Homosexual behavior also had to be held responsible, just like other powerfully influenced behaviors. Responsibility for actions under the law remained a universal principle that CFV could count on from straight thinking people in this election.

Nevertheless, after sorting it and re-sorting it, everyone in CFV wanted to avoid the question of behavior if at all possible. The path held certain risks. Perhaps it also held rewards, but all discussions usually ended with, "Let's keep it on the back burner. Hold it in reserve until we are forced to bring it up."

It is also safe to say that, early on, most of the decision makers believed they would eventually be forced to bring it up. Already, the opposition had unleashed virulent telephone and mail harassment against CFV leadership, including numerous death threats. Will Perkins' Chrysler dealership had been picketed by men in drag, dressed as nuns, and dykes on bikes. Meanwhile the gay lobby enjoyed the automatic media status of "poor defenseless gays, only guilty of the pursuit of same-gender happiness." For CFV to reveal hard, researched facts about the dangerous behavioral trends among their numbers seemed the only way to eventually break through their lockup on the media.

FINDING THE RIGHT SPOKESMAN

The first Colorado attempts to mention homosexual behavior and health had been made early-on by Tony Marco in his debate against the Ethnic Harassment Bill. Even though his behavioral comments had helped defeat the law in committee, the news media had painted him as a bigot and a homophobe for the inflammatory facts and questions he had posed. Every time he defended himself thereafter, his public image was made the issue.

After a '92 University of Colorado address his photo was

published to appear as if he had doubled his fist against an opponent, when actually he was pointing over his shoulder with his thumb. The article's first paragraph set forth the bias of the reporter: "Tony Marco launched into his own anti-homosexual campaign Thursday at the University of Colorado." Nothing in the article, nor anything that happened at the event, backed-up this inflammatory statement. In this particular debate, Tony had delivered a quiet, reasoned explanation of Amendment 2. During a question period afterward, his address had been commended as impressive by an opposing college professor who had co-authored the Colorado Springs Human Rights Ordinance.

At another event, a high profile debate between Marco and Rabbi Steven Foster, a former friend distanced himself from Tony with the comment, "This guy fulfills the worst stereotypes of Christian hatred toward homosexuals." The man who said this was an esteemed member of the Colorado Springs evangelical community.

Why had he said it? Because Tony had dared to argue aggressively and win? He had clearly come to the debate better prepared. He had demonstrated a command of his facts concerning the civil rights argument. He had exhibited assertive debating skills which would have been lauded if he had been on the other side.

The comment by the local evangelical pointed to the extent of the intimidation problem Amendment 2 faced: even the Christian community had been cowed by the trend of political correctness. Truth did not matter as much as perception. Anyone opposing homosexual rights laws, or addressing homosexual health and behavioral statistics, would not be judged by the merits of their arguments but by their style. Being nice to the poor, victimized homosexuals counted more than research and relevant arguments. One of Tony's maxims, "Facts don't hate, they just are," while true in print, would not be perceived as true when coming from his mouth.

Another serious attempt to address behavior and health came during the summer months. A research psychologist, Dr. Paul Cameron, Chairman of the Family Research Institute in Washington, D.C., had compiled a devastating brochure titled *Medical*

Consequences of What Homosexuals Do. CFV leadership thought that perhaps the body of evidence it contained would let the facts of homosexual behavior speak clearly from the printed page, rather than from any CFV spokesman's mouth. Unfortunately, this medium proved troublesome, too.

The simple facts of the *Medical Consequences* research were overwhelming, covering the incredible numbers of partners both male and female homosexuals average per year. Though the numbers had diminished under the threat of AIDS they remained shockingly high, far above any comparable heterosexual average. The high incidence of sex-related drug use was outlined, including the use of a pill called "ecstasy" designed to maximize climatic sex (as if sexual pleasure itself were not addictive enough).

Rates of anal trauma, anonymous oral intercourse, torture sex, orgies—practices too pornographic to name—not to mention their medical consequences, high rates of hepatitis A & B, gay bowel syndrome, intestinal parasites, worms, flukes, ameba, giardia, shigella infections, and HIV transmission . . . homosexual sex appeared to be a veritable biological swapmeet, as the brochure described it.

Most compelling of all, the brochure charted a study comparing male homosexual lifespans with the life expectancies of heterosexual single and married men. The study revealed that homosexuals had been dying young long before HIV came along. Medical literature on the subject had been researched as far back as 1858. Most were shocked to learn that AIDS deaths, for example, had only reduced the lifespan of modern homosexuals by an average of 3 years. The study showed that if gay men don't die of AIDS by the median age of 39, they will die of other health hazards by 42.

These figures are down from those of married men who die at the median age of 75 years; single heterosexual men at 57.[129] How can such a lifestyle be called gay? Or worse, healthy, safe, and normal? If cigarette smoking carried these hazards it would have been outlawed long ago.

"Facts like these don't hate, they just are," Tony had said. If anything hates young men it must be the politically correct, who in the name of love, engage in a conspiracy of silence concerning this sexual deathtrap. The Cameron brochure revealed that modern gayness had reduced the advantages of modern medicine to the median lifespans known to be present in ancient Greece. Mummies of the period reveal 40-something bodies riddled with similar parasites and infections. By the best scientific evidence, society is not evolving through homosexuality, but truly devolving, winding itself backwards.

And so the media committee of Colorado for Family Values met to consider Dr. Cameron's brochure, *Medical Consequences of What Homosexuals Do*. They thought they could light a fire under their own network of supporters by distributing 100,000 of these informative publications through the mail, and through petition volunteers.

But after learning more about Dr. Paul Cameron, I and others suggested that his name be removed from the material. Even though his facts did not hate, the media had labeled him a homophobe for many years. As an early researcher on the subject of homosexual behavior and health, one who had born for decades the full impact of the cynical *Overhauling* lies and tactics, he had been denounced under gay extremist pressure by the American Psychological Association, and had even been alienated from Surgeon General C. Everett Koop. Possibly, neither Cameron nor his research deserved this attack. But as Will Perkins said, modern politics is not about "what should be done, it's about what you can do."

Cameron carried far too much political baggage, or so it seemed to some of us who predicted that *he* would become the issue rather than the facts and figures of his research. Still, after careful consideration, the decision of CFV went the other way and Cameron's name went out on the brochure distributed in Colorado.

Intercepted by homosexual sympathizers, the *Medical Consequences* brochure was immediately vilified in the press. They concentrated on Cameron's disputes with the American Psychological Association, which had declared homosexuality no longer a disorder. Though his past controversies amounted to political attacks, the media hue and cry had managed to keep the public from dealing with the real issues.

Beyond that, many of CFV's own supporters were so shocked

by the frankness of the facts and figures of homosexual behavior that they, too, chose to attack the source of the information rather than deal with it. CFV's telephone rang too often with the outcry of offended amendment supporters.

Meanwhile, in every interview and debate situation, Dr. Paul Cameron would be manipulated into defending himself and his own credibility, rather than explaining the dangerous issues of homosexual behavior as it related to the Colorado election. Under the media pressure, he sometimes made harsh statements that were then used out of context to paint the entire issue. Everything he said played into the *Overhauling* strategy. He could be made to look like a "ranting homophobe" and thus be discounted.

If Tony and Dr. Cameron had become easy targets for media distraction, Kevin Tebedo had too. In many speaking situations his youthful mannerisms tended to work against him. Most of the quotes that found their way into the press from his mouth were combative. The board noticed and put out the suggestion that a chief spokesman should be chosen who would not give the press so much of what they were looking for in an amendment representative.

This hot seat thrust Will Perkins reluctantly to the forefront. Realizing the very real antagonism of the press, he warned everyone who would speak for the issue, "You have to watch out for the 'whale syndrome' on this thing. That's where you get to the top, start to spout—and you get harpooned."

As Will began to field press duties midway through the campaign, it became apparent that the same behavioral and health information from his mouth had a more favorable impact in the public arena than it had from any other spokesman. Being a simple-is-better sort of public speaker, he articulated the difficult civil rights issues behind the amendment with clarity. Many times the wisdom of the things he *didn't* say in a given situation, weighed as heavily as the words he chose to speak. Under his discretion, more and more, people seemed ready to see past their own prejudices and hear the truth on the subject of Amendment 2.

An added area of real impact was Will's credible explanations of the negative impact of gay rights laws on free enterprise. "New costs and red tape," he would say. As a successful business owner he could command the respect of other business leaders on this subject.

Until this point in the debate, CFV had outdone itself with substance, now with Will Perkins, for the first time it gained the style it so desperately needed. Even though the media attacked Perkins' character with statements such as: ". . . [he] makes hatred palatable to the general public . . ." and ". . . [he is] able to persuade voters to embrace a philosophy they would have rejected were it coming from anyone else . . ." or ". . . [he's] convincing audiences by blurring the line between debater and salesman . . .", all such criticism contained an element of jealous admiration. Bruce Loeffler, a Colorado College professor and gay rights activist, said simply, "We're in trouble—this guy is impossible not to like."[130] Indeed, Will provided the media harpoon a frustrating target.

After the election had passed and the boycott and media assaults had increased dramatically—Will Perkins remained standing, his business actually booming in spite of—or perhaps because of—all the negative attention. It was then the Sunday *Denver Post Magazine* hailed him begrudgingly on its cover as "THE MAN WHO SOLD AMENDMENT 2" to Colorado.

In the feature's descriptions of Will, quoting both friends and foes, the article listed comments such as: ". . . one of the nicest men one could ever meet . . ." "Will Perkins is a decent man . . ." "A devout Christian who was never heard to employ an angry word throughout two years of campaigning for Amendment 2 . . ." ". . . a 'transparent' man of faith and integrity." "I've seen him run his business and he runs it the way he runs his life. He lives his religion." "Perkins has given away more of his own fortune than anyone [I've] ever known, often to bankroll shelters for the poor . . ."

As Loeffler had said, ". . . this guy is impossible not to like."

If Tony Marco, Kevin Tebedo, Mark Olsen, and everyone behind Colorado for Family Values could speak in unison, they would say, if you should attempt an Amendment 2 style campaign in your state, pray to find someone like Will Perkins as a spokesman.

RELIGIOUS RIGHT, RELIGIOUS LEFT

Throughout the campaign Will Perkins handled the religious question this way: "There are religious people on both sides of our issue. Our amendment is smack in the middle."

This answer was true, as well as prudent. Amendment 2 remained morally neutral, but religious people were deeply divided over the issues it raised. The first and most obvious division occurred between the religious left and right. This split in theology, or philosophy, paralleled the conservative-liberal split in American politics.

What distinguishes the religious left and right? For the purpose of simplification, the right are those Jews and Christians who accept the authority of the Old and New Testament. They look up to the Bible as the inspired Word of God and attempt to submit to it, whether they like it or not. They accept the Biblical theme that all human beings are sinful and rebellious by nature and that God will hold them accountable. They believe God gave his laws to the world for its own good, to protect it from its natural depravity. Under this high respect for Scripture, verses which condemn homosexuality in plain language are accepted without argument.

The religious left, on the other hand, dares to argue with Scripture. They look on it as imperfectly inspired, needing the filter of modern scholarship to be properly understood. They do not necessarily accept the notion that man is sinful and rebellious by nature, nor do they think a "loving" God would possibly condemn anyone for their natural condition. Biblical authority, in their view, arises from an enlightened interpretation of God's Word, which reveals an evolving moral standard. Bible passages condemning homosexuality as an "abomination," or calling the practice "detestable," are generally explained away by the left.

How do the religious right and left play out politically? Glenn Tinder, professor of political science at the University of Massachusetts, wrote eloquently "on the political meaning of Christianity" for *The Atlantic Monthly*. He explained how the Biblical concept of original sin produces an extremely cautious view of society on the religious right:

> The Christian concept of sin is not adequately described . . . by saying that people frequently engage in evil actions. Our predisposition toward such actions is so powerful and so unyielding that it holds us captive . . . . In the Christian view . . . [every] society is placed in question.[131]

True to Tinder's observation, the religious right trusts neither human nature, nor government. In this, their values match those of America's founding fathers. In the words of James Madison:

> It may be a reflection on human nature, that [checks and balances] should be necessary to control the abuses of government. But what is government itself, but the greatest of all reflections on human nature? *If men were angels, no government would be necessary.*[132] [emphasis added]

Madison's Christian caution is also evident in the writings of Jefferson, Hamilton, Jay, Washington, Franklin, and many others. In the words of Jewish conservative Don Feder, "By today's standards, the founding fathers were the religious right."[133] This cautious Christian world view held by America's founders produced the political principle known as "ordered liberty." As later restated in Katherine Bates' immortal hymn, *America the Beautiful*, "confirm thy soul with self control, thy *liberty* in *law*." In order to secure the blessings of liberty for the largest number of people, the great American experiment in freedom wisely limited itself with checks and balances. Due to its Biblical understanding of human nature, it recognized that liberty *must* be restrained by law, both civil and moral. (Laws like Amendment 2 notwithstanding.)

The religious right points to the fact that the founding fathers equally distrusted government and human nature. That is why they placed the standards of Biblical authority above civil documents, including the Constitution.

Religious righters believe the founder's view of Scripture is still good for America. In this they often join forces with political conservatives who also wish to preserve America's best traditions, though not always for religious reasons. Within the concept of ordered liberty the religious right today believes that it is good for society that some laws, like sodomy laws, come directly from the standard of Scripture. They often quote the Old Testament Proverb in this regard, "Righteousness exalts a nation, but sin is a disgrace to any people."[134] They are also concerned that the political and religious left has been discarding these moral standards from public life in recent decades, making morality a purely private matter. They fear that America will reap a chaotic harvest from the loss of public morals, forfeiting the fruit of ordered liberty in this culture.

Who are the religious right? Aside from their noted clergy, they might include influential conservative Jews like Ruth Wisse and Michael Medved, Christian Coach Bill McCartney, and family activist Phyllis Schlafly. People know where these opinion leaders stand on most issues because they are not inventing the wheel of morality as they go. They look back to their Biblical standard for guidance. Because of this, a set of unchanging Biblical morals flow from their positions that can stabilize the culture that holds them sacred.

The religious left, on the other hand, views all of that religious right stability as dangerous rigidity. They think the ten commandments would work better as ten suggestions. As Don Feder has said, one can imagine their God at Sinai commanding: "Are you comfortable with not stealing?"[135] They think it is bad for society that some laws, like sodomy laws for example, come from Scripture. They would never think of imposing a Biblical command on a secular population. To them the Bible has little or no public relevance. Its meanings are entirely subjective and private. They have subsequently cooperated with humanist efforts to banish religious standards from public life.

The religious left would include influential Jews like Rabbi Harold Kushner and Barbara Streisand, and Christians like Bill Clinton or Pat Schroeder. You can't be sure where these people will make a stand because they have an evolving standard of decency. They can make hard decisions and define hard positions at times, but not based on any absolute values. They freely pick and choose such things. Barbara Streisand, after the passage of Amendment 2, publicly condemned the "moral climate" in Colorado. The left does not hesitate to make up really high sounding "morals" when it suits them. For America, a set of cultural values flows from the religious left that allows almost anything to flourish in time: good or bad. Under its shelter, diversity—a form of unrestrained freedom which castigates traditional moral ideals as "unloving"—becomes highly valued, ironically for its values-free qualities.

Religious left values not only shelter other faiths—they embrace them fully so as to offend none (except for Biblical Judeo-Christianity, which is *anathema*). If Native American religious values, for example, should suddenly request their turn at interpreting the Constitution of the United States, the religious left would be hypocritical not to give it serious study. "What gives us the idea that we know better than they," they ask? "Our moral interpretations are no better than anyone else's." The values of the religious left are relative. They change with the forces of evolution. This makes them completely compatible with polytheistic or pagan societies worshipping any god but the Judeo-Christian God. Religious lefters find their political expression mostly (not totally) through America's liberal wing today.

Amendment 2 in Colorado forced the religious right and left to examine anew their beliefs concerning homosexuality. The right found the Bible clearly condemning the practice in both the Old and New Testaments. The left initiated a new spate of sensitivity training seminars to educate their people lest they be misled by the ancient language of Scripture.

In the Old Testament the classic passage of discussion was the story of two angels who were sent to destroy the city of Sodom for its wickedness. They arrived and spent the night at Lot's house. Genesis records, "before they had gone to bed, all the men from every part of the city of Sodom—both young and old—surrounded the house. They called to Lot, 'Where are the men who came to you tonight? Bring them out to us so that we can have sex with them.'"[136] As the story goes, God was not pleased. Neither were the angels. They supernaturally blinded the mob, sent Lot and his family out of the city, and rained fire and brimstone down on it. Sodom is alluded to throughout the Bible as a warning against what happened there.

For the religious right, Sodom has become a synonym for homosexuality. For Western Civilization, *sodomy* has become the definition of the homosexual act itself. In the words of Colorado Springs Presbyterian pastor Bernhard Kuiper, "If you believe the Bible, homosexuality is a very grievous sin against God and nature."[137]

However, the religious left begs to differ with this understanding of Scripture. They ask what God *really* meant by all of that fire and brimstone? It doesn't automatically occur to them that God opposed homosexuality. They refer to another Old Testament passage addressed to apostate Israel that says, "Now this was the sin of your sister Sodom: She and her daughters were arrogant, overfed and unconcerned; they did not help the poor and needy. They were haughty and did detestable things before me. Therefore I did away with them as you have seen."[138] From this, the religious left claims that the real sin of Sodom was "inhospitality." John Boswell of Yale says, "not in a single instance is the sin of the Sodomites specified as homosexuality." Dr. Ralph Blair of Evangelicals Concerned adds, "The Bible is an empty closet. It has nothing to say about homosexuality as such."[139]

The religious right asks; what about those "detestable things" mentioned just before the part where God "did away with them"? And what about the Old Testament law that says, "Do not lie with a man as one lies with a woman; that is detestable"?[140] Isn't the Bible clear enough there? And what about the New Testament passage that says: "Sodom and Gomorrah and the surrounding towns gave themselves up to sexual immorality and perversion. They serve as an example of those who suffer the punishment of eternal fire"?[141] Was it speaking of inhospitality? And what of the New Testament description of perversion in which lesbianism is condemned along with other sins: ". . . God gave them over to shameful lusts. Even their women exchanged natural relations for unnatural ones"?[142] The Bible is an empty closet? It has nothing to say about homosexuality? Either embrace the Bible or throw it out, challenges the right. It is hypocritical to twist its clear meaning.

The religious left remains unflappable. They have consulted scholars at seminaries throughout the world who have handed down very enlightened views of these references to homosexuality in the Bible. They've written book length explanations.

Following the Amendment 2 win, this religious debate increased all across the nation. Finding no common ground in the negative disputes sweeping the church, the Episcopalian Theologian John Stott exhorted Christians to argue the positive side of the Biblical account. "What we need to do," he said, "is to argue that Creation establishes heterosexual monogamy as the norm. In Genesis 2:24, which is the biblical definition of marriage ('Therefore a man leaves his father and mother and cleaves to his wife, and they become one flesh'), we see that the only 'one flesh' God approves or intends is in monogamous, permanent heterosexual marriage."[143]

This argument gives high theological treatment to the common truism one often hears: "God created Adam and Eve, not Adam and Steve." As in most cliches, a multi-layered truth can be found here. Stott emphasizes that Jesus endorsed only the male-female union in the New Testament. No other. "What God has joined together, let man not separate."[144]

But the left thinks such ideas are quaint. One of their pro-gay documents declares: "The issues about homosexuality are very complex and are not understood by most members of the Christian church."[145] After all, they say, some of the best minds in the religious world were required to justify homosexuality from Scripture. It would seem that only the ignorant would refuse such expert knowledge.

Perhaps the most incredulous thing about the religious left during the Colorado campaign was that, given their intellectual proclivities, they did not appreciate the moral neutrality of Amendment 2. In fact, more than any other group, they found great moral fault with it. Time after time they hurried across the neutral zone to attack CFV and the amendment in the public square.

The most common accusation went like this: "Homosexuals are God's children. What gives Amendment 2 the right to take away basic rights and freedoms from those you disagree with?" (This is, of course, the argument to expect from a person who believes morality should remain private. However, the left went on to declare Amendment 2 *immoral* . . . publicly, not privately.)

Apparently the religious left had never read the text of the Ethnic Harassment Bill to see who had been the aggressor in Colorado. Nor had they bothered to notice that Amendment 2 took no basic freedoms from homosexuals. Rather it restored rights and freedoms that had been taken away from God's *straight* children in Denver, Boulder, and Aspen. As the terminator of gay rights laws, one would think the amendment would have been hailed by the religious left as a liberator, restoring equality and plurality to the state, moral and sexual freedom to the private sector.

Sensing the media's willingness to vilify the religious right and lionize the left in these arguments, homosexuals courted every possible religious left association during the amendment campaign. Occasionally they did their own brand of moralizing. Robin Miller, a self-proclaimed "born again" homosexual lawyer from Colorado Springs (also a radical feminist), didn't hesitate to reproach Will Perkins' personal faith: "The things he is saying are untrue, and it's not walking the Christian walk to lie about that."[146]

An unnamed "evangelical" parent of homosexual children, added, "What he is doing is evil."[147]

Not only did Colorado for Family Values find the left shooting at their flanks, surprisingly early in the campaign, they totally miscalculated the response of the religious right. Primarily, they had false expectations of support from evangelical pastors. They believed that these men and women would want to do everything in their power to see Amendment 2 pass. They believed that as soon as CFV mentioned government threats to moral freedoms, religious right pastors would be motivated to engage in the political process, even from the pulpit. Not so.

Letters sent to pastors seemed to fall off their desks and into the round file. Out of 400 initially contacted, only two pastor's assistants bothered to reply at all. This became a major source of disappointment within the ranks of CFV. They were in the public square alone, being shot at by the most powerful media guns in the state. It would have been nice to have had these voices of moral support behind them, but they were unable to rally the troops.

Failing to rouse evangelical Protestants in the state, CFV next lost the support they had counted on from the powerful Catholic

Church. After unsuccessfully opposing Denver's gay rights ordinance the year before, Colorado's Archbishop J. Francis Stafford declined to take a position at all regarding Amendment 2, calling it "too ambiguous."[148] (He would later learn that the Vatican had no similar feelings of ambiguity regarding the issues it raised.) Nevertheless, in the early going, the powerful Colorado representatives of the religious right deserted CFV.

Will often referred to this period of time saying, "I knew how Custer felt the day he modeled the first arrow shirt."

No one seemed more disappointed than Kevin Tebedo who had entered the political fight believing that churches and pastors would supply his much needed ground forces statewide. Perkins, a man of maturity, seemed determined to learn the truth behind their reluctance. The younger members of the team quickly took his lead and began to do the same.

As they looked around for what they had done wrong, they stumbled onto what someone else had done right. The National Association of Evangelicals (NAE) and the Southern Baptist Convention had provided a good model for political action on the religious right. During 1992, they had jointly tried to increase evangelical involvement in public issues through a Christian Citizenship Campaign. Meeting the same kind of reluctance, they had found a middle way. The heart of the program followed two simple thrusts:

1. to distribute, through churches, side by side comparisons of the issues and candidates for the November ballot, and

2. to encourage aggressive voter registration through church facilities.

"Evangelicals generally acknowledge that government is ordained of God," Tim Crater of the NAE explained, "but they seldom appreciate that in America the people govern. . . . Far too many evangelicals have buried this important talent in the ground when it needs desperately to be used."[149]

CFV settled on the NAE approach. First, they distributed information about the amendment for comparison. In Colorado's public atmosphere, saturated with more homosexual information than anyone wanted to hear, CFV leaders encouraged pastors to teach their congregations whatever they believed the Bible taught about the practice. Their messages carried an automatic political implication as far as any law normalizing and accepting sinful behavior was concerned. CFV also encouraged and reminded Pastors and churches to be involved in voter registration.

During their annual convention, the Southern Baptists stopped short of endorsing Amendment 2, voting instead to affirm Biblical prohibitions of homosexuality. They sought to defend their historic beliefs against the modernist reinterpretations of Scripture. In reasserting this position, they did not need to address the amendment. Likewise, within the state, very few pastors took a public stand on the amendment. Instead they preached the Biblical standards and let their people decide the political implications for themselves.

Will Perkins became completely taken with the wisdom of this approach. Because of his own rough-and-tumble media exposure, he knew that anything a pastor might say publicly would be quoted out of context in the media. The press would cast both the pastor and his church as "homophobic" and "hateful." The church would not be able to completely erase the public perceptions created by such a hard shot from the media.

The instincts of religious right churches to guard the integrity of their spiritual mission seemed best for an even greater reason: religious right clergy endorsements would have turned the debate into a religious war after all. The media continued to portray the campaign as if it was primarily fought over religious lines in Colorado. (This missed the entire truth of the amendment's civil rights case.) If religious right pastors had directly addressed the amendment, then some of the media charges would have held water. The campaign would have pitted the morality of the hard driving left directly against the right. This was avoided.

At this point it must be added that the rank and file of both the religious right and left did not think and vote in solidarity with their leadership. Religious right congregations did not remain as silent as their leaders. Individual members campaigned actively and voted for the amendment. Likewise, a significant minority on the religious left campaigned and voted in favor of Amendment 2 against the expressed wishes of their leaders. So the religious division over Amendment 2 was not strictly left and right. Both the right and left were profoundly divided among themselves. This aspect of the religious split followed the values gap in the general culture between the elite and the grassroots. (See study in endnote #204.)

The campaign brimmed with religious language. Nearly all of it from the religious left. But the news media found only one term in its politically correct lexicon: "religious right." It seemed the left did not exist to them.

Will kept calmly repeating his line, hoping the wisdom of it would somehow sink in: "You just have to understand, there are religious people on both sides of our issue. Amendment 2 is smack in the middle."

Will's position did finally come through to the people of Colorado. They read the amendment and understood that it did not address the religious or moral issue. It did not coerce, it removed coercion. This truth became Amendment 2's "Teflon coating": none of the religious right accusations would stick to it, though they were constantly repeated. The amendment's language addressed the cultural question, Whose rights would be upheld by the law? Would it be homosexual minority? Or the rights of everyone, both homosexual and those who objected to homosexuality for whatever reason? By attacking the amendment, the religious left favored the rights of the homosexual lobby and the cultural elite over what turned out to be the Colorado majority.

Conservative Jew Dennis Prager, a respected author and scholar, expressed his puzzlement at this religious left militancy: "The Greeks assaulted the family in the name of beauty and Eros. The Marxists assaulted the family in the name of progress. And today, gay liberation assaults it in the name of compassion and equality. I understand why gays would do this. . . . What I have not understood was why Jews or Christians would join the assault."[150]

Meanwhile, religious groups endorsing gay rights laws proliferated, including many Jewish and Christian organizations. The American Academy of Religion and The Society of Biblical

Literature among them. In Colorado, homosexual religious groups such as Evangelicals Concerned, Dignity (which advertises Catholic masses for gays and lesbians, held at Denver's Capitol Heights Presbyterian Church), and congregation Tikvat Shalom, exclusively for Jewish homosexuals, were publicly visible and vocal against the amendment.

Rocky Mountain United Methodist Bishop Roy Sano sent a letter to 290 Methodist ministers urging them to defeat Amendment 2. (After the election, The Rocky Mountain United Methodist annual conference voted again against the amendment, as if their first signal hadn't been clear enough. Also, during the later injunction hearings, three Jewish and two Christian associations joined in "friends of the court briefs" on behalf of homosexuals.)

The National Council of Churches (whose membership is generally from the religious left), took off the gloves just days before the election, threatening the religious right with this dire warning: "It is blasphemy to invoke the infinite and holy God to assert the moral superiority of one people over another." (In other words, they were saying, "It's immoral for religious people to call immorality immoral in public." Even though all the moral assertions were coming from leaders of the religious left.)

Two days before the election CFV received a surprising boost from the Bishop of Rome. The Vatican roared on the subject of homosexuality in roughly the same terms Coach McCartney had used during the petition drive. The Church did not address Amendment 2, but made clear that the Roman Church teaches that homosexual tendencies are not sinful, but homosexual behavior is (preserving the distinction between actions and personhood). Furthermore, the Church forcefully stated "Sexual orientation does not constitute a quality comparable to race [or] ethnic background" but "homosexual orientation is an objective disorder. There are areas in which it is not unjust discrimination to take sexual orientation into account, for example, in the placement of children for adoption or foster care, in employment of teachers or athletic coaches, and in military recruitment."

Of course, under the concept of religious freedom the Catholic Church has every right to stand up for its faith. Not without consequence, however. This official Catholic document was hailed with the following front page headline in the *Rocky Mountain News*, VATICAN ENDORSES BIAS AGAINST GAYS; DENVER-AREA HOMOSEXUALS CRY FOUL OVER CATHOLIC CHURCH'S OK OF DISCRIMINATION IN EMPLOYMENT, HOUSING AND ADOPTION.[151]

Though the Vatican statement no doubt influenced a number of "yes" votes for Amendment 2, the amendment itself made none of the moral pronouncements of Rome.

Will kept repeating to the last, "There are religious people on both sides of our issue. Our amendment is in the middle."

POLITICAL POLLS

During the summer of '92, before the election, two consultants from one of the largest conservative organizations in the nation visited a meeting of CFV insiders in Colorado Springs. They came with a serious request: "We think you should discreetly withdraw Amendment 2 now and avoid a humiliating defeat in November."

Will Perkins, Kevin Tebedo, Mark Olsen, and Tony Marco, who were present at the meeting, were stunned. Considering the size and clout of this national organization, the words nearly took all the heart out of them. Polls showed Amendment 2 lagging behind the opposition. CFV had doubts about the validity of these polls, but they simply had not raised enough money to commission polling of their own. What did these political biggies know that CFV did not? Was the fight as good as over?

"Isn't it a bit soon?" Will asked incredulously. "Why quit now?"

"Because trying and failing is worse than not having tried at all," came the politically astute reply. "Very few efforts succeed in their first attempt on an issue as big as this. You guys have done a great job getting this thing off the ground. Why not fold now and build your strength for next year?"

Tony Marco and Mark Olsen each gave an opinion that, though the issue lagged in the polls, they didn't see an automatic defeat just yet. Kevin added that he could not forget the miraculous way the petition signatures had come in when all had seemed lost. He was not ready to call it quits by a long shot.

After a long and thoughtful pause, Will spoke up again. "Gentlemen. Winning and losing is in God's hands. I don't know if he wants us to win this thing, but I sure do know he wants us to fight it."

To express his personal feelings on the matter, he paraphrased the story of the Old Testament priest Eli, whom God had severely punished because he knew that his sons were committing sexual sin but he did nothing to warn them. "I think I will answer to God, like Eli," Will said, "if I don't fight these homosexual rights laws. That's what I believe."

He went on to acknowledge the political credentials of his two visitors and the conventional wisdom of making sure the fight was winnable. But then he said, "I didn't get in this to pull out because of the polls. If we fail in November, I will just try again. Even if I am the only one left doing it. But I won't be quitting now. No way."

Looking back, the CFV core recalls this visit as the turning point in their resolve. Never again did they let the polls and the news media dictate their responses, even when the polls became much worse. Never again did they consider stopping short of winning the election. Furthermore, the two political consultants who had raised the question in the first place seemed impressed with Will's answer. They solidly supported CFV all the way to Election Day thereafter.

Mark put it this way: "The conversation with these guys refocused our efforts and our commitment to finish this job and finish it right. Perhaps that was our visitors' true mission after all."

POLITICAL RALLIES

From the beginning CFV debated whether or not to hold public rallies for their supporters. The homosexuals were marching at every opportunity. They held parades and protests, occasionally picketing Will Perkins' Chrysler dealership in drag to gain more media exposure for themselves.

CFV developed a different strategy. The first step in avoiding confrontation came when Tony and friends had boycotted the gay pride parade during the early campaign against Colorado Springs' Human Rights Ordinance. Something about this early tactic rang bells. It spoke of confidence in the arguments, not in media exposure or perception. It also seemed to produce the right results, contributing to the ultimate defeat of the local law.

As the amendment campaign gained steam, CFV backers all across the state began to urge for public demonstrations. Emotions ran high against the homosexual provocations. Invitations to march and assemble came from many groups. CFV declined them all. The only strategy they embraced was to quietly hold small seminars and press conferences. They had already learned that homosexual activists would infiltrate and try to provoke violence. Activists had already disrupted with loud noises, whistle blowing, picketing, and other forms of unrest during their press conferences. Why invite such hate baiting on a large scale?

In May 1992 a major pollster in Boulder conducted a survey that lent weight to this gut decision on CFV's part. They published a report that predicted the Colorado "gay rights fight to be a brutal brawl in the mud . . . . Like two slam-dancers waiting for a beat, the supporters and opponents of the Colorado for Family Values anti-gay rights initiative are poised to start bashing each other."[152]

The rationale behind the pollster's dire prediction came from a poll on the moral beliefs surrounding Amendment 2. Their survey had found that in Colorado 34% of the people expressed strong moral objections to homosexuality, and 26% strongly disagreed. Lots of strong emotion here, they warned. The moderates in between amounted to roughly a third of the population. To the pollsters, this was a recipe for disaster. CFV thus proceeded with great caution. They did not want their good arguments obscured by "a brawl in the mud."

While homosexual activists continued to seek every opportunity to get these two explosive sides into a public fight, CFV worked to avoid that possibility. All political rallies in favor of Amendment 2 were nixed.

NO ROOM FOR HATRED

It seemed almost impossible for Amendment 2's principal framers to see their motives vilified in the media as hateful or as spawning violence against homosexuals. This defamation tactic had begun with the very first announcement of the amendment's language. They knew Amendment 2 did not deserve the charges. Still, the attacks hurt because those who had put forward the amendment were Christians of the religious right persuasion. Accusations of violence and hatred struck close to the core of their creed—"love your neighbor as yourself."[153]

As the hate-crime statistics and alleged gay bashing stories continued to escalate in the press, Mark Olsen proposed a strategy called "No Room For Hatred." The essence of his idea was to take the hate argument away from the opposition by actively and loudly opposing hatred through CFV's own position.

"When we defend ourselves against hate or gay bashing we are hurting ourselves," he argued. "It is like Nixon when he said, 'I am not a crook.' He dignified the charge by repeating it in reference to himself."

Later, to keep CFV on this positive track, Tony Marco suggested that CFV propose the signing of a joint "Resolution in favor of a principled debate" with the leaders of the opposition, EPOC, and other prominent gay rights leaders statewide. Mark drew up the resolution in June 1992. It stated, among other things, that:

> . . . hatred toward those you disagree with has no place in a principled difference of opinion. Aggression against another human being is always wrong. No matter the issue, no matter the differences, those we disagree with are still people. People with feelings. People with a fundamental right to live in peace and dignity.

In fact, this resolution was signed by CFV's leaders and presented to the opposition at a press conference. The press ignored the resolution and so did the opposition. This seemed to confirm the impression arising from reading the *Overhauling of Straight*

America, that all the hate talk had been a deliberate tactic by the homosexual lobby. Hate served their political agenda of vilifying the opposition.

Internally, however, Mark's No Room for Hatred campaign served CFV well. It stirred a healthy debate among the staff. It forced them to look at themselves from the outside, constantly re-examining their message and its meaning in the public square. "Was Amendment 2 hateful?" they asked. "Are our methods communicating hate?" No Room sharpened their decision making skills to the point that, when they finally decided against implementing the campaign, they did so in favor of the simple truth: nothing about CFV nor Amendment 2 had anything at all to do with hatred toward homosexuals.

More than that, by this time CFV had become convinced of their best weapons: the amendment and Will Perkins. The truth would perhaps not have broken through the opposition's irrational hate talk if Will had not embodied *reason* so very well.

As time passed, CFV learned that things could get much uglier than they did in the Colorado campaign. In Oregon, where the level of emotion had remained high, homosexuals deployed "anti-bigot goon squads" which disrupted—sometimes violently—the petition process for Measure 9. In Oregon, also, extremely violent and threatening posters appeared, promising violence to the state if it passed the measure.

CFV would simply advise anyone taking on this issue that, in the absence of a spokesman like Will Perkins, a No Room For Hatred campaign might have much to recommend it. Especially as a means to lower the tensions and the accusations of hatred which will come against anyone opposing gay rights.

Since the Colorado election, the churches of Lewiston, Maine picked up on this idea. They publicly invited both sides in their local gay rights election issue to come to a specific church, sit down, and sign a commitment to conduct a reasoned, non-hateful debate. The homosexual lobby did not show up. They also lost the election.

THE TABLOID

Long after the No Room For Hatred approach had been shelved by CFV, Mark Olsen subbed its ideas into perhaps the single greatest contribution to the '92 campaign. It was an 8-page tabloid newspaper that presented the Amendment 2 arguments as the media never could, or would. Staying up all night for two nights in a row, he laid out a barrage of information so devastating that it received mention in the opposition's subsequent election night speech.

Seven-hundred-fifty-thousand of these Amendment 2 tabloids were printed and drop-shipped to CFV volunteers across the state. Each area leader was given a walking list of all the registered voters in their targeted zone. Will Perkins suggested that the tabloid be packaged in water proof blue plastic and thrown on the voter's porches like a newspaper. The job was monumental, but with Kevin Tebedo's army of volunteers, it was completed one week before the election.

The two-color, easily read paper followed under the headline: "Equal rights—not special rights! Stop special class status for homosexuality. Vote Yes on Amendment 2." The entire list of charts, graphs, and short items proceeded under the civil rights arguments. All behavioral and health statistics used were related to these issues.

In the bastion of political correctness, Boulder, Colorado, in voting districts where the tabloid was carried door to door, Amendment 2 won. The same held true in the suburbs of Denver, where Amendment 2 won four of six counties, though losing the inner city in a close race. Six-hundred-eighteen volunteers in the Denver area met and distributed tabloids door-to-door in 1,100 voting precincts. All-in-all, no one with CFV would have wanted to see election day without that tabloid out there doing its job.

TV, BEHAVIOR, AND CENSORSHIP

I had worked for a year in the Colorado television industry and anticipated helping CFV with the production of television commercials. Throughout the campaign I had received warnings that a disproportionate number of people employed in production and broadcast television were living the homosexual lifestyle. "Flaming" was the adjective used most often in this regard. Of course, the same thing had been said of the television industry in Texas, Canada, New York, Atlanta, Los Angeles, and other places where I had worked in the past.

It is taken for granted that homosexuals have found an economic and philosophical home in all of the communications arts. But like their own 10%-of-the-population-is-gay myth, (which turns out to be somewhere between .5% and 1.5%)[154] their numbers in every area of life have been vastly overestimated. Still, I took extra precautions against reprisal. I sought and obtained a confidentiality agreement with a production house in advance, binding its employees to professional silence as I prepared to produce TV commercials for Amendment 2.

As the campaign neared its final weeks, the polls showed Amendment 2 losing by 46-54 percent. I grew worried and lost confidence in my original high-road approach to TV commercials. The lock-step thinking in the news media seemed impervious to the truth. CFV's good arguments were not making headlines, not getting through. I feared that Colorado's voters were being bullied and intimidated by all the hate, bigotry, homophobia, and discrimination talk, in spite of the amendment's excellent arguments. The discussions about civil rights law had failed to excite a strong response from the conservative population. I sensed that something dramatic would be required to break through the media mirage, something to boldly challenge the bullying cultural elite of the state in the last days of the campaign—or all might be lost.

I called Mark and Will, who were focused on distributing the tabloid at the time. The tabloid would be the only thing in print representing our side against the media lock-out. I suggested we produce hard hitting TV commercials based on homosexual behavior. These would light a highly visible fire for our arguments, I said. We had obtained and viewed an incredible number of hours of public domain gay pride parade footage in which thousands of homosexuals put their lifestyle, most vulgarly, in the faces of the citizens of those California cities where they had been given special protections for many years. The parades featured the kind of public nudity and lewdness that would otherwise have landed people in jail. In San Francisco, then Mayor Diane Feinstein rode in a gay pride float, boldly endorsing these outrageous exhibitionists. The gay pride parades caused us to recall an instruction from *The Overhauling of Straight America*, in which the authors say:

> In the early stages of any campaign to reach straight America, the masses should not be shocked and repelled by premature exposure to homo*sexual* behavior itself. [emphasis theirs] Instead, the imagery of sex should be downplayed and gay rights should be reduced to an abstract social question as much as possible. First let the camel get his nose inside the tent—and only later his unsightly derriere!

How incredibly disgusting and cynical. Several things seemed apparent: One, the homosexual community had followed the *Overhauling* plan to the letter. Only in San Francisco, New York, and other cities where they had long ago established protected class status, did they parade the full diversity of their sexuality in public. In Colorado they had reduced gay rights to an abstract social question, i.e., "the nose of the camel." The Colorado news media and social engineering establishment, if they had not read *The Overhauling of Straight America*, could have written it. They had certainly been used as the willing vehicle for its agenda. Until now, everything had gone according to the homosexual script. They looked like a bunch of nice guys, while Colorado for Family Values was being smeared as the aggressors. "Why not show the footage?" I asked. "What can we lose? They call this stuff gay pride. If they are so proud of it, let's show it to the state."

My friend Tony Marco was not present to hear this. He told me later that he viewed my advice as a big mistake. From the very beginning, Tony and CFV had been careful not to overexpose the gay pride footage. They had presented it to leaders for evaluation, but did not advise public showings. What I suggested came from my own susceptibility to the opinion polls showing Amendment 2 losing the election. Fear had motivated me.

In that mode, I suggested that the gay pride footage would have to be edited for decency, but argued that it was important to show because it represented the camel's "unsightly derriere." It was the hidden part of the gay agenda. Why should we let the homosexuals reveal their real lifestyle on their own terms, I suggested? Especially when such an unhealthy lifestyle had nearly obtained the power to "make us learn that they were just like anybody else?" (Except for their average lifespans, and their unhealthy sexual practices, and public lewdness, which of course, according to the politically correct, didn't relate to our issue.)

Meanwhile, CFV had fallen critically short of funds. The budget for our commercials would have to be lower than low, I was told. A tenth of my original estimate was suggested to me. Kevin put forward the idea of using simple 10-second commercials. Very short, to the point. Less costly for production and time buying. This sounded good to me and to Will Perkins. Will said that the only possible way we could get enough saturation of the market would be with 10-second buys anyway. Another political decision determined by a lack of funds.

Since I had another production going at the time, I figured that, if I could piggyback the costs of production with my existing sessions, we could get the spots on the screen within the paltry budget.

Some of our political consultants informed us that 10-second TV spots simply wouldn't get the job done. At least 30-second spots would be needed, and even those would be doubtful, unless strategically planned. We had no polling data to direct our messages. We were flying blind again. Considering their advice carefully and soberly, we decided to go ahead anyway.

For one thing, they did not know exactly what we had proposed. They had not seen the potential of that public domain gay pride footage in our files. I had a good idea of how I wanted to assemble it. "No one will need more than 10-seconds of this stuff," I said, "in order to make up their minds to either hate us or support us. This issue may lend itself to the only 10-second political commercials in election history. Besides, more than 10-seconds might offend too much, like the Cameron brochure."

Will Perkins did his usual soul searching, and more. He called the San Francisco police department to get the low-down on the footage from that city's gay pride parade. He asked first if what he saw was trick photography or the real thing? Did the homosexuals really do all that lewd stuff on the streets?

"Yes, they did, and more."

"Do you guys have laws against public lewdness and indecency in San Francisco?"

"Yes."

"Why didn't you make arrests? These people were grossly indecent."

After an awkward pause the police official said, "Our main concern is keeping peace. These people can't be controlled if you cross them. Besides," he added, "we all wanted to keep our jobs. Did you see Mayor Feinstein in that parade? What are *we* gonna do?"

Following this conversation Will found the ability to make his decision about the TV commercials. He felt a new level of conviction that this kind of behavior would overwhelm every social structure in the country, once given the advantage of protected class status. "Colorado must be warned," he said. "Let's do it."

The TV commercials seemed the last card in our hand. Once they aired, we would feel that we had at least done everything we knew how to do to overcome the media bias and see Amendment 2 stop forced affirmation of homosexuality in Colorado.

Faxing scripts back and forth for days as I flew to and from my other production site in Florida, Will and I collaborated on a series of very simple 10-second scenarios. (As we both believed, simple is better.) Kevin and Mark had stressed that one of our greatest problems would be confusion in the voting booth. We could lose the election simply because people might not understand the ballot question. "Should I vote yes or no on Amendment 2?" That's really all many voters wanted to hear from CFV. Their minds were made up long ago. They just didn't want to make a mistake on the ballot by misreading the language of the amendment and answering "no" when they meant "yes."

It seemed to us that people needed one set of instructions that they would easily remember, "vote yes." The punchline of our commercials would have to repeat this information. We would include it at the end of every spot. We decided to strengthen the instruction with a little ditty, a little rhyme to trigger memory. Each commercial would pose a different question, but end with the same answer: "Yes we do . . . vote Yes on 2."

Here's how it worked:

(1) 10 SECOND SCENE: we see outrageously provocative "in-your-face" poses from a San Francisco gay pride parade; VOICE OVER: "This city gave 'special rights' to homosexuals and now they can't stop *this*—! Do we want to stop it in Colorado? *Yes we do, vote Yes on 2."*

(2) 10 SECOND SCENE: more of same from several other city parades; VOICE OVER: "These people would call it a 'hate crime' if you spoke out against their lifestyle. Do we want to protect freedom of speech in Colorado? *Yes we do, vote Yes on 2."*

(3) 10 SECOND SCENE: small children with parents in close proximity to sexual degradation in a gay pride parade. We see male and female S&M role models, Dykes on Bikes, leather and bondage displays. This is the gay answer to family values, *Gloria Goes to Gay Pride*. VOICE OVER: "Where gays have special rights school kids are taught that this lifestyle is healthy and normal—*by law!* Do we want to protect our children? *Yes we do, vote Yes on 2."*

At the end of this spot we found a shot of a little oriental girl, perhaps six or seven, being literally dragged along the San Francisco parade route by her lesbian mother. The child is screaming and crying as all around her adults with whips and chains celebrate their gay pride. The expression on the little girl's face is frozen and brought full screen at the end. "*Do we want to protect our children? Yes we do, vote Yes on 2.*"

I cannot imagine a right thinking person who would consider these gay parade scenes a proper environment for children. The picture says more about the threat this lifestyle poses to America than any words we could say. It is an image that burns through all of the media sweet talk about gays being just like the rest of us. This spot alone, in my opinion, would win any election in any state of the union . . . if allowed to air.

When Will Perkins purchased time on the TV stations in the Denver market, which represented 70% of the state's electorate, every station's "standards and practices" committee previewed the spots. Seeing their incredible impact they cried, "Foul!" "Indecent!" "Poor taste!"

Of course, to us these remarks coming from TV executives carried about the same moral weight as an airborne virus. Nevertheless, these strangely moralistic gatekeepers piously refused to air our spots, claiming them to be "indecent."

Will commented, "If they used the same criteria for network TV shows as they used against us, they'd be showing test patterns 50% of the time."

Even though the CFV commercial scenes had been heavily censored with black-out blocks covering exposed body parts and other obscenities. Even though the scenes were not staged but recorded in broad daylight on the public streets of American cities. Even though we had ordered the spots played only late at night to avoid younger audiences. Even though the news media claims to be virulently opposed to censorship—they dared to censor Colorado for Family Values with impunity. And the liberal elite applauded.

Not only did they refuse the spots in the face of our good arguments, they made the ban stick. The Federal Communications Commission would have overruled them in our favor, except Amendment 2 was a state issue, not federal. It remained beyond the feds' jurisdiction. Thus, we were drummed off the air before 70% of our voters in the final 10 days before the election. (Might we say again, "Welcome to the gay '90s?")

The sickening arrogance and hypocrisy of political correctness hit us like a kick in the stomach. This mental lock-step has no standard, if no morals. It only gives lip service to ideas such as censorship.

On a 1-to-10 scale, normally censorship rates a 10 as a news story. Of course, newsmen always assume censorship to be in the other direction. They look for those incidents where a concerned parent tries to remove *Heather Has Two Mommies* or *Gloria Goes to Gay Pride* from grammar school library shelves, upon which, you'll read a high decibel denunciation of the evils of censorship from every news source in the land. But CFV? Amendment 2? Gay Pride? Are you kidding?

How much did CFV lose through censorship? We know we lost the metropolitan Denver area where our opposition spent much of their bigtime TV budget. Prevailing wisdom said that if Denver is lost, the state is lost. However, the CFV tabloid distribution in Denver's suburbs seemed to overcome the effects of the blackout there. All the counties surrounding Denver metro voted in our favor. We also know that where the television commercials aired in the rest of Colorado, Amendment 2 won 67% of the counties. Our opinion is that the TV spots did not convince many voters to vote for the amendment. Rather, the spots motivated them to get out and make their vote count on both sides of the issue. There were simply more people on the amendment's side.

As an interesting sidebar to this story, two months after being censored from TV in Denver, NBC aired "The Gay '90s: Sex, Power and Influence" using several of the same gay pride scenes used in CFV commercials. The only difference, our scenes were dressed up for public consumption with censored blocks on the screen. NBC's footage included a scene in which a man walked along the street displaying a 16 inch replica of his genitals (something we had blocked out for decency sake). But the Denver NBC affiliate had no problem with the footage in "The Gay '90s" because, by their standards of decency, it had been used in good taste to present homosexuality as a legitimate lifestyle.

"The Gay '90s" production shamelessly venerated domestic partnerships, even lesbian insemination for the obtaining of children with two mommies. "These images," wrote Matt Roush, *USA Today*'s TV reviewer of the show, "should help deflate the arguments of the underinformed."[155]

Apparently NBC News executives assumed that America was underinformed as well. At the show's conclusion that night, Maria

Shriver spoke for them: "For *all of us* here at NBC News, good night." This phrase could not have been uttered without full network approval. Media executives were once again demonstrating their elitist attitude.

One would hope Denver TV management would show vigilance and courage against this high-handed network treatment of their viewers. But they did not. The Denver affiliate, which had banned Colorado for Family Value's commercials for indecency, raised not a single eyebrow to Maria's naked use of the same scenes. Their double-standard showed that their original ban on CFV had not been honest.

I called the *Gazette Telegraph*, *Denver Post* and *Rocky Mountain News* asking them to report on this media hypocrisy. "Here's a censorship story with pictures," I said. I offered them video tape of our commercial and "The Gay '90s" scenes side-by-side for comparison. The pictures could have been printed in the paper to illustrate how Amendment 2 had been discriminated against by Denver's TV broadcasters. Clear-cut censorship.

"Sorry," the editors of all three papers replied. "It's not news."

Returning from Denver discouraged and trampled in spirit by the arrogance and impunity of television censorship, Will Perkins had another idea. Why not capitalize on the TV censorship issue via radio?

RADIO

Something new is happening in the media these days. It's called talk radio. Oh, there are loose-lipped shock-jocks like Howard Stern spewing around out there, but we are talking intelligence, values, and "mega dittos buddy"—Rush Limbaugh. The voice of conservatism, shut out of the media (in the same manner that Amendment 2 was shut out of Denver TV) are finding their voice in Mr. Limbaugh, who has tapped a powerful reservoir of frustration with the news media.

During the Colorado campaign, Amendment 2 found a similar local conservative voice in Denver's Mike Rosen, who presented his astute observations and arguments on radio KOA. In Colorado

Springs, Chuck Baker performed the same kind of service on KVOR. These hours-long talk radio formats guaranteed that at least an intelligent presentation of Amendment 2 would be made possible in any given debate.

The other radio bonus came through Christian and conservative stations. We had found this group of broadcasters essential in locating our petition volunteers early in the campaign. As the campaign drew to an end, Will had placed a sixty-second Amendment 2 commercial on these friendly stations in Denver and around the state.

Now, with the extra money available from aborted TV ads, Will proposed we spend it on a new version of a sixty-second radio ad. Since our censorship story had been shut out of the press, we had one last chance to tell the people about it through Denver radio.

"No one likes censorship," he said. "Especially when the so-called champions of 'free speech' are guilty of it."

We took the master of the original 60-second radio spot running in Denver and interrupted it for maximum effect:

> I apologize for interrupting folks, this is Will Perkins. I've interrupted this commercial because channels 2,4,9 and even the cable TV companies in Denver have refused to air our commercials showing homosexuals 'acting up' in public streets. We figure if you see what the homosexuals really do when you give them special rights, you'll agree with us that we've got to stop it here in Colorado. But the TV stations have said 'no' to our commercials. We don't know if they have received pressure from the opposition, Governor Romer, congresswoman Pat Schroeder, Denver Mayor Webb who has voiced his opposition, pressure from the homosexual community, or if it is an agenda of the station management. In any event, it's an unprecedented action, prohibiting your right to know the facts about Amendment 2. Why don't they want you to see these spots? Ladies and gentlemen, if for no other reason than this blatant act of censorship, Colorado needs you to vote Yes on Amendment 2. Paid for by Colorado for Family Values.

We played the interrupted commercial on every available Denver radio station until we ran out of money.

ELECTION DAY SURPRISE

November 3, 1992 brought a feeling of gloom to nearly everyone associated with CFV. It went with the exhaustion. But even more, it went with the headlines: POLLS SHOW AMENDMENT 2 GOING DOWN TO DEFEAT.[156]

"It should lose, 47% to 53%," said pollster Floyd Ciruli, who conducted polls for 9News in Denver. *Denver Post* business editor, Henry Dubroff, boasted, "Give them credit—polls show that the 'Vote No on 2' campaign is way ahead. They've enlisted support from companies ranging from US West to Apple Computer to The Greater Denver Chamber of Commerce . . . [they've] mounted a powerful argument that passing an anti-gay rights law would hurt Colorado's image nationally and damage our booming tourism business."[157]

The last minute feeling for Amendment 2 supporters was that all had been done, and it still was not enough. However, I am told that in a morning prayer meeting in the CFV offices the mood was upbeat. One of the volunteers, an elderly lady, predicted victory. She pooh-poohed every suggestion that the odds were against the amendment. She simply believed in none of the polls, she said. She believed in prayer. With no anxiety, she simply went home to watch the returns.

Will Perkins believed in victory, but he remained realistic. He had prepared both a winning and losing speech for the press. His losing ideas went something to the effect that it had been important to fight the issue, even to lose it, in order that future generations facing the strange new world of forced homosexual affirmation would look back and appreciate the effort at least. And he had expressed some thoughts to the press about blaming Denver's TV censorship for the election loss, and mounting another campaign.[158]

Regardless of the outcome, he had booked a flight to South America the following week. He planned to visit one of his daughters in Santiago, Chile, feeling the need for a complete change of scenery. After that, he expected that he would return to the routine of running a car dealership for a while, playing a round or two of golf with his son, Tom, and playing the grandfather role again, albeit with more concern for the future if the polls proved to be correct.

The CFV office staff went about making plans to watch the final election returns from Perkins' showroom floor, where they could lend moral support to each other at the actual hour of the dark revelation—or victory.

The news media would be on hand for one purpose only: to record the expected defeat. Especially focusing their closeup cameras on the faces of the Colorado for Family Values' principal bigots, as the gay community found the homophobic shoe to fit them, and then proceeded to "*. . . make them try it on for size, with all of America watching.*" What a night of anticipation for politically correct Colorado!

Having cast my ballot ahead of time, I hid out in the deepest forests of the Colorado mountains from Halloween until election day, searching for elk with a 30.06 rifle. Accompanied by two Air Force captains, we left camp each day before daybreak and did not return until well after dark. I never saw an elk, but I never thought about Amendment 2 for three full days. Then came election day. I felt like a coward. Riddled with guilt, I drove home to face the returns.

Reaching home at midday, I showered, then called Mark Olsen. He informed me that we were losing in Denver. No huge surprise. Seventy percent of the state lived in the region that had been banned from viewing our TV spots. "But the other counties aren't in yet," he said. "Don't count us out."

Whistling in the dark, I thought to myself. "Yeah. Listen, if you don't mind, I won't be coming into the showroom. I think I'll just watch it here on the TV. I'm really exhausted from hunting and I'll be going back out in the morning, so I'll call you when its over." Perhaps no one felt more sure of defeat than I did.

Toward early evening a small earthquake rattled the state. Not a literal quake, but a social tremor. Call it an act of God. Call it Wiley Coyote noticing suddenly that the fuse on the bomb he is holding has mysteriously burned to its detonation, as in the distance he hears a familiar "beep, beep." El Paso county, seat of bigotry and hatred, where Colorado Springs reigned supreme, had not just voted favorably for Amendment 2, but had delivered a whopping 2-to-1 margin! If the far flung counties of the state followed anywhere close to that trend, or even approximated it . . . hello Amendment 2!

I suddenly glued myself to the TV. By early evening the vote counters in Denver were excusing themselves, counting and recounting the tallies from what *Overhauling* had called the "antiquated backwaters" of the state. Oh yes, Amendment 2 country! The *Denver Post* reporter Michael Booth ran to his news desk and hastily typed out the opening line for the morning paper: GAY-RIGHTS BAN NARROWLY WINNING, AMENDMENT 2 OPPONENTS STUNNED: "In a potentially stunning defeat for backers of gay rights," he wrote, "voters last night were narrowly approving a constitutional amendment. . . ."[159] Of course TV reporters were on the scene live, reporting everything that missed Booth's deadline late into the night.

An hour later, Bill Clinton's victory was hailed. In Colorado he won, as across the nation, with a minority of 40-something percent of the vote. Let the celebration begin at Democratic Headquarters in Denver. Strike up the band!

Whistles blew, horns blatted, champagne corks popped, aerosol confetti sprattled the chandeliers.

But wait! What's this? Some livid gays from the streets have taken over the Democratic stage? What? They are ordering us to stop celebrating? There is nothing to celebrate? Why? Because of some tragedy? An airline crash? An assassination? What tragedy?

Amendment 2! What? It won? By how much? 51%? Impossible! Why even Clinton didn't get that much. (False low reporting begins here. For months, no Colorado news source would correctly report the 53.4%.) "How could this happen in liberal Colorado?" they asked. Never mind that a majority vote is democracy in action, to the gay lobby something had gone terribly wrong here. Dim all the lights. Pour out the champagne. Mourn, wail, rend your garments.

At which point the angry homosexuals on stage announced their official version of how it could happen—Colorado for Family Values had run a slick campaign that had fooled people into thinking they were voting against special rights by voting for Amendment 2. But wait, CFV's TV ads had been banned in Denver. EPOC had swamped the airwaves with anti-amendment spots. How could this be? Surely you can't simply fool *that* many people, *that* much of the time, can you? Maybe the voters knew what they were doing! Soon someone shouted through a bullhorn (well-named in this case) the real reason Amendment 2 had won was because—"Colorado has become a 'State of Hate!'"

(For those completely paralyzed by political correctness, please remember that is not hateful to pause for a laugh at this point.)

"Boycott the State of Hate," screamed someone from the crowd.

GOVERNOR ROY ROMER, left, and Denver's MAYOR WELLINGTON WEBB, right, march to the state capitol with 400 people, angry over losing their election issue.

"Punish the State of Hate!" cried another.

This angry mob poured into the streets of Denver and marched on the capitol. They would not celebrate a Democratic victory on this night. No way! They could not conceive that the same state that had elected the Clintons had rejected the notion of giving them protected class status. The state that had sent Pat Schroeder to Washington, Roy Romer to the Governor's mansion, and Senator Ben Nighthorse Campbell to the halls of Congress—this state, which had been the first to legalize abortion, the first (among the very few) to approve former California Governor Jerry Brown in the '92 presidential primary—had now ratified Amendment 2?!?

Impossible.

The obvious answer lay in the fact that Amendment 2 had been an issue to transcend party politics. It could not have won without Conservatives and Liberals, Democrats, Libertarians, Independents as well as Republicans voting for it. Something in the Amendment 2 logic had broken through to the people. The Achilles heel of gay politics had been rightly exposed. But the truth seemed simply too painful to bear. Better to declare bigotry and ignorance as the winners on this night.

Feeling betrayed and alone, near the morning hours gay activists threatened to do violent things to city property if someone didn't get out of bed and show they cared. At which point the police informed Denver Mayor Wellington Webb and the honorary chairman of the homosexual campaign, Governor Roy Romer, that they were being summoned. Romer and Webb returned to the scene of the near riot and marched to the capitol in solidarity with the angry gay mob. Along the route, the governor grabbed a "No on 2" sign and waved it before rolling news cameras. So did Denver's Mayor Webb. The *Rocky Mountain News*, carried their pictures on the front page.[160]

Irony of ironies, this governor carrying the "No on 2" sign had sworn on a Bible that he would faithfully defend the state constitution. Amendment 2 was now a legitimate part of that constitution—voted into place by the will of the people. Did the constitutional part of Romer's sworn duty give him pause? No. The governor took the bull by the bullhorn and pledged himself to overturn Amendment 2. He claimed sadly that Colorado needed to be "educated" on the issue and, furthermore, he would lead the charge to remove their ignorance. Thus reinforcing the standard homosexual perception from *The Overhauling of Strait America* that all who opposed homosexual rights were intellectually backward.

Newly doctored protest signs appeared: "Hate is *NOW* a Family Value." (During the campaign the sign had read, "Hate is *NOT* a Family Value." Amendment 2 supporters had completely agreed.) The ever-faithful press took closeup pictures of the newly doctored sign and televised the slogan nationwide. (The effect of the message? . . . Colorado had voted for hate.)

Will did not declare victory until 12:30 am, determined not to suffer some kind of last minute reversal. He gave his speech to the subdued and stunned news cameras.

Meanwhile, the victory celebration in Perkins' showroom swung between moods of disbelief, elation, and sobriety. Disbelief as the size of the victory continued to grow; elation as well wishers and volunteers came by the dealership to congratulate the tenacity of Will Perkins and Colorado for Family Values; sobriety every time any of the CFV insiders stopped to realize they had made no plans for winning. They had spent their last dime getting to election day. Not only money, but energies had been exhausted. Having won the battle for the hearts and minds of the state in spite of the odds seemed a bit much to comprehend.

"What do we do next?"

"Take some time off," Will replied. "Let them sort it out." Perhaps the most naïve thought CFV's chairman harbored, bordering on wishful thinking, was that he could simply walk away after November 3rd. Win or lose, his duty to his grandchildren and to the state would have been fully rendered. He confesses that, yes, he may have still had that thought as he boarded an airplane for South America.

7

Fallout from a surprising victory

In a final CFV media committee meeting before the election, a volunteer posed the question: "If by chance Amendment 2 wins, what do you think the opposition will do?"

After a short silence another volunteer replied, "I think they will self-destruct."

Several laughed, considering it a remark to break pre-election tension, nothing more.

But the speaker interrupted again. "Wait now. Think about it. It is a matter of expectations. We know we are in danger of losing, but our opponents only expect to win. If this election forces them to face the fact that the majority is not with them, they might do something really indiscreet."

Eyes glazed over. "OK, next item of business." No one suspected that this off-the-cuff commentary would prove prophetic.

SELF-DESTRUCTION & GAY POLITICS

The angry explosion at the Democratic celebrations on election night gave the first clue that Colorado gays were seriously out-of-touch with reality. The next night, 7,000 homosexual supporters gathered at the state capitol again, nearly equalling the size of CFV's core list of supporters statewide. Governor Romer and Denver's mayor showed up, sowing seeds of disrespect for the election. Romer hinted that the amendment might be found unconstitutional. Mayor Webb told the crowd that he thought the amendment was invalid in the city of Denver. The homosexual lobby applauded these elected heros, and gay leaders vowed a lawsuit and a boycott on the spot.[161]

Only five days after the election the *Denver Post* reported that a group of psychologists who cater to Denver homosexuals reported that their clients were in shock, realizing that most of their friends, co-workers, and acquaintances had voted with the majority. This part of the response seemed normal. Certainly it takes time to adjust to any significant loss. However, this particular report ended with the words of a psychologist who said, "It's sort of like being thrown out of your family."[162]

Good mental health demands that reality be faced squarely. While it is understandable that homosexuals would lose touch with reality following an election defeat, it is reckless for authorities who supposedly care for them to reinforce their worst paranoid fantasies. Losing an election may feel like being thrown out of one's family but this feeling should stay on the couch. It has no basis in reality, therefore it is dangerous and inflammatory to make it the bottom line of any credible commentary. Perhaps an unstable gay person who could no longer distinguish between rhetoric and reality would read this and be pushed to desperation.

One Colorado Springs homosexual spokesperson lamented excessively following the election vote, "You don't know what it feels like to walk into the local supermarket, look around at the people you thought were your friends, and suddenly realize everybody hates you."

"Everybody hates you?" Perkins replied. "That doesn't make any more sense than for me to walk out into the parking lot, look at all the cars, and say, 'anybody who didn't buy a Chrysler hates me.'" With tongue-in-cheek he added, "I could say they didn't show good judgement, but I couldn't say they hated me."

Apparently this kind of logic no longer occurs spontaneously among journalists. Following the vote, national TV coverage displayed a young homosexual in Denver responding to Amendment 2. "To us it means the beginning of gay ethnic cleansing in this country." No qualifying of this statement followed. No challenge or examination of its idiocy.

This is where political correctness betrays everyone. It confuses reality and fantasy. It has no principles, only an agenda that blinds its true believers. Even a psychologist cannot discern between an electorate and a family. Newsmen cannot distinguish between disapproval and hatred, race and sexual preference, legal constraint and ethnic cleansing. How can homosexuals be expected to grasp the difference between tolerance and affirmation? With this sick reinforcement from the cultural elite, the off-the-cuff prediction that militant homosexuals might self-destruct suddenly became no laughing matter in Colorado.

The next Sunday, a long-haired '60s holdover columnist, Ed Quillen (who had opposed Amendment 2), wrote angrily in the *Denver Post*: "Gay-rights activists are often their own worst enemies, as they demonstrated Tuesday night when they stormed the Democratic victory celebration in Denver. Watching in amazement from Salida, I got this message from them: 'We don't care about anybody else's rights of speech and assembly. Nor are we going to build a coalition to repeal this hateful amendment in 1994. Instead, we're going to shout and stomp and destroy the evening. Nobody has a right to celebrate unless we approve.' The gay fascists set the cause back by at least a decade . . ."[163]

Denver Post columnist, Tom Gavin wrote: "I, apparently unlike homosexuals of the state and nation, was raised to respect things like majority rule. Like the free vote. Like democracy. Me 'lose' elections? You bet. . . . But never—no never!—did I get out of bed after yet another vexing election defeat and stamp my little foot. And make a little mouth. And throw a little fit. And agitate for a boycott. What is there about homosexuals that makes them so petty? So vindictive? So, yes, intolerant? And why are politicians so quick to cave in, to kowtow, to genuflect, to bow and scrape . . . ?"[164]

In spite of their apparent disorientation, within days social activists and homosexual leaders seemed ready to launch a counter offensive. First, a Los Angeles group asked entertainers to stay away from Colorado. One national homosexual group telephoned Chrysler headquarters and asked them to "do something" about Will Perkins' in Colorado Springs.

"I understand the art of intimidation," Will responded. "This is a typical tactic that the homosexuals choose to use."[165]

The *Denver Post* carried a Sunday, November 8th, feature

headlined: SHOCKED GAYS LOOKING TO GOVERNMENT FOR VICTORY.[166] The great revelation in this *Post* article came from the mouth of the civil rights director for The Gay and Lesbian Task Force: "We are ready to take the next step, to move on the federal government." He explained that homosexual activists would now demand "pay back" for their multi-million dollar Clinton campaign donation, asking the President to make good on his promise to add homosexuality to the Civil Rights Act of 1964.

Colorado citizens are not stupid. Alarms rang here. Even gay supporters felt something strange in this statement, though they couldn't put their finger on it. The problem with homosexuals coming out boldly for the Civil Rights Act of 1964—now that they had lost the election—lay in the fact that they were betraying a loud and long public stand for "home rule."

Using home rule during the campaign, the gay lobby had argued that local city governments should be allowed to decide their own fate concerning gay rights laws. Thus, Denver, Boulder, and Aspen's gay ordinances should be left unmolested by a statewide law like Amendment 2. The principle of home rule demanded it. This had been a most effective argument used against Amendment 2. Home rule is, after all, a conservative principle, a live-and-let-live idea. Colorado had automatically loved it.

Home rule would have continued to be a very strong argument against Amendment 2 if the gay lobby had embraced the true principle. But they had not. They had only been hypocritical about it from the beginning.

CFV had been the first to point this out. They continued to remind the state that the gay lobby's Ethnic Harassment Bill (H.B. 1059) had been the first violator of home rule in the state. (Many had forgotten this.) The gay attempt to force all the local cities of Colorado to kneel beneath a statewide gay rights law had revealed a total lack of commitment to home rule. Indeed, CFV and Amendment 2 might not have come into existence if the homosexual lobby had not tried to run rough-shod over local autonomy with this legal weapon. CFV continued to claim that no one who had ever supported the Ethnic Harassment Bill could honestly embrace home rule. Therefore, they claimed, the gay lobby had only used it as a campaign tactic. Now, as their spokesman quickly deserted home rule for the Civil Rights Act of 1964, everyone could see who had been telling the truth. CFV.

One year after the Amendment 2 win, a more important lesson about home rule has become apparent. The lesson begins with the idea that there are two levels of home rule:

(1) home rule for laws enacted by a majority vote of the people, and

(2) home rule for laws enacted by the cultural elite. (This is the path gay rights laws have used to advance their agenda over the heads of unsuspecting populations.)

These two levels of home rule are not equal under our form of democracy. The vote of the people takes clear precedence over the vote of the cultural elite. What are the people continuing to say at the ballot box? How are they establishing the highest value of home rule? In Cincinnati on Election Day '93, the people overturned their city council's gay rights ordinance by a whopping 62 percent. In Lewiston, Maine the people overturned their city council's gay ordinance by 67 percent. In Portsmouth, New Hampshire the people ordered their city government *not* to enact a gay rights law by 59 percent.[167]

The issue of home rule belongs to the people first, city councils, governors, and legislatures second. If, in any contest, the gay lobby argues home rule, it can only be seen as a tactic of convenience. They have no real commitment to it.

On November 9, six days after the election, Governor Romer convened a meeting in his office with Rabbi Steven Foster and Jack Lang y Marquez. Marquez reported on the meeting in a memo to the Colorado Civil Rights Commission as follows:

> 11/9: Attended meeting in governor's office regarding Amendment 2. Attendance was at the request of the governor and was also attended by Commissioner Foster. Outcome of the meeting was the *formation of a task force of business and community leaders* to minimize the effects of the passage of Amendment 2 and *develop a strategy for*

> *reversal of the amendment.* Governor Romer stated that *his official position* would have to be to uphold the will of the people and to see to the implementation of the law.[168] [emphasis added]

This cabal of zealots directed by the governor actually conspired to overturn a part of the law the governor had sworn to uphold. "*His official position would have to be to uphold the will of the people?*" How could he actually do that and at the same time convene a meeting to reverse Amendment 2? In this meeting he had instigated the formation of a task force and a strategy to do just that. This was no casual discussion of a potential problem. Could this same governor be trusted to put the state's best defense behind the amendment in a court of law?

The arrogance and elitism represented in this meeting is revealing and appalling. It shows the desperate risks the political elite are sometimes willing to take to advance their social agenda. Romer's conduct of this meeting flirted dangerously with an impeachable offense![169]

On November 11, Marty Booker took his life in Colorado Springs because of Amendment 2. Well, perhaps not *just* because of Amendment 2. He had AIDS, too. He was only 26. A close friend had committed suicide two months before, and that had depressed him. But he blamed Amendment 2 in his suicide note and gave the Colorado newsrooms just the story they were after: "I refuse to live in a state where a few people can make my life a living hell," he wrote the day after the election. "Thanks to CFV, hell was delivered to my very front door! I suppose I'm weak but it took a lot of courage to get out before I would have to live through the 'Auschwitz' CFV has in mind for people like me! I love you all. I'm sorry my crime in life was LOVE—albeit to the same gender."[170]

Gazette Telegraph newswriter Angela Dire reinforced the demented reasoning in Booker's suicide note, commenting, "Not even his best friend or the aunt who raised him knew just how powerful a symbol Amendment 2 was for Booker."

What did she mean? Most people understood Amendment 2 as a powerful symbol of democracy in action; like the "powerful symbol" of the election of Bill Clinton (depressing stuff for conservative Americans. Should they end it all too?). The truth is, the news media themselves had hyped Amendment 2 into a symbol of hate for unstable souls like Marty Booker. Now they were determined to pass the buck.

Booker's story was picked up and wired coast to coast, finding its way into the *Denver Post* as an Associated Press article the next day: GAY MAN'S SUICIDE NOTE CITES PASSAGE OF AMENDMENT 2.[171] (Newsroom appetites had become truly conscienceless.)

The *Denver Post's* version of the suicide story, published the next day, arrived in former Senator Bill Armstrong's office with a note attached: "You are a murderer. As one of CFV's leaders, you are morally responsible for a young man's death. How many human lives are you willing to sacrifice to your Amendment 2?" A copy of the same note arrived at the home of Barbara Sheldon.

News organizations played Booker's suicide shamelessly for about 48 hours, then suddenly stopped. A widespread rumor put a lid on it. A reliable source had claimed that a politically motivated suicide pact had been plotted. From this rumor, a police probe followed information that Booker had allegedly threatened suicide well before November 3 due to his deterioration from AIDS. AIDS being an overwhelming factor, his claim to have ended his life due to a campaign of Amendment 2 hatred seemed highly suspect. It had also been rumored that the sick man was suspiciously acquainted with Colorado Springs homosexual activists, and that he might have been coached as to the timing of his terminal event. Possibly the content of his note had been suggested to him to make his death mean something heroic to the gay community. The investigation at least stopped newsrooms from mindlessly using this pitiful AIDS-suicide story to further discredit Amendment 2.

A remarkable thing to see was the similar reasoning of the press and that of a suicidal man dying of AIDS. Blame Amendment 2 for his suicide? That made as much sense as the fifty ACT UP billboards placed in Denver displaying the pictures of AIDS victims, now dead: "AIDS is not killing Gordon Bourne," they read, "you are!" Did Denverites seriously feel guilty for killing Gordon Bourne? If so, no wonder Amendment 2 supporters were construed to be the murderers of Marty Booker.

On November 12 the homosexual lobby filed a lawsuit to put Amendment 2 on hold (requesting an injunction). The case became known as *Evans v. Romer*. The plaintiffs were a group of homosexuals, together with the cities of Denver, Boulder, and Aspen. Governor Roy Romer who had been the symbolic head of the anti-amendment crowd, was officially named as defendant. (Things in Colorado just got "curiouser and curiouser" after the election.) The state attorney general prepared to defend the amendment under the governor's direction. (Yes, the governor who had started a task force to overturn it.)

CFV knew that their amendment had passed the scrutiny of eight nationally known constitutional lawyers. Now it would face its first Denver judge. A sense of impending doom fell over the amendment supporters. It appeared that the whole election might now end up in the hands of the cultural elite after all. Not exactly the best group to decide the merits of Amendment 2.

On November 13, the *Denver Post* carried a front page picture of a homosexual man enduring a mock crucifixion at a gay rights rally.[172]

On Sunday evening, November 15th, 300 religious left Catholics, Protestants, and Jews gathered at Denver's Central Presbyterian Church on Capitol Hill to pledge themselves anew against Amendment 2. Rabbi Foster of Temple Emanuel addressed the group in deflated generalities, "You and I, dear friends, we're going to make it happen." Reverend Marshall Gourley of Our Lady of Guadalupe Catholic Church added, "CFV, I would suggest, doesn't stand simply for Coloradans for Family Values but Coloradans for Fear and Vindictiveness, Vengeance. People once again feel that they have license to call people names that reflect hate."[173]

On November 17, the city of Atlanta banned city funds for travel to Colorado. November 18, Barbara Streisand stood at an AIDS benefit to declare that the State of Colorado's "moral climate" had become unsuitable for travel. New York City Mayor David Dinkins suggested a travel boycott of the state. High level talk of an organized boycott against Colorado's democratic election surged nationwide, fanned by the eager press.

On December 1, Catholic worshippers arrived for mass at Denver's Basilica of the Immaculate Conception only to find that the statue of the Virgin Mary had been desecrated in the night. (By those hateful homophobes from Colorado For Family Values? No.) The vandals removed all doubt as to their political sentiments. Mary's statue had been draped with a huge condom, a penis had been molded of clay and positioned near her head, then blood colored paint had been thrown over her body. Near the shrine a sign bore this message: "Pope, you are wrong! Condoms save lives." A rainbow of multi-colored condoms were stapled to the protest sign and scattered across the grounds so that none would miss the point. (One cannot help but wonder if Rev. Gourley from Our Lady of Guadalupe Catholic Church figured out from this event just who it was in Colorado who felt they had a "license to call people names that reflect hate?")

An hour earlier the *Denver Post*[174] had received a telephone call: "Today is World AIDS Day," the proud caller had announced. "We threw blood on the steps of the Cathedral, the Basilica I mean, and also on the Virgin Mary there. . . . We're just concerned citizens, concerned about AIDS deaths and the church, you know."

The *Post*'s opinion editor, Al Knight, boldly observed that this kind of tactic ". . . is only slightly different than full-blown terrorist thinking, the kind that advocates an occasional car bombing or random kidnapping, all in the interest of getting someone's attention."

Denver's politicians seemed speechless, having no moral code that would allow them to condemn the sin here, without condemning the sinner. After testing the political winds, they issued statements of condemnation and regret, mostly implicating Amendment 2 and the climate of hatred it had spawned—even as they distanced themselves from the actions of a few homosexual extremists.

But were the desecrators extremists? Or merely activists playing out the collective fantasies of political correctness? Homosexual leaders seemed to confirm the latter. Tom Witte, former editor of the gay magazine *Quest*, used the event as a bully pulpit to tell the Pope that he should cancel his planned '93 summer visit to Denver on World Youth Day. The desecrated Virgin carried the message, he said, "[The Pope] is not welcome."

World AIDS Day organizers excused the vandalism. "There is a lot of anger out there," they sighed, as if such indiscretions just can't be helped. Scott Little of Denver's ACT UP chapter flat out blamed the vandalism on the Catholic Church and the people who had voted for Amendment 2.[175] The impressions left from these remarks made any condemnations of extremism seem as if the political elite were laughing behind their hands.

These antics began to reveal two things:

(1) the homosexual lobby had truly not prepared itself for the realistic possibility that they might lose this election, and

(2) the news media (more shocked than anyone that their propaganda campaign had failed) became even more cooperative in casting Amendment 2 as the instrument of trouble and hatred.

Amendment 2 began to dominate every Colorado news source. According to Denver political consultant Dick Waddams, Amendment 2 spawned more post election news coverage than any item he had seen in his career. In a matter of weeks he had collected 4,000 news items attacking the results of the election.

Every conceivable crackpot story was pursued to prove that the amendment had spawned hatred. If a quote could be found to impugn the motives of the Colorado voting majority it was put in a bold sidebar: "It seems to me Amendment 2 is mean-spirited," the *Gazette Telegraph* quoted a Republican Representative from Leadville as saying, "It legalizes discrimination." Said another, "a bigoted law."[176]

The press turned next to celebrity mouthpieces in order to show Colorado to be out of step with the social evolution of America. For a while any lesser star from Hollywood (that city of indecent proposals), could be seen on Donahue, Arsenio, CNN, Hard Copy, *Entertainment Tonight*, network news shows, *A Current Affair*, Oprah, "E" network, and the entire circus of *Talk Soup* fame, pontificating against Colorado's vote for hatred.

By January, a few homosexuals were seeing past this bandwagon of mindless Colorado bashing. Pro-homosexual agenda writer Dana Parsons of the *Los Angeles Times* warned his fellow homosexual campaigners: "Amendment 2 wasn't passed by a right-wing phalanx that sneaked in while no one was watching to win a fluky victory."[177]

Were his words heeded? Apparently not. No one in the homosexual lobby seemed to care how this vilification of Colorado played, even in their own backyard. Thus emboldened by the mass outpouring of media condemnation for Amendment 2, a Denver organization plunged ahead to launch a nationwide boycott to punish the State of Hate.

One had to ask, How many logical contradictions can the public endure? How can a class of victims in need of protection under the Civil Rights Act of 1964 possibly punish an entire state? Where's the so-called gay oppression in this forceful action? Where's the powerlessness in need of special rights and protections? Where's the impoverished gay ghetto?

Of all the self-destructive milestones reached in this campaign, Boycott Colorado scored off the chart. The people of the state could only become furious with the boycotters. "You don't make friends by using bully techniques," said one Denver PR man. But the homosexuals trotted out a Harvard School of Government grad, to assert, ". . . publicity is almost always a good thing even if it doesn't say precisely what you want it to say." (Which made about as much sense as the notoriety gained through state-sponsored terrorism. Or pasting condoms on a statue of the Virgin Mary.) Nevertheless, the boycott began in earnest.

Without Colorado for Family Values making a single public statement in its own defense, the core activists of the homosexual community seemed determined to follow Marty Booker into political oblivion.

"We didn't really have a long range plan for winning," CFV Communications Director Mark Olsen said, "but then, we didn't really need one. We just regrouped and scratched our heads as our opposition shot themselves in the foot."

THE BOYCOTT BULLET

In the meantime, the gay lobby's call for political IOU's went out to city mayors and city councils who had enacted gay rights ordinances across America. These pliable bureaucrats turned out to be the homosexual lobby's very best friends.

Mayor Bradley of Los Angeles asked his city council to ban travel to Colorado. They did. The cities of San Francisco, San Jose, Berkeley, New York, Philadelphia, Seattle, Boston, Detroit, and many others followed suit.[178] Soon, the U.S. Conference of Mayors, scheduled to meet in Colorado Springs in June '93, cancelled their convention at the request of the supposedly powerless homosexual lobby.

These elected officials seemed incredibly willing to betray the democratic election process that had put them in office, for the sake of political correctness. Some opponents questioned the legality of their actions. Unfortunately, no one stepped forward in any of the boycotting cities to challenge these boycotts in court.

Meanwhile, each boycott victory received full news coverage in Colorado. The American Public Health Association cancelled a Denver convention. The American Association for the Advancement of Science cancelled. The American Association of Law Libraries, the American Library Association, the National Council for Social Studies, the American Mathematical Society, the Latin American Studies Association, the Coalition of Labor Union Women, the National Coalition Against Domestic Violence. After a short look at this impressive list, one might wonder, who's left who hasn't turned their back on Colorado? Boycott success figures were given heavy press even when they applied to the year 1999. The cumulative effect of this onslaught against the state would have been demoralizing, except for the fact that huge fissures began to appear in the Boycott structure very early on.

Two months after the election, on Sunday, January 2, 1993, the *Denver Post* announced: AMEND. 2 BOYCOTT SPURS BACKLASH. The article described a survey of Colorado voters revealing that, ". . . there's a backlash in Colorado to the growing national boycott of the state over Amendment 2, the citizen initiative that barred laws protecting gays." (Notice the double message here? Insisting that Amendment 2 removed protections from a group of gay victims, which made the boycott seem justified.) "People are more angry than ashamed . . . 94% said they haven't changed their minds about

Amendment 2 . . . the majority rejects the 'hate state' label and charges of bigotry . . . they see themselves as tolerant . . . [the majority was] against laws that would give homosexuals a type of special or protected status."

Not only did the boycott appear to be backfiring, this study also indicated that CFV had run a good campaign. At least some of the amendment's major points had been understood by the people in spite of the negative press. For example, the people seemed to agree that the homosexual lobby wanted special rights, not equality under the law.

This became a strong indicator for the wisdom of Amendment 2 over Oregon's Measure 9, at least when using the "special rights" campaign slogan. Both Colorado and Oregon ran heavily on the idea that homosexuals wanted special rights. However, Oregon lost with the same argument. The difference had been in the language of the laws themselves. Amendment 2 had left moral judgements about homosexuality in the private sector. Oregon's Measure 9 had asked the government to call same-sex attractions unnatural, wrong, and perverse. For Measure 9 to accuse gays of wanting special rights while asking for a moral law against them, rang an alarm for Oregon voters. It seemed unfair.

Of course, Oregon's "unfairness" problem would not have existed forty years ago when America still accepted biblical morality by consensus. In those days of moral absolutes, nobody would have debated the fairness of a moral law; calling homosexuality wrong, abnormal, perverse, and unnatural made perfect sense then. Even today, for those who embrace biblical morality, questions of sin remain untouched by questions of fairness. For traditional Jews and Christians alike, the Old Testament story of Job has always illustrated that God's judgements do not always seem fair. In fact, they do not always make sense. In essence, God's perfect justice, seen in a fallen world, must of necessity appear unfair at times. This belief in God's ultimate goodness, in spite of temporal appearances, is a central principle to a Judeo-Christian heritage.

But biblical morality has become a minority position in modern times. Under the guidance of the ACLU, notions of sinfulness are being jettisoned from the law. In place of morality, fairness has become the dominant issue. Sometimes, it is the *only* issue. The consequence is that an issue like Measure 9 is doomed if it attempts a fairness argument. Arguing morality and fairness in the same breath doesn't succeed in today's America. With the special rights campaign, Measure 9 actually lowered itself from its moral perch.

Even so, Oregon's moral language won 43% of the vote. This came as a surprise to most political observers who had predicted a far greater beating for this law in the public square. One wonders how Oregon's approach might fare someday if it is argued as a purely moral law, not compromised by special rights, or any other fairness theme? Former secretary of education William J. Bennett has perhaps caught an early trend toward a return to morality in public life. In his 1992 book, *The De-Valuing of America,* he dared to speak boldly about morality in our nation's history:

> "We cannot deny . . . that our values, our principles and the spirit of our institutions all come from the Judeo-Christian tradition. That tradition and the American Tradition are wedded. When we have disdain for our religious tradition, we have disdain for ourselves."[179]

The framers of Colorado's Amendment 2 agreed with Bennett's statement about moral history, and for that matter with the language of Oregon's Measure 9. However, Colorado took into account America's moral present. That allowed them to make, and win, the fairness argument. Post election polls in Colorado show that a full 60% of the general population believe that when homosexuals talk about gay rights, what they really mean is special treatment.[180] Special rights remains a powerful fairness argument against gay politics for anyone not pushing moral laws.

Based on the same *Denver Post* poll, a second major point of the Amendment 2 campaign seemed to have succeeded as well: namely, that Amendment 2 represented less government interference in the private sector. In that sense, the voters had seen it as a law in the conservative tradition. Polling executives agreed that, after this finding, it would be unconscionable to go on labelling Colorado the "Hate State."

Did the homosexual lobby recognize their error? Change their ways? No. Nor did their supporters.

Immediately after the release of this poll, Governor Roy Romer adopted a new stratagem against the amendment. His tactic might have been lifted from a page of *Overhauling of Straight America* (or perhaps hatched in a high level meeting with Marquez and Foster?) The governor's new tactic was to directly blame Amendment 2 for the boycott. (Which made as much sense as blaming Amendment 2 for Marty Booker's suicide.)

Speaking to the City Club of Denver, Romer said, "Amendment 2 is affecting Colorado's economy." He then cited the case of Ziff-Davis, a large New York publishing firm which had planned to move to Colorado but "is now considering other options. We would have had it in the bag," Romer claimed, "were it not for Amendment 2."[181]

Upon his arrival in Colorado Springs the next day for the Chuck Baker radio show, a caller confronted the governor with his accusation. The caller said that, first of all, it only seemed logical to blame the boycotters for the boycott. To blame Amendment 2 for the actions of gay radicals impugned legitimate voters. These people had done nothing worthy of economic terrorism, the caller asserted, they had merely voted their conscience. "This is democracy you're attacking, governor."

The governor replied that he actually *believed* that the amendment had caused the boycott. (Was he pleading ignorance?) Apparently his cause-and-effect logic button had developed a glitch, similar to ACT UP's: "AIDS is not killing Gordon Bourne, you are!" The governor called this an honest difference of opinion. The caller admitted to the difference of opinion but said the honesty seemed up for grabs.

In the days following, the news media picked up the governor's new line of attack. Blaming Amendment 2 for the boycott became a plague. A *Denver Post* headline read: AMENDMENT 2 SCUTTLES LIBRARIAN MEETING.[182] The *Rocky Mountain News* announced, AMENDMENT 2 MAY KEEP ZIFF OUT OF STATE.[183] An *Associated Press* version appeared in the *Denver Post* under the title, ROMER: ZIFF-DAVIS SURE THING BEFORE AMENDMENT 2.[184] In Colorado Springs the *Gazette*'s business editor, Jerry Mahoney, titled a

January 10 piece, AMENDMENT 2 WON'T HELP THE ECONOMY.[185] (Wouldn't it have been more honest and accurate to have said, *BOYCOTT* WON'T HELP THE ECONOMY? This kind of deliberate manipulation of the truth seems to only hurt the cause of journalism.)

But even with the media and a governor in one's pocket, it doesn't help much if a cause is not founded on sound principle. As Boycott Colorado got under way, hypocrisy in the boycott ranks set-in. Perhaps this is because the morality of the political left is so totally *relative*: it means one thing to one person, something else to another. At any rate, two events accelerated boycott duplicity before the eyes of Colorado residents:

(1) the Good Lord saw fit to bless Colorado's ski slopes with a 40% above average snowfall, and

(2) the holidays in Aspen and other excellent slopes belong to the rich and famous (straight and homosexual), who do not part with their comforts easily.

In spite of Barbara Streisand and Liza Minnelli's visible disapproval, Colorado saw the following Christmas list of guests in Aspen: George Hamilton, Sally Field, Kurt Russell, Goldie Hawn, John Oates, Anthony Zerbe, Don Johnson, Melanie Griffith, Robert Wagner, Jill St. John, Jimmy Buffet, Don Henley, Cher, Jack Nicholson (who called the boycott "rubbish"), arch lesbian Martina Navratilova, Marvin Davis, and Chris Evert—the appearance of these stars on the slopes shot moral holes in the boycott's circus tent. One Aspen hot spot owner whined, "It's hard to ask people to give up their home [read here, second home] and their holiday."[186]

What seemed good for the celebs, seemed good for the populace. A liberal schoolteacher from the mid-west confessed, "We discussed the boycott but family tradition and great snow persuaded us. Colorado has the best skiing in the world."[187] SKI AREAS SEE RECORD SEASON, blared a post-holiday headline.[188]

Hidden away in section D of the *Denver Post,* a few of us found the story of ultimate hypocrisy: Terry Schleder, the leader of Boycott Colorado, had been seen by a reporter enjoying herself on the ski slopes of Breckenridge, Colorado.[189] Schleder, the one who had told the nation to ski Utah until Amendment 2 was repealed, had in this incident demonstrated that her personal principles were exempted in the face of five inches of fresh powder.

The Colorado ski revenues, and boycott hypocrisy, both went-on to break all records in the '92-93 season.

Nevertheless, the homosexual boycott continued to present itself as a righteous cause. They turned next to professional organizations most "friendly" to their agenda, asking them to cancel conventions planned for Colorado. They did. News organizations touted each new boycott victory like nails in CFV's coffin, eventually listing 29 of them: HISPANIC GROUP VOTES TO MOVE CONVENTION;[190] LIBRARIANS JOIN AMENDMENT 2 BOYCOTT;[191] COLORADO LIBRARY ASSOCIATION VOTES AGAINST HOLDING ANNUAL MEETINGS IN YES-ON-2 COUNTIES.[192]

The boycott list grew. The Universal Unitarians, National Council for Family Day Care, Western Alliance of Arts Administrators, AIDS Medicine and Miracles, Land Trust Alliance, Lotus Development Corporation, National Education Association, Chamber Music America, United States Student Association, Western States Humanities Council, the *Self Magazine* advertising convention.[193] The published tally amounted to at least 39 million lost to Colorado (if you counted into 1999).

CFV representatives asked members of the news media not to report these figures of boycott losses without a side-by-side balance of how much the state had gained through skiing and through replacement convention bookings. Nothing doing. The boycott victories were trumpeted alone each day as if they existed in an economic vacuum.

Perhaps swelled with a 39 million dollar inflated sense of momentum, early in '93 the homosexual lobby took out its big boycott gun, placed it carefully against its own head and pulled the trigger—all the while smiling like Alfred E. Newman on a *Mad* cover. *Nothing amiss here.* From Colorado Springs, we watched, slackjawed as details of the incident leaked-out. A New York Boycott Colorado group had strong-armed a Boulder Tea Company called Celestial Seasonings.

If it could be suggested that the media is gay, then it could be equally suggested that Celestial Seasonings is a gay tea. The company's founder, Mo Siegel, is a solid Bill Clinton Democrat. He had voted against Amendment 2 and supported Boulder's gay rights ordinance. The homosexual lobby could not have asked for a better friend. He employed homosexuals in his tea making company with full acceptance (not mere tolerance). In other words, this man and his company embodied everything activists said they wanted in America. But no, they actually wanted more. How much more? One-hundred-thousand dollars more. Homosexuals are big Celestial consumers. Perhaps the New York group had consumed so much of the stuff that they now simply felt they owned a majority share of Celestial stock?

The New York City homosexual consortium threatened to dump Siegel's tea into the East River, banish Celestial from every Greenwich Village tea shop, and ruin his business with a highly visible boycott unless his Colorado company put up $100,000 to fight Amendment 2. He said that he couldn't quite believe what the New Yorkers were threatening at first, then he suddenly woke up to the fact that it was not a *boycott*—it was *blackmail*. If he paid them off, they wouldn't boycott his products. Perhaps this qualified under the term "extortion" because the price of peace with the homosexual lobby was $100,000. The charge made enough sense to the FBI that they began an immediate criminal investigation of the New York gay group.[194]

If arch conservative Coach McCartney had ignited the Amendment 2 petition process in Colorado, arch liberal Mo Siegel's clash with the homosexual Mafia mobilized Colorado against the boycott.

As a sidebar here: all of the Celestial Seasonings news clipping in my extensive collection show that the extortion stories did not make front page. Politically correct egg-on-the-face apparently rates section B & D coverage only (for those following along in your media imbalance notebooks). These stories achieved six or nine inches of news space, no more. Nevertheless, they played front page banner headlines in the minds of a wounded Colorado public, and to conservatives nationwide. Rush Limbaugh and others picked up on the phoniness of this deal. The boycott now engendered some righteous anger and derision against the homosexual lobby.

As a result, the homosexual community began to divide up and attack each other. Linda Fowler, head of the Denver Mayor's Gay and Lesbian Advisory Committee, complained against the New York group, saying, "What doesn't make sense is targeting the people

AP/WIDE WORLD PHOTOS

NEW YORK BOYCOTT COLORADO marchers prepare to dump Celestial Seasonings Tea, Holly Sugar and Coors Beer into the East River, perhaps to prove that they had not targeted Celestial Seasonings for extortion.

who have been our friends and supporters."[195]

Did she mean it? She wouldn't mind an extortion attempt against Holly Sugar? Coors? Gates? Montfort meats? They had also been targeted by the New York group. But if she had meant targeting for the *boycott*, not extortion, then her comment revealed how the homosexual lobby treats its best friends. They had pulled off their own "no win" situation. They were self-destructing.

Perhaps out of embarrassment, perhaps coincidence, the next day the *Denver Post* dumped on the Colorado homosexual lobby. The featured front page headline blared: BOYCOTT'S BARK WORSE THAN BITE.[196] The article went on to reveal the other side of the boycott story (at last), the side CFV had been insisting would balance the overestimated boycott losses: ". . . growing convention business in some areas has compensated for any boycott-created losses," the article said. "The $93 million [the new bookings] spend dwarfs current boycott losses [$39 million]. . . . In Colorado Springs where Amendment 2 was launched, convention bookings are $2 million ahead of projections . . . even Pope John Paul II's visit this summer could pump more money into the state than the boycott takes out."

Two days later Colorado Springs' *Gazette Telegraph* sneaked-in an Associated Press version of the story, watered down to an unapologetic four inches of back page column space: CONVENTION SURGE SEEN AS MAKING UP FOR BOYCOTT. Of course, never one to neglect headline campaigning, they linked the article with a second one about Colorado ski resorts enacting gay rights laws in defiance of Amendment 2: MORE TOWNS URGED TO DEFY AMENDMENT.[197]

Three final signals seemed to break the back of the Boycott Colorado effort. The first was a demonstration of blatant homosexual hypocrisy. This example could not be hidden on the opinion pages or back pages of the news (like Terry Schleder's violation of principle in Breckenridge). This one took place in front of all, in a big way in Denver—GAY GROUP DEFENDS COLORADO MEETING,[198] the headline read.

Yes, the so-called National Gay and Lesbian Task Force (which had compiled all of those heavily quoted hate crime statistics, remember?) and had actively promoted Boycott Colorado to every other enterprise in the country, now exempted itself from politics and held its convention in the home of "the best skiing in the world."

Even homosexuals saw through this hypocrisy. Boycott Colorado believers screamed. Did the National Gay and Lesbian Task Force apologize for their lack of principle here? No. They came up with a lame justification for what could only be viewed as a cheap betrayal. (One wonders if their call for one million marchers in Washington, D.C. in April became "payback" for this double dealing? Only 300,000 gays showed up.)

Second death knell to the Boycott: Ziff-Davis, the large New York publisher, came back to Colorado sniffing around for a site for their national headquarters. The company made noise in several sites until finally rejecting the state in May over tax disputes.[199] Tax and other financial incentives ruled the Ziff-Davis decision, not the boycott as Governor Romer had claimed.

One begins to suspect the true depth of politically correct scruples in the bottom line world of business anyway. If Ziff had been committed to real moral objections to Amendment 2, they wouldn't have spent so much time trying to make the Colorado location work for them. An issue is a matter of principle or it's not. This was one of those issues. Does a huge company like Ziff operate differently from the family of the Midwestern school teacher? *"We talked about the boycott but the snow is so great out here, and the state is so beautiful, and wonderful to look at, and . . . and . . ."*

Not to mention what this said of Colorado's Governor Roy Romer. One is left to suspect that Ziff-Davis had been undecided all along, and the governor had merely used their indecision to stick the blame for the boycott on Amendment 2: *"We would have had them in the bag were it not for Amendment 2,"* Romer had said to The City Club of Denver. Perhaps now he would reconsider? Perhaps now he would blame the boycott for the boycott? (*Nah!*)

Third fatal blow to Boycott Colorado: the city of Colorado Springs stood up to the Colorado Bar Association. The state Bar had caved in to boycott pressure and had cancelled its convention at the famous Broadmoor Hotel to protest Amendment 2. The Broadmoor meeting site had been a 75-year tradition for them. When the city asked them to come to their senses and return to the site, the Bar tried to extort a politically correct "letter of welcome" from Mayor Bob Isaac. His words only had to mention "gay and lesbian" members of the Bar specifically, they said. In exchange for this concession they would change their minds.

The mayor was not the kind of man to enjoy watching the tail wag the dog. He refused. He welcomed the Bar Association as he usually did, but refused to bend to their politically correct language. The Bar took their convention and walked.

But Colorado Springs wouldn't take it lying down. Leading members of the city mounted a letter campaign. The pressure of the Colorado majority began to be felt at the Colorado Bar Association offices. LOCAL LAWYER GROUP RIPS STATE BAR, read a *Gazette* headline. A local attorney was quoted as saying, "The Colorado Bar Association has no business endorsing a boycott of Colorado Springs."[200]

On March 21, 1993, under an onslaught of negative mail, the state bar broke ranks: BAR TO MEET IN SPRINGS; LETTERS HELP SWAY LAWYERS.[201] Voting on the boycott issue once again, the Bar decided to keep their convention in Colorado Springs after all.

Sanity returned. The boycott ended with a whimper and a noticeable media silence.

In June of '93 an Associated Press article appeared measuring the boycott's impact: "A brokerage firm's economic report says Colorado posted more rapid economic gains than any other state during the past year. Kemper Securities, which released the report last week, rated Colorado No. 1 on its list for the first quarter of this year [it's hard to argue with being number 1]. The weakest states were California, Hawaii and New Jersey."[202] Not only did this report reveal the media hype on the boycott, it is interesting to note that the states rated dead last in economic performance (California, Hawaii, and New Jersey), are ranked at the top for embracing gay rights laws. Could there be more than a casual connection between economic misery and the success of the gay agenda?

On November 14, 1993, the *Denver Post* decided to take another look at the boycott from the safe distance of eight quiet months in which no new boycott victories had been announced. The results? Colorado had boomed. Particularly, Celestial Seasonings Tea revenues had risen over 8% to $59.1 million. After the record ski season, summer tourism in the state had also flourished. *More* people had decided to make Colorado their destination, not less. Colorado had logged a double-digit increase in state sales tax collections for the year. Denver hotel occupancy in August had been 81%, up from 77.5% . . . before the boycott had done its supposed damage.

One had to chuckle reading a quote from Boycott Colorado's Terry Schleder, trying to put a positive spin on her double-digit embarrassment: "the problem with boycotts is, if you do a good job, you work yourself out of a job." (One could almost hear the nervous coughing in the room full of journalists.)

The only true evangelist for the boycott was someone named Rich Grant from the Denver Metro Convention and Visitors Bureau who said, "This thing hurt."[203] One had to wonder how an 81% hotel occupancy rate might have hurt the Convention and Visitors Bureau? Grant then predicted that the boycott would be much worse in Cincinnati, where voters had recently repealed a gay rights law by a whopping 62%, fueled largely by a family oriented inner city black vote.

Will Perkins said it best, when interviewed in Cincinnati shortly after their win: "Pray for a boycott."

Cincinnati may soon suffer like Colorado. Another Terry Schleder may work herself out of a job in Ohio.

MEET ME AT THE INJUNCTION

In January 1993 Judge Jeffrey Bayless prepared to hear arguments about imposing a temporary injunction against Amendment 2. The injunction would order the state not to enforce the law until its constitutionality could be decided in the trial of *Evans v. Romer*. Colorado for Family Values was not named in the suit. The election had made Amendment 2 a part of the state's constitution, therefore the homosexuals sued Colorado, ironically naming their friend, Governor Romer, as defendant.

The actual defense of the amendment would be handled by the staff of Attorney General Gayle Norton. Solicitor General Tim Timkovich was named lead counsel. In a pre-trial motion, Timkovich moved to dismiss the hearing as irrelevant to the legal facts involved in the defense of Amendment 2. This made sense to a lot of folks who figured the hearings would prove unworthy and frivolous. As it turned out, the motion gave a hint as to the social agenda of Judge Bayless. He ruled for the gay plaintiffs against every objection the defense raised at this time. He ruled as if his mind had been made up long ago about how he would run the hearing. This judicial lock-out had the effect of intimidating the attorney general's team, dampening their hopes for lodging future objections with this high-handed judge.

Solicitor General, TIM TIMKOVICH prepares to defend Amendment 2.

What exactly was at stake? Time, mostly. If the amendment was placed under an injunction until its constitutionality could be decided, the process would take years. Meanwhile, it would be placed in a prison of sorts, held there like a murderer, too dangerous to be let out on bail until the trials and appeals were done. These years of appeal would be handed to the media, Governor Romer, and his task force, allowing them every opportunity to "educate" Colorado voters, and perhaps to overturn Amendment 2. Under the injunction, the will of the people of Colorado would be effectively held hostage to the gay agenda.

In other words, an injunction gave Bayless the power to turn *Evans v. Romer* into *The Cultural Elite v. The People of Colorado*.

This situation played heavily in favor of the gay lobby. They tended to fare well in elitist situations—courts, governors' mansions, news rooms, city councils, educational establishments, and the like. Only the man-on-the-street had opposed them. As the injunction hearings drew near in Colorado, a feeling of impending doom settled over the electorate. The whole show had shifted into the hands of the cultural elite. Most citizen voters felt that the higher matters of the law, judges, and court rulings were hopelessly over their heads.

This split between the elite and the people had been well noted in the mid-'80s by researchers Stanley Rothman and S. Robert Lichter. Citing their studies, George Gilder, the father of Reaganomics and the acclaimed mentor of Rush Limbaugh, wrote: "Private opinion diverges widely from establishment opinion on every major sexual question, from special gay rights to adultery."[204] In Colorado, as across the nation, elite sexual values seemed destined to win in the courts.

In order to finesse an elite social agenda, however, Judge Bayless would first have to find something terribly wrong with Amendment 2. What could possibly be found wrong with it? Unless one assumed that the Colorado majority hated homosexuals and wanted to discriminate unfairly, the amendment itself seemed legally sound.

What might the plaintiffs say to help Bayless find this terrible wrong? They had been working for months, preparing their court case even during the campaign. From campaign rhetoric it was expected that they would probably enter the courtroom claiming that Amendment 2 had been hatched by a bunch of religious fanatics in Colorado Springs who wanted to use the government to punish gayness. They would make these empty accusations, no doubt, encouraged by the ACLU.

The ACLU preferred to make moral charges against any law they opposed. They had pioneered the use of the idea of "separation of church and state," applying it to the Constitution until they had effectively banished morality from public life—something the founders never dreamed. In their official *Guide to a Gay Person's Rights,* the ACLU expanded this moral attack, writing, "The law has only begun to jettison notions that a person's homosexuality reflects sinfulness . . . ."[205] If the law had only begun this process, then by golly, you could bet the homosexuals and the ACLU would do everything in their power to hasten it in Bayless's court. At the very least they would do all to jettison—if not notions of sinfulness—Amendment 2 from the law. And who could blame them? It was merely self-serving to use the courts in this way. Without a moral rudder, the law had, in effect, "laid down" for this sexual agenda.

Knowing this, the ACLU handbook encouraged homosexuals to bombard the courts, exploiting its moral vacuum. They predicted that gays would eventually wear out the system and have their way, even against the will of the people. "Rights," they said, "if they are rarely used . . . may become forgotten and violations may become routine. These laws may change, and in some [instances] they change quite rapidly. . . . Even if the laws remain the same, their interpretations by courts and administrative officials [like Bayless?] often vary . . . there are wide variations in the ways in which particular courts and administrative officials will interpret the same law at any given moment." The ACLU advice column ended with this emphatic, and dire promise, ". . . the law *will* change."[206] [emphasis added]

These comments reveal that the ACLU is guided by an irresponsible and self-serving agenda of discovering, inventing, and exploiting an endless list of new rights. Gays are a natural ally to this aim. Unfortunately, so are many judges. The ACLU assumes government and courts should solve *every* human ill and too many judges seem ready to oblige. All other institutions—family, church, business, military—are assumed inferior to this enlightened circle of demigods. The lordship of America's values belongs to the courts, or so assumes the cultural elite.

Lawyer John T. Baker, debating on church and state in Colorado Springs, declared the ACLU's cornerstone assumption beneath these elitist attitudes: "The Constitution is an 'evolving' document,"[207] he said. Obviously, the homosexual lobby went into Judge Jeffrey Bayless's courtroom with the ACLU point of view: the law is evolving, changing. They were there, in fact, to change it.

Most people depend on the law remaining relatively the same. They do not want to wake up one day to find a murderer's rights have evolved so that he may now prowl the streets again. Nor do they expect assault, battery, and harassment convictions to become something more complicated, and malleable, like a harassment or hate crime. Likewise, Amendment 2 supporters in Colorado trusted the law to remain true to its clear principles. They had read Amendment 2 and understood it: no more gay rights laws in Colorado—period. They knew that it did not do the bad things that the news media and the homosexual lobby claimed it did. They trusted the state to defend the amendment with the vigor it deserved, and depended helplessly upon the justice of the court to decide its true merits. CFV itself relied principally—and perhaps too much—on the amendment's well-researched wording. After all, eight Constitutional lawyers had given it a clean bill of health.

In retrospect, these attitudes may now belong with the dinosaurs. The competence of the state attorney general's defense of the amendment is open to question. Even worse, the judges involved with the case went out of their way to cripple the defense. The ACLU's advice to gays reflected a sad reality: The Constitution *is* evolving under social pressure. Consequently, our entire system of law can be twisted and bent to fit one judge's opinion. The personal agenda of a Jeffrey Bayless can make all the difference in the outcome of a case. Even the homosexual lobbyists are admitting this now. In a recent National Public Radio report on gays in the military, one activist claimed that a liberal judge is all a discharged gay needs to be reinstated.[208]

Columnist Joseph Sobran observed, "The idea of 'evolving standards' does have one, albeit sinister, advantage: It removes all limits on power. It lets the state define its own authority, without the restraint of inherited meanings and shared understandings. It annihilates legal tradition and makes the interpretation of law a game without rules."[209]

A game without rules was exactly what Bayless needed in order to find something terribly wrong with Amendment 2. In an analysis of the hearings by National Legal Foundation lawyer Robert K. Skolrood, ". . . virtually all of the plaintiff's testimony was irrelevant. In the thirty-six years I have been practicing law," he wrote, "I have seen the law all too often become a tool of manipulation rather than a force for good."[210] He spoke of the proceedings in Bayless's courtroom, which provided a prime example of manipulation.

Anti-amendment forces entered the courtroom with a coalition of social pressure groups. Their testimony was speculative, having nothing to do with the amendment's legal standing. The social pressure came through written testimonies called *Brief Amicus Curiae*, or "friends of the court briefs." The anti-Amendment 2 briefs included: "the National Education Association, the Colorado Education Association, the International Association for Supervision and Curriculum Development, the Colorado Bar Association, the Coalition of Associations of Mental Health Professionals, the AIDS Action Committee, a major labor union, and a coalition of three Jewish and two Christian associations."[211]

Make no mistake, these groups had come together to overturn the will of the Colorado voting majority on Amendment 2. How could they do this? Only in a game without rules. If the Constitution is evolving, then it is naïve to believe that a judge will not be affected by elite social pressures of this magnitude. Winning an election is a good thing but not the *only* thing. It seems that an aggressive challenge in the courts will also be necessary to bring legal values back into line with the will of the people. Judges who will interpret the Constitution rather than evolve it will have to be appointed to the bench by elected officials, or such manipulation will grow like an unchecked cancer.

Judge Bayless proceeded to find the following two things terribly wrong with Amendment 2:

1. that homosexuals would be in danger of "real, immediate, and irreparable harm" if Amendment 2 became law, (most amendment supporters laughed at this idea, never believing that the courts would buy into the gay lobby's own hate propaganda), and

2. that the amendment had a possibility of being ruled unconstitutional for violating homosexuals' basic rights. (Those with legal understanding did not give this idea serious consideration. It is simply not in the rules of a Colorado court to find such a

fundamental right for homosexuals. The federal court had rejected the idea repeatedly, how could Bayless presume to invent it?)

On the question of "real, immediate, and irreparable harm," it seemed the press was eager to add their own version of a *Brief Amicus Curiae*. Perhaps they believed that coincidental stories of immediate danger to homosexuals would cause a judge to find evidence that they *were* in grave danger?

Whether intentional or not (you be the judge), after laying down a barrage of gay bashing and hate crime stories for weeks, the *Gazette Telegraph* of Colorado Springs put these two headlines side by side, days before the court hearings began: RULING DUE NEXT WEEK ON AMENDMENT DELAY . . . WHITE SUPREMACIST GROUP PUTS OFF RALLY: AMENDMENT 2 HAILED.[212] Obviously, the racist headline was placed strategically to rub-off on the amendment.

The out-of-state racist quoted in this story had nothing to do with Amendment 2. He was merely an opportunist. Only 32 people showed up at his stupid rally.[213] But the *Gazette* deemed it necessary to mention that this do-nothing white supremacist had "hailed Amendment 2." Anyone supporting or "hailing" Amendment 2 now seemed brother to a racist. By inference, opposing the homosexual agenda was tantamount to opposing black civil rights laws.

That was not the end of the *Gazette*'s real, immediate, and irreparable harm stories. In the same issue, this headline blared: BIZARRE DETAILS OF ATTACK ON THERAPIST PUZZLE POLICE: RELIGIOUS SLOGANS SPRAY-PAINTED ON WALLS. This so-called story concerned an alleged attack on an openly pro-gay psychotherapist who said she was knocked out and tear-gassed in her office by someone who spray painted religious slogans on her walls. The slogans read, "Seek God," "Repent," and "Stop Evil" and the perpetrators had defaced her "Celebrate Diversity" bumper sticker with a Christian cross.

(There you have it! The kind of hatred from the religious right we always knew to be there, lurking beneath the surface of Amendment 2. Closely linked to this white supremacist stuff, too.)

Unlike the politically motivated attack on the shrine of the Virgin Mary, however, this crime had no proud telephone caller claiming credit. The police found no signs of forced entry. They scratched their heads, calling it the strangest assault they'd seen in a long time. Finally, they considered filing charges against the therapist herself, before quietly closing the file.[214] But the story had already done its damage. Judge Bayless wanted to know if Amendment 2 threatened homosexuals with real, immediate, and irreparable harm? All he had to do was read this issue of the *Gazette Telegraph* and answer "yes."

The *Gazette* was hardly alone in this agenda. The following are more of the "irreparable harm" headlines published in Colorado just before Judge Jeffrey Bayless began his hearings: 4 GAY MEN'S SLAYINGS MAY BE WORK OF 1 KILLER, *Denver Post*, December 31; CITY MARKS 4TH SLAYING OF GAY IN '92, *Rocky Mountain News*, December 31; SLAYING OF 4 GAY MEN AREN'T WORK OF SERIAL KILLER, DENVER POLICE SAY, *Rocky Mountain News*, January 1; POLICE: GAY SLAYINGS NOT LIKELY RELATED, *Denver Post*, January 7; THERAPIST ATTACKED; RELIGIOUS NOTES LEFT, *Denver Post*, January 7; CHILD WATCHED BASHING OF HER LESBIAN MOTHER, *Denver Post*, January 7; VICTIMS DETAIL TRAUMA OF HATE CRIMES, *Denver Post*, January 7.

After a weekend to ponder these hyped stories of criminal violence against homosexual people, Judge Jeffrey Bayless entered his courtroom. In a pre-trial motion, the defense raised a "blanket objection" to the range of irrelevant testimony the homosexuals planned to bring into court. Nearly all of the gay lobby arguments were legally objectionable to the actual merits of the case. Bayless again overruled the attorney general's blanket objection.

As promised, he then proceeded to listen to every conceivable ranting from the homosexual plaintiffs. The courtroom was packed every day. TV and news cameras whirred and clicked. This was the show trial. The anti-amendment testimony ranged far from legal matters, speculating as to what homosexuals thought about themselves and what the public thought about them. Even non-experts were asked to speculate about how many homosexuals existed in the population. Non-scientific ranges ballooned high.

Witness after witness came forward to testify to the fanatical nature of the religious right and their sinister involvement with Amendment 2. News stories quoted this anti-amendment testimony heavily. No one from CFV was asked to testify.

As the irrelevant testimony proliferated, the attorney general's lawyers made perhaps a fateful decision, one that, in some opinions, banished all hope for the amendment in the state thereafter. They decided not to stand and object to this ridiculous testimony every time it came up, which was constant. Since Bayless had emphatically overruled them in pre-trial motions they felt it would make them look bad. Either way, it seemed a no-win situation, they thought. To let the opposition run with their testimony would give the impression of a weak defense. To be repeatedly overruled by Bayless would give the impression of an incompetent defense. The defense team opted to keep quiet, believing that later appeals to higher courts would show that they had objected in principle, but had been overruled by Bayless. In retrospect, displays of indignation by the defense lawyers might have mattered more in this trial than jurisprudence.

With the media eyes of the state focused squarely on the courtroom, the defense lawyers sat quietly, conferring behind their hands as the entire gay pride parade took the witness stand, weeping, wailing, and claiming one terrible Amendment 2 offense after another. Newsmen mentioned that Timkovich and company seemed strangely quiet, failing to make objections to much of this testimony. They characterized them as passive and weak.[215] Meanwhile, Bayless let the anti-amendment testimony ramble on for extra days. On the last day of the hearings the defense was allowed a few hours to make a rebuttal. By now the entire state had developed a political migraine headache, not to mention a legal bleeding ulcer. What *ever in the world* had happened to their fine amendment in that courtroom, they wondered?

At the last possible minute on Friday, Judge Bayless rose to the bench to explain it all. He read an hour-long decision on statewide TV. From the polish of the document, he had obviously been working on it for a long time, though he claimed to have stayed up all night getting it ready. His ruling amounted to a politically correct magic show, complete with disappearing logic and legal procedures-sawn-in-two. The hour drew one of the largest TV audience in Colorado history, most of whom had little idea of what they were hearing, or had heard. In the deliberately tangled legal web he wove, Bayless dropped three telling ideas that became his formula for putting Amendment 2 on ice:

(1) He referred several times to "society's evolving standards of decency." A very bad sign for Amendment 2. This meant the judge looked to society for standards, not to the Constitution. The phrase also betrayed his ACLU mentality, assuming evolution of the law to be an automatically good thing. The other side of Bayless's motive was revealed with his use of the word "decency." Ironically, decency can only be determined if one makes value judgements. But in a court that had (according to the ACLU) "jettisoned notions of sinfulness," whose values would guide Bayless's judgement concerning gay rights laws? Those of the Bible? Of Judeo-Christian morality? Of the founding fathers? Of Western Civilization? Of the Colorado voting majority?

As feared, Judge Bayless chose his values from the politically correct grab-bag of the cultural elite. Still, his hand-picked standards of decency would have to be justified on some legal pretext (no wonder the speech took an hour). On he rambled, shuffling papers and glancing repeatedly over his glasses as if everyone *should* be following along perfectly now, listening numbly, swallowing this legal sleight-of-hand like sheep before a shearer. Finding no basis for his decision in existing laws on homosexuality, he selected his legal excuses from two obscure California racial discrimination rulings, *Reitman v. Mulkey* and *Hunter v. Erickson. (Of course! Who wouldn't have thought of this?!)* To use these precedents the man had to leap a huge chasm of legal logic, a leap which essentially ruled, without trial, that homosexuality was equal to race under the law.

(2) As the TV audience sat scratching their collective heads, the judge next applied these two racial cases directly to homosexuals affected by Amendment 2, as if homosexuals qualified for "minority or protected class status." Never mind that the federal government criteria have never been met for adding sexual orientation to this

list. Never mind that the U.S. Supreme Court has refused to acknowledge homosexuality as a protected class in other rulings (see Appendix D). He merely assumed what he needed to assume in order to overturn the will of the people on Amendment 2. "His decision," wrote one analyst, "came down to what appears to be a newly constructed legal theory never tested by higher courts."[216] (That put it politely.)

(3) The third blow the judge gave to the amendment came from a most surprising source. First, he proclaimed that the religious right motives of the amendment's founders had no bearing on the case at all. CFV's founders had done no wrong. They had created a civil law. He agreed that Amendment 2 contained not one trace of moral or religious sentiment. For a moment the hearts of Amendment 2 voters went pitty-pat. Maybe . . . just maybe this judge had ruled in their favor? (*Watch out. All of this is called in basketball, a 'head fake': "Michael Jordan looks left, the defense freezes, then he goes right—score!"*) In order to trash Amendment 2, Bayless now fabricated an argument out of thin air: He used the two California racial discrimination cases to construct the idea that Amendment 2 would "give effect" to something called "private biases," which violated a heretofore unknown "fundamental right."[a] *What? He didn't even have the power to invent a new fundamental right! How could he do this?*

Hearing this, I recall feeling like I'd been hit in the stomach with a fifty-pound anvil! Later I realized why I had felt that way. Bayless's so-called private biases could include every opinion that remained free in the private sector once notions of sinfulness and morality were jettisoned from the law. Nothing remained sacred,

---

[a] FUNDAMENTAL INTERESTS, RIGHTS, AND PRIVILEGES: In modern constitutional parlance, a fundamental interest—sometimes also called a "fundamental right"—is one that triggers STRICT SCRUTINY of a law to see whether it violates the EQUAL PROTECTION CLAUSE. Usually the courts will strictly scrutinize a law that establishes SUSPECT CLASSIFICATION [or PROTECTED CLASS STATUS]—that draws a line on the basis of race or ethnic origin for example. If a fundamental interest or right is at stake, the Court may invalidate a law. (From *The Evolving Constitution*, Liebermann, 1992: Random House.) See also Appendices D & E for Bayless's violations of guidelines.

nor even private. Bayless wanted to become the new "thought police" making the world safe from private opinion. If he is right, if the system of American law no longer bows to a higher Judeo-Christian code of morality, then everything, *every private opinion* can be made subject to his judicial power. Bayless made his ruling as if this was a given fact, as if the law, even now, regards no higher authority. His decision did not reflect the values of the Constitution; he imposed his own wishful thinking on it. That is why he invoked an "evolving" standard of decency. Given the trend to jettison morality from the law, the private biases Bayless ruled against must of necessity include morality. Unless corrected by the people, Bayless and judges of his like will cause the law to swallow its maker. (During future election campaigns, people need to remember that judges are appointed and approved by elected officials. Someone must begin to answer for the way the Constitution is being trampled in court.)

Heedlessly, Bayless plunged ahead, concluding without any real evidence, except for the complaints of homosexuals themselves, that dangerous private biases against homosexuals would flourish under Amendment 2. (Biases like those of the white supremacist who had "hailed Amendment 2" in the *Gazette* article, no doubt.) This situation, in his opinion, would cause "real, immediate, and irreparable harm" to homosexuals. At last he had found the second terrible thing wrong with Amendment 2.

Just before making his injunction official, the judge dealt the amendment a final blow. He did this in his rules for deciding its constitutionality. Because he had ruled without trial that gays were equal to racial minorities, and because of the new fundamental right he had invented for them, the state would now be subject to "higher scrutiny." Talk about making an uneven playing field! This meant that Judge Bayless would not have to prove his unproven claims, but Amendment 2 would have to *scale Pikes Peak with a broken leg* in order to prove its very right to exist. The amendment would have to meet more than a reasonable, or "rational" test in proving its case, he said. By his decree, it would have to prove what is called a "compelling state interest."[b] The expert analysis on this ruling concludes: "as soon as the Court announces that it is applying strict scrutiny, it is a foregone conclusion that the state will not be found to have had a compelling enough interest to justify the law."[217] Counsel Timkovich added, "Such a standard is *never* met." In other words, one man, one Judge named Jeffrey Bayless had just made sure that the law created by the Colorado majority would not be found constitutional in his state. With that, he granted his injunction, bringing the gavel down—(*Slam-dunk!*)

The courtroom erupted with screams, laughter, and tears of joy as the homosexuals danced and hugged each other. They spilled into the hallways and lobbies, weeping before TV cameras. "I've been waiting to hear that all of my life," gushed plaintiff Evans, of *Evans v. Romer* fame.[218] One would have thought from the show of emotion that the homosexuals from the "State of Hate" had been waiting in line for the gas ovens, or for "ethnic cleansing" orders, forced to wear hot pink triangles so that they could not hide. One of the celebrants leaned over to Kevin Tebedo, sitting beside National Legal Foundation counsel, Miss Tracy Winn, hissing "Take that, you f____s!"

Now it was the Colorado majority's turn to try to get in touch with reality. What had happened? Somehow the court had asserted itself above the will of the people. Voters seemed numb with shock. None claimed to feel "thrown out of their family," but many felt like a legitimate election had just been hijacked—a feeling based in solid reality.

That Sunday, January 17, 1993, *Gazette Telegraph*, printed the following citizen comments, among others: "I think the judge just caved in to pressure." "Why did they let us vote if they were going

---

[b] COMPELLING STATE INTEREST: a reason for a state law, regulation, policy, or action that is strong enough to allow it to limit a person's constitutional rights. This is the most difficult level of interest for the state to prove. Most analysts concluded that it is not only impossible in the case of Amendment 2, it is unnecessary. Because of this ruling the citizens of Colorado wrote-off all subsequent trials of Amendment 2 in the state. The next legitimate trial of its merits, in their view, will not happen until it is appealed to the U.S. Supreme Court.

to turn around and say the vote didn't count?" "I have two children and I have always taught them that the most powerful thing you can do is this country is vote. What do I tell them now? Do I tell them the system lied?"

As a sidebar here, the *Gazette* went on to feature 11 comments against the judge's ruling and 8 comments in favor.[219] Nothing wrong with this on the surface, but the editors had admitted that the public response ran "5 to 1" against Bayless.[220] Given this ratio, they should have printed 40 comments against his ruling to balance the 8 comments they printed in his favor. Apparently the press only observes quotas and parity when the issue is politically correct.

For the public good then, Bayless's ruling needs to be put into perspective. What does his injunction mean? In basketball parlance it means that the people of Colorado have been delivered a blatant three-shot foul, and, instead taking a trip to the free-throw line, the referee has ejected them from the game. Meanwhile, the perpetrators have been sent to the line where they will be allowed to shoot "technicals" for the next several years. Bayless's social activism has stopped a good and valuable law from taking effect until a bunch of malcontents have been given every chance to strip it of its constitutionality. (Like the assumption of innocence, why can't a good law be constitutional until proven otherwise? Perhaps because our courts are playing games without rules.)

Attorney Robert K. Skolrood of the National Legal Foundation added his dire view: "it is very probable that the injunction will be in effect for several years before a final decision is rendered. All the while, the sovereign power of the people of the State of Colorado is crippled"[221]

Since the injunction, the people of Colorado have been forced to watch helplessly as the cultural elite have devoured Amendment 2 like feeding sharks. A form of official anarchy has been encouraged by this political carnage. Unable to wait for the legal process to conclude, the ski resort of Telluride passed a renegade gay rights ordinance. Crested Butte followed with their own version. These city councils acted in complete contempt of the state constitution, the courts, and due process of law. The fact that they were not reprimanded by the governor or other political leaders, signaled to the state that Amendment 2 was fair game, *a bad law,* deserving nothing but ridicule.

But even under injunction the amendment has legal teeth. The last line of it reads: "This section of the constitution shall be in all respects self-executing." These words mean that the amendment can legally work for anyone accused under gay rights ordinances in the meantime. Amendment 2 has been voted into the state's constitution by the will of the people, and as such, it is *self-executing*. While the amendment may not yet nullify gay rights laws, it can still be used against them as a defense. Such a law is despised only by those ignorant of its power.

Meanwhile, the arrogance of the cultural elite has rolled on unabated. With the amendment held under injunction, a state senator has insolently drafted a proposal to repeal it. Another effort has been made to expand privacy laws to circumvent it. Other politicians try to compromise, clarify, or replace it with new amendments.

All of this aggression against the amendment has been allowed to go on with impunity. State officials stand back like passive police in a riot, letting the anti-amendment crowd bludgeon Colorado with political bricks (it's Reginald Denny on skis). A certain amount of respect for the law has been sacrificed in the process.

The good news is that the attempts to repeal Amendment 2 are failing. Popular support for the amendment is actually increasing statewide. Voters are failing to rally to the anti-amendment grandstanders. A recent effort seeking to overturn the amendment through a referendum process fell apart for lack of support.

THE 6-TO-1 COURT INSULT

Bayless delivered only the first courtroom foul to the people of Colorado. Six-months later, the state Supreme Court added their special insult to his injury. In a 6-to-1 ruling, they upheld Bayless's eccentric judgement and invented their own fundamental right in order to do so: "the right for gays to participate equally in the political process."[222] No court anywhere has ever recognized such a right under their definition.

AMENDMENT 2 FLAWED,[223] declared news headlines as soon as this ruling came out. (Indeed, if anything was flawed it was the ruling itself!) News writers seemed to be desperately seeking courtroom approval for their own anti-amendment prejudice. Front page pictures of happy gays, hugging and celebrating were prominently displayed again. Opposite them appeared a somber Will Perkins, answering impossible questions about Amendment 2's newest courtroom setback.

The National Legal Foundation subsequently explained the Colorado Court's faulty reasoning in a *Brief Amicus Curiae Of Colorado For Family Values*, submitted to the U.S. Supreme Court in October of '93. (For the full text of this analysis, read Appendix D.) In this brief, attorney Robert K. Skolrood lodged a list of five main offenses committed by the six justices of Colorado. His list demonstrates how very far afield the court roamed in order to hold Amendment 2 in its social and legal prison:

(1) to make its ruling the Colorado Supreme Court seized power that only belongs to the federal courts,
(2) the Colorado Supreme Court violated the U.S. Supreme Court's specific standard for recognizing a fundamental right, (in this, they joined Bayless in "inventing" a fundamental right so that they could subject Amendment 2 to higher scrutiny, demanding that it prove a compelling state interest),
    a. in order to do this, they relied on cases totally irrelevant to the Amendment 2 case,
    b. they stretched something called *The Hunter Doctrine* from *Hunter v. Erickson* to fit their decision, going directly against the U.S. Supreme Court's specific instructions for using the doctrine,
(3) to make this unorthodox ruling, the Colorado Court was willing to paralyze the sovereignty of the people of the State of Colorado,
(4) the Colorado Justices furthermore made the state government dangerously vulnerable to litigation in order to favor the gay lobby in this ruling, and
(5) the Colorado Supreme Court ruling made a mockery of all

subsequent Amendment 2 trials to be held in the state.

This bizarre example of bending-the-court-backward for political correctness is hardly the mandate of the Colorado justices. If any

JUSTICE WILLIAM H. ERICKSON stood alone against his colleagues on the Colorado Supreme Court in their social activism against Amendment 2.

other decision-making body had violated its principles in such a reckless fashion—especially for such a doubtful cause—they would simply be fired.

Justice William H. Erickson stood alone against his rash colleagues. He wrote:

> I respectfully dissent. . . . In my view, the district court's underlying legal premise that the Supreme Court has recognized a fundamental right not to have the state endorse and give effect to private biases is erroneous. Similarly . . . the legal premise that the Supreme Court has recognized a fundamental right to participate equally in the political process is erroneous. Because Supreme Court precedent does not support the evaluation of Amendment 2 under the strict scrutiny standard of review, I would reverse and discharge the entry of the preliminary injunction.[224]

Erickson's courageous dissenting opinion should become a part of Colorado history long after the politically correct ruling of his colleagues is overturned. (For those sufficiently aroused by the court's activism, a list of excerpts from Erickson's arguments can be found in Appendix E of this book. His complete 38-page dissenting opinion can be obtained as a matter of public record through Colorado county court law libraries.)

From my own study of these documents I find it impossible to believe that Bayless's ruling or the Colorado Supreme Court ruling will stand before the U.S. Supreme Court, providing the High Court accepts the case. In the meantime, these socially aggressive judges have expanded their powers in order to frustrate a perfectly good law. In my opinion, these rulings will bring their final insult home to the State of Colorado when they are reversed by the U.S. Supreme Court (providing they are allowed to get that far). How then will the people of Colorado feel about these justices who held their democratic process hostage—for no good reason at all?

But an even more sinister question looms before the State of Colorado as their amendment trials proceed. Have Bayless and these six Colorado justices prepared a "poison pill" for Amendment 2? Have they managed to doom it from ever reaching the U.S. Supreme Court? Or worse, when it reaches the federal court, have they placed it on a false foundation so that it cannot be properly defended? It would appear so.

PERVERTED JUSTICE

It is accepted that a referee should not write rules during the course of a ball game. To do so would unfairly advantage one team or the other, and the referee would bear the blame for the resulting feelings of unfairness. Rule books are established in advance so that referees will not have to face this situation.

In Colorado, Bayless and the six court justices deliberately placed themselves in this untenable position concerning Amendment 2. They invented rules as they went, giving an unfair advantage to the gay lobby against the people of Colorado. The rule book of the U.S. Supreme Court was readily available to them. They could have used it to give the state and nation a coherent decision. But they did not. Why didn't they?

Perhaps because the clear precedents of the nation's highest court favored Amendment 2, as seen in the *Brief Amicus Curiae of Colorado for Family Values,* and in the many legal citations of Justice Erickson's *Dissenting Opinion* (Appendices D & E). To follow the rule book would have meant overturning Bayless's injunction, allowing Amendment 2 to become law. Instead of following the path of reason and fairness here, the Colorado justices invented dubious rules, allowing them to nullify Amendment 2.

Bayless's invention was that first fundamental right he "discovered" during his injunction hearings. This impromptu rule was then used to impose the impossible test of compelling state interest on the amendment, dooming its hope of constitutionality.

Strangely, the Colorado Supreme Court liked his style. They followed the Bayless formula 6-to-1, inventing their own fundamental right, which again, forced compelling interest on the amendment. Then they handed the case back to Bayless, knowing that they would see it again on appeal. By this time, whether constitutional or not, they had sentenced Amendment 2 to several years on a legal treadmill. (If one wanted to torment an enemy, this would be a very effective way of doing it.)

As the next Bayless trial began, who could blame the people of Colorado for deserting the courtroom? Standing-room-only crowds had hung onto every word of the original hearings. During this trial, barely a half dozen spectators could be found dozing in their seats. Of course, the press crowded into their own privileged gallery, hungry for any excuse to make the proceedings seem more than a travesty.

Tony Marco provided them a small opportunity. On the witness stand, he took occasion to criticize CFV for using behavioral statistics and gay pride footage in their TV commercials. "The case in favor of Amendment 2 was even stronger without such material," he said. He also took a swipe at the successful "special rights" slogan CFV had used.

"You believe the idea of 'no special rights' is irrelevant to the debate?" the gay lobby lawyer quizzed.

"I believe it is," Marco replied.

This testimony played the press like the sweet kiss of Judas: 'SPECIAL RIGHTS' TACTIC NOW CALLED IRRELEVANT, AMENDMENT 2 AUTHOR TESTIFIES.[225] Other versions of the story characterized him as slamming his former colleagues at CFV. The one thing Tony did not slam, however, was Amendment 2. He believed in it so much that he didn't mind telling the world that CFV could have done a much better job of winning their election.

Later he clarified, saying that he had not criticized special rights as a campaign tactic. On the stand he had been explaining that special rights was meaningless as a legal argument, which of course, everyone with CFV already knew. Nevertheless, "no special rights" remained the best civil rights slogan Amendment 2 and similar laws could hope to find. The sensation of his witness stand remarks caused more confusion for the state's voters to sort out.

By far the strangest aspect of the trial was in the two legal questions the Colorado justices imposed on the proceeding. (At this writing, the trial has concluded and is pending a Bayless decision.) The first question the judges set for Bayless to decide went as follows:

> HAS THE STATE SHOWN A COMPELLING INTEREST FOR AMENDMENT 2 TO IMPINGE FUNDAMENTALLY ON THE RIGHT OF HOMOSEXUALS TO PARTICIPATE EQUALLY IN THE POLITICAL PROCESS?

A moment of stunned silence would be an appropriate response to this question . . .

What?! This is the question upon which the constitutionality of Amendment 2 now rests? By all means, let it be *unconstitutional!* The assumptions of this question have nothing to do with Amendment 2; they were cooked up in the brains of six like-minded Colorado justices. No matter how it is answered, Amendment 2 cannot win this contest. Game, set, match. This question makes a farce of the trial. It must be left for the reader to decide if the Colorado justices intended to do exactly that.

One is uncomfortably reminded that the attorney general's staff spent this state's resources attempting to answer this worthless question. Why waste the effort? They flew-in "expert witnesses from myriad universities and institutions to testify about morals, history and politics,"[226] in order to prove that Amendment 2 had a *compelling interest to impinge a fundamental right that doesn't exist!* They submitted a stack of depositions on the subject four feet tall, about the size of my research for this book. Talk about dancing on Bayless's string! All to prove a question that insults Amendment 2, and the voters of this state. Figure it out.

What exactly is wrong with the trial question? Let's read it again: *"Has the state shown a compelling interest for Amendment 2 to impinge fundamentally on the right of homosexuals to participate equally in the political process?"* First, it assumes that homosexuals are a legally recognized class. The U.S. Supreme Court disagrees. Amendment 2 disagrees. The Colorado voting majority disagrees. Who, on the side of the amendment, would agree to defend this false assumption?

Next, it assumes that a fundamental right can be claimed *based on homosexuality*. Again, the U.S. Supreme court disagrees. Amendment 2 disagrees. The state's voters disagree.

The question further assumes that equal participation in the political process is a fundamental right in this case. In court history, this right has never been stretched even near to the broad definition set for this trial. The burden of proof for this question should be on the justices who invented it, not on the attorney general.

Finally, the question illogically demands that the amendment prove a compelling state interest to violate rights that do not exist!

Requiring the amendment's defender to prove this question can only be seen as unfair. It makes as much sense as The Grand Inquisitor asking the heretic to recite the Apostles Creed so that he can be assigned to the rack for falsely embracing orthodoxy. If American law has become so confused, it is due to the evolutionists who have twisted it from its moorings. It is time for a return to the original meaning of the Constitution.

Perhaps the greatest mistake of the legal proceedings in Colorado was for the amendment backers to simply write off the trials following Bayless's first injunction speech. Understandably, few people could care after that, but something more important than winning or losing remained at stake: just *how* did the legal elite plan to kill Amendment 2? Did they plan to load it with a "poison pill?" Did they plan to assign it to a hopeless treadmill? Or did they plan to honestly try it on its own merits? Asking these questions now, while awaiting Bayless's rulings, raises the more disturbing possibilities.

The first possibility will be that Bayless rules that the attorney general did not prove "a compelling state interest for Amendment 2 to impinge the fundamental right of homosexuals to participate equally in the political process." This ruling would remain true to his injunction reasoning. Amendment 2 voters could heave a sigh of relief and say with Limbaugh, "See? I told you so. Bayless is driven by political correctness. What else would one expect, considering the source?"

But—one must assume that an honest court asks trial questions that can be decided both ways—what if Bayless suddenly changed his mind and decided that Amendment 2 had won this trial question? The very thought of it is an outrage. Winning this question would place the amendment itself on a false legal foundation. The false foundation invented by the Colorado judges, who were so fond of inventing fundamental rights. Homosexuals do not qualify for protected class status (or a suspect class) under the law. Amendment 2 does not need to prove a compelling state interest. No fundamental right has been violated here. Winning this trial question would in effect nullify the rationale for the amendment itself. Winning would in effect, saw-off the limb the defense stands on. Did the Colorado justices intend to do this? Did they intend to create a poison pill?

If Amendment 2 arrived before the U.S. Supreme Court on appeal, after having won this question in Bayless's Court, it would hand the gay lobby every legal precedent necessary to overturn the amendment itself. If Skolrood is right and the law is "all too often . . . a tool of manipulation rather than a force for good," then this case would top them all. It is one thing for judges to have a social agenda, it is another to manipulate the law to pervert justice itself.

No matter how Bayless finally decides to rule, the fact remains that in framing this trial question the Colorado justices invented rules and created an unfair environment for Amendment 2. This fact alone indicates that a renewed commitment to the Constitution is needed to restore order to the court. The present situation threatens to plunge respect for the law to an all-time low.

Unfortunately, this is not the end of the court manipulation in Colorado. The judges of Colorado created a second question for the attorney general's team to defend on behalf of Amendment 2:

> ARE HOMOSEXUALS A SUSPECT CLASS UNDER THE FEDERAL LEGAL PRINCIPLES?

What a relief, you might say. Here's a reasonable question. (Suspect class is roughly equal to "protected class status.") This is the only question raised by Amendment 2 itself. The amendment said flatly, "no." Deciding the amendment's constitutionality based on this question would be a legitimate endeavor. But this second question is completely compromised by the first. The constitutionality of the amendment is tied to *both* questions, therefore, this one becomes a cynical joke. At best, if the amendment defenders win this question, it will be a bone thrown by the court to the people of Colorado. They can say they won something . . . but it just wasn't *worth* anything. Winning this question would not reverse the injunction. It would not release Amendment 2 from its legal prison. What's the point?

How is Bayless likely to rule? From the style he has shown so far, I would expect him to make a split ruling on the two questions.

This would amount to a political ruling, not a judicial one. I would expect him to toss a "bone" to the Colorado majority by announcing that the state had won question number two. (Yeah, hooray.) There would follow a moment of rejoicing across the state. But this would merely be another Bayless "head fake." Taking a large breath, he would then rule that the state lost question number one, which, alas, was the only question that really mattered. Amendment 2, therefore did not meet the test of constitutionality. Then, with authority, he would once again let the gavel fall.

[NOTE: As this manuscript went to press, I reserved this space for comment on the judge's subsequent ruling. On December 14, 1993 Bayless issued a split ruling exactly as predicted above. Bayless wrote: "Amendment 2 is found to be unconstitutional and the court orders that the preliminary injunction be made permanent." (*Slam-dunk!*) After absorbing this largely irrelevant 17-page ruling, it is evident that the court aggression against the people of Colorado can be laid completely at the feet of Colorado's socially aggressive judges. Every argument that stood the test against Amendment 2—at least in Bayless's mind—came from the "fundamental right" the judges created out of thin air . . . a "fundamental right" not recognized by any other court of the land.] —S.B.

THE COURT VS. THE WILL OF THE PEOPLE

Bayless and six Colorado Justices have ruled directly against the will of the people. What will this mean in the long run?

The homosexual lobby claims that it will mean everything. They point to the fact that judges in the '60s used the power of courts to force busing, desegregation, and affirmative action on an unwilling Southern majority. As for black Americans, so it will be for homosexuality in Colorado and elsewhere, they say.

Amendment 2 backers disagree. First, judges do not successfully impose values on a dissenting majority *except* for reasons of highest moral imperative. Those reasons do not exist with the gay lobby. The fundamental rights they invented will not stand. When judges dare to take such novel action from a misguided sense of mission, it is the duty of the people to reverse the court. As in the Dred Scott decision of 1857, in which the U.S. Supreme Court supported slavery and denied citizenship to Negroes, morally outraged Americans rose up and corrected the Court by passing the 14th Amendment to the Constitution guaranteeing civil rights to blacks.

A similar situation exists in the rulings of Bayless and the six Colorado Justices. These men have stretched and bent the power of the laws of our land to serve homosexual politics. In doing so, the judges appear to be nitpicking against the democratic process itself. This is an outrage. It is dangerous judicial activism. The Colorado majority feels it, and they will continue to respond at the polling booth.

Beyond Colorado, it now appears that a national voting trend is emerging in solidarity with the sentiments of Amendment 2. Sample populations in Oregon, New Hampshire, Cincinnati, and Maine have spoken overwhelmingly in the '93 elections, rejecting gay rights laws and embracing the civil rights principle behind Amendment 2. In their own adapted languages, these states have affirmed that how a person has sex, or desires to have sex, does not qualify them for membership in any protected class. The Colorado judges need to listen to the people of America as *they* establish current standards of decency.

Secondly, judges do not successfully impose values on a dissenting majority for less than reasons of fundamental justice. Again, if they do such a thing, they can and should be reversed by the people, or by higher courts, whichever comes first. Regardless of Judge Bayless's ruling, and the Colorado Supreme Court's 6-to-1 insult, it may be confidently asserted that gay rights laws *do not* involve issues of basic rights or justice (see again, Appendix E). The entire idea of sexual orientation cannot even be proven in court. How can a fundamental right be established on this inadequate definition?

In Bayless's courtroom the National Gay and Lesbian Task Force, assisted by the ACLU, submitted a five point test one could use to identify someone with a homosexual orientation. They said a person could qualify under *one or more* of the following points:

1. Personally identifying oneself as gay.

2. Identifying with a community defined by a sexual orientation.

3. Establishing a public ID based on one's sexual orientation.

4. An emotional attraction to and desire to share emotional intimacy with a person of the same gender.

5. A physical attraction to and/or desire to share sexual intimacy with a person of the same gender.

(Notice, not one of the five criteria involves behavior. How can mere "desire" or claimed "sexual fantasy" qualify a person for any fundamental right? This is "touchy-feely" law. Behavior seems the only legally sane proof of same-sex attraction, and behavior itself turns out to be a no-win legal definition, too! The whole gay legal issue is a bottomless pit.)

After seeing the Gay and Lesbian list, Tony Marco began to claim to be homosexual. Tongue-in-cheek, of course. He would explain that he could construe the legal definitions to qualify himself as gay under all but the last criteria. (He then claimed that he could legally take advantage of definition number five too, by telling a simple lie.) If the courts bought into this list, he said, he could twist protected class status from its moorings and use it for himself.

The point is that sexual orientation does not belong in court. It's too easily manipulated. One only has to recall the heterosexual young men who avoided the military draft in the 50's and 60's by claiming to be homosexual. (The image of "Clinger" in the TV series *M*A*S*H* comes quickly to mind.) Orientation can be disguised, faked, changed, cross-dressed, or claimed by anyone who feels it is to their advantage to do so.

Both orientation and behavior can be arguably altered. Disregarding the politically correct American Psychological Association, clinical psychologist Joseph Nicolosi calls homosexual behavior a "developmental disorder." He is a respected scientist who claims that the condition can be successfully treated and reversed.[227] His study is supported by thousands of case histories of successful transformation from homosexuality to a straight lifestyle. There are no fundamental legal rights to be based on this behavior or orientation. It is changeable.

In contrast, racial identity is not changeable. It is easy to prove in court. It is immutable, visible, and genetically demonstrable if necessary. Historically, blacks could not alter nor disguise their identity to escape slavery. Nor did they have to form a task force and create a toll-free hotline to prove their history of discrimination. For the manifest suffering of blacks, the American people demanded a 14th Amendment to the Constitution.

Finally, the Colorado Court's citing of racial discrimination law to justify gay rights law is completely unfounded. The black American experience and homosexuality simply do not compare on any scale. Southern racism prompted the most *exceptional* use of the law in American history. This group of civil rights laws answered the unique condition of the buying and selling of human beings. Never before, never again, has any evil so deeply rooted itself in our body politic. A half-million soldiers died in a civil war before blacks were freed. The South was brutally plundered. The legacy of hatred left simmering between North and South remains to this day, and it is unparalleled. The civil rights struggle of blacks in the '60s played directly against this painful national wound. Residual discrimination is seen directly in *per capita* income levels among black households today, versus gay households. Homosexual politics is a trivial pursuit by comparison to the real struggles of black civil rights in this country.

It would be well for Judge Bayless, the state Supreme Court, and those on both sides of the homosexual rights issue to heed the words of Abraham Lincoln when evaluating the Colorado Court's ruling against the will of the people. In this sterling quote from his debate with Stephen Douglas over the Dred Scott decision, Lincoln revealed the ultimate winners in a dispute between the courts and the voting majority: "*In this age, and in this country*," he said, "*public sentiment is everything. With it, nothing can fail; against it, nothing can succeed. Whoever molds public sentiment goes deeper than he who enacts statutes, or pronounces judicial decisions.*"[228]

This quote, penned six years before his immortal Gettysburg Address, affirms that Lincoln envisioned America as a nation "of the people, by the people, for the people"—all along. The 14th Amendment bears testimony to his prescient wisdom. After his death the people corrected the error of the Supreme Court. And in Colorado, Lincoln's wisdom declares that Amendment 2 has struck a far deeper chord in the national soul than the rulings of Bayless and six other misguided justices.

The Colorado majority can take comfort from Lincoln's quote. On issues not affecting fundamental rights, or moral imperative, the courts will eventually follow the will of the people. Not the other way around. Even if, in the interim (as during the reign of the Dred Scott decision) a few years of struggle must pass.

An indication of the High Court's recent commitment to Lincoln's principle is seen in the U.S. Supreme Court's *Bowers v. Hardwick* decision. In this ruling the High Court upheld Georgia's sodomy law. In the resulting opinion, Justice Byron White appealed to "a majority of the electorate in Georgia" as a guiding authority for the decision. He acknowledged that when the people of Georgia upheld a moral and criminal definition of homosexuality by consensus, the High Court would not violate their standard. Therefore, in matters affecting "evolving standards of decency" in Colorado, the federal court is likely to honor the values of the voting majority above the opinion of state justices.

The Colorado Court's decision on Amendment 2, however, will test the U.S. Supreme Court in ways different from *Bowers v. Hardwick*. The question of whether or not homosexual's will be given protected class status, and whether or not they have thus been dealt an infringement of a fundamental right, are at stake. If for some politically correct reason, the High Court finds that homosexuality can be defined as a minority group—and if they subsequently find that Amendment 2 denies some fundamental right to this ill-defined group—then the only thing the people of Colorado can do is redraft the law according to the changing rules of the court—*and pass it again!* It is not likely that any judge, no matter how committed to social activism, would have the unmitigated gall to enjoin such a law. This is the process by which the people communicate to the court the ultimate principles of Constitutional meaning.

The question remains: How is the U.S. Supreme Court likely to rule on Amendment 2? Before the Colorado law was placed on the original petition, eight constitutional lawyers scrutinized it and said that its language would pass every Supreme Court test in existence. These men had made careers studying the High Court.

They all ratified the present language of the amendment. It seems improbable that the nation's top justices will rule against it.

Improbable—but not impossible—as long as this nation continues to allow its Constitution to be evolved.

In the meantime, there will continue to be a struggle between the courts and the people. In fact, unless the homosexual lobby stops its campaign for forced acceptance through protected class status, this struggle is guaranteed to extend beyond the Colorado courts, engulfing the courts of other states. In Cincinnati, Ohio where a large majority voted to overturn the city's gay rights law, the homosexual lobby immediately took the people to court. A local judge was found who would rule in their favor. For gay politics, this is a fool's quest. Taking the people of America to court is betting on the wrong horse.

THE "CHRISTIAN" COMPROMISE

Beware any form of compromise in a battle over gay rights laws. Either homosexuals deserve protected class status or they don't. It is not a multiple choice question.

Early in February 1993, with Amendment 2 under injunction, a would-be hero emerged in Colorado Springs with something called a clarification of Amendment 2. He had been working for weeks behind the scenes to gain key support for his plan to scrap the hard won amendment, receiving support from a few key businessmen, community leaders, and city officials. His name was Greg Walta, a 51-year-old lawyer who had served on the ACLU's national board of directors. He claimed that he held the key to stopping bad feelings between the amendment majority and the homosexual lobby. Who wouldn't want to hear this?

His proposal seemed seductively simple. It stated that common ground existed between Amendment 2 voters and homosexuals. Ground on which a new amendment could be written to "clarify" Amendment 2, replacing its (supposedly) badly written wording. As one Walta supporter vaguely lamented, "there is something wrong . . . everything is not fine with Amendment 2 . . ."[229] Walta claimed that what was wrong could be fixed on the common ground of "no special rights" for homosexuals. He had listened to both sides throughout the campaign and had heard as follows:

> a) The proponents say they oppose discrimination against homosexuals, but are fighting against "special rights," presumably quotas and affirmative action.
> b) The opponents say they only want protection from discrimination, not special rights, quotas or affirmative action.[230]

Therefore, Walta challenged, why not hold both sides to their words? If they meant what they said, they should be able to compromise concerning "no special rights, quotas or affirmative action." In a press conference on February 7, Walta unveiled the basics of his proposal:

> The clarifying amendment should repeal and reenact the present amendment by prohibiting discrimination based on sexual orientation, with the following exemptions and provisions:
>
> a) An exemption for apartments below a certain number;
> b) An exemption for businesses below a certain number of employees;
> c) An exemption for churches and religious organizations;
> d) A provision against quotas, statistical evidence and affirmative action.

Responding to his press conference with immediate enthusiasm, the *Gazette Telegraph* launched Walta's campaign the next day with these glowing words: "He is a born-again Christian and a card-carrying member of the American Civil Liberties Union [ACLU]. He's a straight, white male from Colorado Springs who never gave much thought to gay rights until six months ago . . . 'I just can't stand the fighting going on anymore,'" Walta was quoted as saying. "'I love Colorado Springs and want to stop the acrimony in the community.'"[231] Walta then claimed that his clarification of Amendment 2 amounted to a peacemaking "compromise." It would serve both sides, he said. Anyone who opposed compromise, he implied, was not serious about the public good.

The next day Colorado for Family Values prepared a reply. It did not take long. They had only to look at the clarification's premise to reject it. The assumption that Colorado for Family Values had opposed discrimination against homosexuals was a trap: Amendment 2 had said they didn't deserve protected class status; discrimination remained a separate issue. No one knew that better than Greg Walta. In CFV's view, he was not a good-willed compromiser after-all. He was a poor imitation of 'Brer Rabbit,' asking the people of Colorado to toss Amendment 2 into a "briar-patch" of legal thorns. (As if the amendment supporters were not intelligent enough to understand the elements of their own victory.)

Beyond that, the idea that both sides were against "special rights, quotas and affirmative action" did not fly either. CFV maintained that Walta's so-called compromise would "willy-nilly" *grant* protected class status to gays in its very language. The phrase, "prohibiting discrimination based on sexual orientation" would do exactly that. That phrase—in any law—implied that homosexuality *deserved* protected class status, something totally unfounded and rejected by federal civil rights authorities. If CFV had conceded those words, quotas and affirmative action would have followed as night followed day—regardless of Walta's wording against "special rights, quotas and affirmative action."

The way Walta's law was written, the only part written in stone was the part that guaranteed gay rights. The rest of it had been written in pencil, easily erased or altered. As a former ACLU board member, Walta must have known that his colleagues would, in fact, jettison these "distasteful" compromises from the language as the law "evolved" through time. Such action had become the ACLU's very reason for existence: ". . . the law will change . . ."[232] they had promised the homosexual lobby. In fact, they had become committed to changing it like the boundaries of a frontier land treaty. The gay lobby would get the affirmative action they wanted if only they would have patience.

CFV made a bet with themselves that patience was one quality the gay lobby did not possess. They further ventured that Walta would fail to win gay allegiance precisely because of this fact. Homosexuals would never delay their gratification on the issue of affirmative action. This belief had come from months of CFV campaign experience. Gays simply showed no willingness to wait for their agenda anymore. They would not wait for the ACLU either, even if Walta swore on a stack of Bibles to eventually overturn the language in their favor.

CFV also rejected Walta's compromise because it violated a common sense principle which Amendment 2 supporters upheld: "If it ain't broke, don't fix it." If people claiming same-sex attractions did not suffer enough to qualify under the federal government criteria for protected class status, why write a law "prohibiting discrimination based on sexual orientation," giving them this special status? Why burden Colorado unnecessarily? Amendment 2 had removed the load of "fixing what ain't broke."

In the meantime, the amendment conformed perfectly to the conservative notion of "less government." It had effectively tossed the government out of the business of deciding private sexual values. Nice and clean. But in framing his so-called compromise, Walta had asked CFV to deliberately muddy the waters again. His law guaranteed the need for more laws, exemptions, provisions, clarifications, and compromises in the future. The thing was a tarbaby. Once embraced, Colorado would not be able to let go of it. Only a lawyer could figure it out.

As Will Perkins put it, "This new amendment sounds like the 'Walta and Associates retirement act'."

Finally, each of Walta's exemptions, rather than clarifying anything, betrayed their own absurdity. Landlords and businesses would be allowed to discriminate against homosexuals if they were small enough; Churches and religious organizations could do it if they still believed in the authority of the Bible. Whereas Amendment 2 had been falsely accused by the press of "legalizing discrimination," Walta's compromise *actually did it*! His exemptions amounted to "licenses to discriminate." (Not one watchdog in the news media so much as wagged a tongue on this obvious point.)

Dutifully, CFV put out a written 2-page statement containing its reasons for rejecting the proposal. The Colorado Springs *Gazette*

Telegraph announced the statement with a negative spin, as usual: COMPROMISE CALLED SLAP IN FACE: "Defenders of Amendment 2 lashed out Monday at a proposed replacement as a 'watered-down gay rights bill' and vowed to oppose it."[233]

Without the challenge of press criticism, Walta's flawed compromise began to make many converts. Some business proponents saw it as a way to end the boycott (which still raged at the time), settle all the talk of hatred, and fix what was wrong with Amendment 2 (implying it needed fixing).

"The people who supported Amendment 2 were misled,"[234] Walta said bluntly. Which could only mean that he believed Colorado for Family Values had misled them. Not exactly the words of a man who wanted "to stop the acrimony in the community." Yet a certain contingent of concerned citizens seemed to agree with him, no matter how illogical his position.

Walta's up-front claim to be a "born again" Christian played into his curious charisma. The posture courted the approval of Colorado Springs' so-called religious right. Robin Miller, the leading local homosexual spokesperson had also claimed to be "born again" as a tactic in the debate. The term had worn out its automatic good graces with those of Biblical convictions, however. The claim carried no more weight than the character of the person claiming it. It was not a significant ticket to votes, if that had been Walta's intention.

However, the real power of his declaration of Christianity lay in his "peacemaking" role. Peacemaking seemed religiously and culturally irresistible to other Christians. To dialogue, to forgive one's enemy, to end bickering, acrimony, and divisiveness in the community, as Walta suggested—this seemed a truly Christian thing to do.

Yet peacemaking had to find its proper place in the hierarchy of Christian values. The same Bible that said, "Blessed are the peacemakers,"[235] said in another place, "To every thing there is a season . . . a time to kill, and a time to heal; a time to break down, and a time to build up."[236] What time was it for Colorado? This was the question. With the newspaper carrying bold inset quotes from city leaders like: "In the 20 years I've lived here, I've never seen anything so destructive going on in this community;"[237] the lure of "a time for peace" became nearly overpowering for people of faith.

A number of prominent figures forsook their allegiance to Colorado for Family Values and Amendment 2 during this time. Law Partner Bruce Buell let his support for Walta be publicly quoted: "I'm going at it as a conservative Christian and a lawyer who is concerned with civil rights. . . . I'd like to see a reconciliation, and I think reconciliation demands compromise."[238]

Walta's so-called compromise also captured the imaginations of those who thought they understood the public's perception of the controversy, but didn't. Chief among them, the news department of the *Gazette Telegraph*. The Colorado Springs newspaper plastered headlines, stories, and more full color Greg Walta photographs during this time, than they had for any other single issue of the entire campaign. By the end of it, they had nearly turned Greg Walta into the patron saint of Colorado.

Here's a *Gazette* headline and picture sampler: LAWYER WORKS TO RESTORE HARMONY (Feb. 2—*full color picture of Walta*); LOCAL BACKING CALLED KEY TO NEW PLAN (Feb. 5—*full color picture of Walta*); BUSINESS . . . LEADERS MOBILIZE TO BACK NEW PLAN (Feb. 14); OPPONENTS SEEK UNITED EFFORT (Feb. 15); GROUP SAYS VOTERS WERE MISLED ON AMENDMENT 2 (Feb. 16—*full color picture of Walta*); POLL SHOWS SUPPORT FOR COMPROMISE (Feb. 17—*full color picture of Walta*); WALTA PLAN DEFINES 'SPECIAL RIGHTS' (Mar. 2—*B&W picture of Walta*); FINDING MIDDLE GROUND (Mar. 7—*full color picture of Walta*).

Even with all of this media hype behind him, Walta's misbegotten compromise began to unravel. In a telling face to face debate with Will Perkins, his political pants were pulled to his knees, his saintly neutrality exposed for its true bias: Will held up a paid political announcement from a Sunday newspaper, printed just two days before the November election. The bold headline read, VOTE NO ON #2: CHRISTIANS AND JEWS *SPEAK OUT* ON AMENDMENT #2. Buried in a list of 300 names of people who had gone on record as saying that Amendment 2 amounted to "state-sanctioned discrimination"—Greg Walta had signed his name.

"So you have never really been neutral on this amendment, have you, Greg?" Will asked.

"No," he blustered in reply, "And I'm proud of it."

"Well, you may be proud of it but how can you call what you are doing a true compromise? How can someone who has campaigned against Amendment 2 turn around and negotiate a fair

GREG WALTA, the "born-again" Christian who would compromise Amendment 2, left, confers with JACK LANG Y MARQUEZ, the man who would have been Colorado's Civil Rights Czar if H.B. 1059 had passed in '91.

solution?"

This was another significant turning point in the Amendment 2 campaign ignored by the news media. Walta's compromise had been shown to be insincere from the start. It was merely an ACLU attempt to find a shortcut to victory.

In the days to come the compromise suffered another loss before the Colorado Springs Chamber of Commerce. Walta had counted heavily on businessmen, weary of the boycott, to stand behind him. One fine Sunday the *Gazette Telegraph* did their part to help him collect this important vote. They displayed a large picture of the city's supposed business elite standing by Greg, supporting the compromise beneath the headline: BUSINESS/-COALITION GAINS STEAM.[239] Upon closer examination, the picture presented no one new. Those pictured were local lawyers associated with Holland & Hart, the Denver firm representing the plaintiffs against Amendment 2 in court. Others were known anti-amendment campaigners or big business representatives who had already conceded to the homosexual lobby everything they demanded in the workplace. The idea that this photo represented a group of sincere business leaders who had discovered a compromise to end "acrimony" was pure *mirage*.

Three days after concocting this picture, the *Gazette* announced a front page feature poll revealing 60% of the Chamber in favor of Walta's amendment. (Once again, to believe the press was to be seriously misled.)

Days later, a confidential four-page legal analysis of Walta's proposal circulated to the Chamber's leadership. It hammered the kind of legal confusion Walta's law would introduce into the business arena: lost resources from fighting government red tape outweighing any boycott losses from sticking with the Colorado majority, etc. The memo concluded as follows: "Amendment 2 removed the hand of government from the area of private choice concerning homosexual conduct. Denver, Aspen and Boulder laws are also rescinded under the current amendment, thus, individual freedom of choice is restored. Let's stop the debate and get on with the real issues facing the Chamber."[240]

Will Perkins attended a special Chamber session to add his folksy arguments: "What kind of a compromise is it when they want to overthrow an amendment passed by a majority of the people? Think about it. CFV went through a difficult initiative process. First getting the right language, then signing those petitions. We debated against the press for a year before winning the election. Now Walta wants to compromise this law? He's just trying to get a free ride on Amendment 2 without going through the test of the political process."

As CFV had predicted, Walta's compromise failed to win the homosexual lobby's support. Through a perceived compromise, liberals and moderates had been enticed to come together in Colorado Springs to offer the gay lobby a path into the political mainstream, but Denver, Boulder, and Aspen activists would not unite. Walta and friends had perhaps naïvely assumed that the homosexual lobby would play a reasonable hand. (They should have asked Mo Siegel.) As it turned out, homosexuals wanted protected class status—and affirmative action—with all its power in order to force society to submit to them *now*. Nothing less. They did not like Walta's language against quotas and affirmative action, no matter how concocted for later repeal. Neither did they like the exemptions. And when "gays ain't happy, ain't *nobody* happy."

Robin Miller, Colorado's famous "born again" homosexual, screamed at Walta in one meeting, "You're a bigot!"

"It was an angry meeting," Walta confirmed, deadpan.

His next session with homosexual advocates in Denver began by "butting heads." Jealousy emerged with Denver gays complaining about being brought into the process by Colorado Springs "so late." In an open meeting with homosexuals in downtown Denver on February 28, "the criticism came pouring down. Some people walked out. The meeting broke up late and angry."[241]

Through a series of tantrums, the homosexual lobby talked Walta into adding new exemptions and provisions to his law. These were further clarified, renamed, subtracted, realigned—as feared, the simplicity of the original idea was destroyed in the process. Now it became the nightmare of red tape predicted in the Colorado Springs Chamber of Commerce memo. Walta admits now that the whole attempt was a bad idea.[242]

On March 15, 1993 Walta folded the compromise tent. The newspaper account of his journey to defeat did more to reveal the diverse forms of disrespect latent in the homosexual community than any CFV brochure. (Diversity is not benign after all.) The front page banner headlines carried *a full color picture* of a sad and weary Greg Walta (*composition of picture; an unusual super-sympathetic close-up*); AMENDMENT 2 COMPROMISE FALLS.[243] It made one almost want to weep for poor Greg.

What had happened? How could such a nice sounding idea promoted so heavily by the press, rise so high and fall so hard?

Primarily because Colorado for Family Values had been right in their assessment of the compromise. They had made their case to the community based on sound arguments, and the community had understood these points better than any of the elitists knew. Most CFV backers never departed from their solid Amendment 2 vote. The supportive letters to the editor had come in record numbers during this controversy.

Conservative Christians who had been sucked into the peacemaking effort now stood about scratching their heads or wiping egg from their faces. Law partner Bruce Buell, who had lent his reputation to the compromise effort, now mumbled his official excuse for the front page of the *Gazette*: "I thought it was a reasonable proposal. . . ."[244]

In the aftermath, the compromise proved to be another public relations boon for Amendment 2. The law had stood another public test. It had once again outlasted a full court press by the news media. Business had begun to see the advantage of the conservative language inherent in Amendment 2. Religious people had received an object lesson that peacemaking at any cost is not so "blessed." The homosexual lobby had once again bitten the hand of a friend.

From the outside, homosexual rights issues seem like such a "feel good" cause. But Colorado's experience with Amendment 2 and the compromise effort had brought the quagmire of gay politics out of the closet. It further demonstrated the practical nightmare of forced affirmation for the electorate. In Colorado today, the issue sends politicians running for cover. All of which has tended to deepen the state's respect and appreciation for the good thinking behind Colorado for Family Values, and Amendment 2.

The overriding lesson from Walta's failed effort seems to be: beware any compromise on the issue of special rights for homosexuality. Either same-sex attraction deserves protected class status or it does not. As much as one might wish to hide from the divisive question in compromise, there are no subtle variations of "yes" or "no" that properly answer it.

IN SEARCH OF HATE

"This issue is different from any I've experienced," said CFV Chairman, Will Perkins. "If you don't agree with homosexuals they accuse you of hatred."

It's true. Anyone who opposes the homosexual agenda will be forced to wear the "hate" label like a scarlet letter. At least until a winning conservative momentum forces sanity back into this debate.

In Colorado the label would not have carried much weight without the generous help of the news media. Primarily the hate issue gained credence from the media's decision to describe the amendment as "banning laws protecting gays and lesbians." Removing protection from a supposedly innocent group of victims can only seem hateful.

Will Perkins said it most succinctly in nearly every interview, though his best remarks were often ignored by the press: "Amendment 2 didn't take rights or protection from anybody. It didn't change anything in Colorado except those gay rights laws in Denver, Boulder, and Aspen. Those laws should have been changed anyway."

Heedless of the truth, newsmen continued to promote the impression that the amendment invited and legalized discrimination. In Manitou Springs, a jewelry shop window carried a bitter sign following the election: WELCOME TO COLORADO . . . THE FIRST AND ONLY STATE IN THE UNION TO LEGALIZE DISCRIMINATION.

This wrong-headed impression flew in the face of post election polls. These studies revealed not hate, but that a large middle of Amendment 2 supporters had voted for the conservative principle of limiting government. A principle inherent in the amendment's language. "They don't want to see more laws," said Paul Talmey, whose Talmey-Drake poll concluded that 73% of Amendment 2 voters voted for the idea of keeping government out of private sexual values. This is not a "hate" vote.[245]

Nevertheless, *ABC Nightline* published the following "hate-search" opinions: 10% of those surveyed thought Coloradans possibly hated homosexuals, 7% said they thought they might have voted for hate as well as to keep government from enforcing gay rights laws. Even given these dubious Colorado opinions, it is an obvious distortion to characterize the entire vote by the few who may or may not have felt this hatred.

In California, one observant newsman, a former resident of Colorado's gay community, warned his fellow activists, "it's important that gay-rights supporters not fall into the trap of thinking their opponents are automatically hateful or unenlightened. Surely some are, but it doesn't account for a 53% vote in Colorado, and to misunderstand the opposition in any struggle is a mistake that can be fatal."[246]

Assuming that he meant "politically fatal," CFV could not agree more. But to this day, it appears that the homosexual community and their doctrinaire supporters have been unable to see the plain truth here. They continue to uncritically follow the *Overhauling* strategy of vilifying their opposition as hateful, bigoted, and religiously narrow. Have they looked in the mirror?

In the July '93 issue of *Focus on the Family Magazine*, Dr. James Dobson, whose ministry is headquartered in Colorado Springs, published a letter from an articulate young homosexual: "I write this letter on behalf of my many friends who . . . hate the church because of organizations like yours. . . . You support legislation [meaning Amendment 2] to take away our rights and spread misleading, inaccurate information." To which Dobson replied at length before concluding with this challenge: "Have we brought caskets to your front door? Have we thrown bricks through your windows? Have we left bloody animal parts on your property? Have we spread untrue rumors about your activities and motives? Have we spray painted your buildings or made bomb threats at your offices? No, but all of these hostilities have been inflicted on us by the homosexual community and its supporters in Colorado Springs."[247]

On a quiet Sunday, near the anniversary of Amendment 2's passage, Will Perkins sat in church preparing to listen to the formal reading of scripture. Suddenly among the one-thousand worshippers, a dozen or so members of the Savage Homos Into Truth (do not attempt the acronym) and Gay Avengers stood up, blowing shrill whistles. Will said that he thought that perhaps the youth group had started one of their missionary fund raising skits. They've been known to stage mini-dramas during evening services. Then the activists began to shout in unison, "Gay's and lesbians under attack in Colorado Springs. We act up. This is for Will Perkins." At this point Will knew that it was not the youth group. The activists then pelted the congregation with condoms. As they left, people in the congregation could be heard shouting, "God bless you."[248]

Who is under attack? Who hates whom?

Finally, in a search for hatred, one must look at the homosexual activists themselves. Like children, they have misconstrued disapproval for hatred. They have even confused AIDS with hatred. A sign in a recent gay pride parade said, "End hatred, stop AIDS." Mel White, a homosexual preacher in Dallas, Texas virulently blames Rev. Jerry Falwell and Pat Robertson for AIDS and the high rate of gay suicide. "It's your misuse of the Bible that's causing the death of my brothers and sisters," he howled on National Public Radio recently.[249]

Homosexuals have confused tolerance with acceptance. They call morality discrimination. They reject the notion that their kind of family is a cultural burden, or culturally less than equal to the heterosexual family ideal. They reject all arguments that procreation is of more value than adoption. Or that their kind of sex is unnatural or unhealthy, even in the face of shortened lifespans and a multiplicity of diseases. Could it be that a group so deluded is the source of its own hatred?

Torie Osborn accidentally said so. She's the National Gay and Lesbian Task Force leader who visited Colorado Springs following the homosexual march on Washington, D.C.. The march had been a shocking event in which public lewdness, indecent exposure, disorderly conduct, foul language, disrespect of institutions, and sexual harassment received full equality with heterosexual decency—at least for a day.

Torie, fresh from all that homosexual "pride" on display, promptly made a confession designed to win more media sympathy. She told of lying against her sexual orientation while delivering a feminist speech in her twenties. At the time, she had been living "in the closet as a young lesbian." In the speech, she had declared that lesbians threatened the women's movement. "That same night I was with a woman," she confessed softly to a reverently listening Colorado Springs press corp. Why the confession? "That's how deep a gay and lesbian can hate themselves if they want to conform,"[250] she explained. Sympathetic nods and "hmmms" from news writers as they bent to copy her exact words for the morning paper.

One feels curious to ask: What is the difference between the self-hatred of a conformist and the self-hatred of a nonconformist? Torie Osborn has apparently experienced both. In her early years as a conformist in the closet she dealt with self-hatred inwardly, albeit lying to get ahead. Today, having "come out" as a nonconformist, she turns self-hatred outward on society—specifically, on Colorado Springs. The conformist seems by far the more honest of the two Ms. Osborns, at least not blaming society for her own hypocrisy.

For a study in extroverted self-hate, consider the gross public indecency paraded in the name of gay pride in Washington, D.C.. Consider Torie and other homosexual leaders now claiming that all of that unbridled lust in the deadly age of AIDS was nothing but "campy fun." Only straitlaced homophobes would object to sadomasochistic displays, she suggests, or to pornographic orgies simulated by mostly naked men, or women with decoratively mutilated and tattooed breasts, "dykes on bikes," Lesbian Avengers, cross dressers, and the hauntingly sad spectacle of a self-loathing ethnic woman walking in front of the nation's Capitol with a sign reading, "Eat my big Asian p____." And what of those all-too-often camera documented sex acts that slipped the bonds of restraint among the gay paraders? Who but someone projecting self-hatred on the offended public would turn around and say, "You hate us!" . . .?

Unfortunately this self-hatred is politicized by certain therapists and government bureaucrats for the dollars in it. In Colorado Springs, shortly after the passage of Amendment 2, the El Paso County Health and Environment Department issued an announcement concerning the high rates of homosexual teen suicide. (Not in

Colorado Springs, mind you, but nationwide.) Mercedes Harden, the local department director used the suicide rates (like AIDS death statistics are used) to advance the homosexual political agenda of forced acceptance:[251]

"The root of the problems of gay youth suicide is a society that discriminates against and stigmatizes homosexuals," she said. (An unproven and unwarranted accusation.) ". . . legislation should guarantee homosexuals equal rights," she said (. . . pure agenda. The suggestion has no place in a public health document). "Helping professionals need to accept and support a homosexual orientation in youth," she concluded. (Wrong. No one needs to accept what is culturally unacceptable in order to give therapeutic help.)

According to the standards of society, if one desires to engage in an unacceptable sexual behavior, that person must run the risk of feeling anything from guilt, to pain, to shame, to full blown self-hatred. This is reality. It is cause and effect. The condition is true of adultery, incest, pedophilia, and homosexuality among other forbidden indulgences. Homosexuality is not singled-out here.

But what is the "cause" of the self-hatred? Is it society's standards? Or does society at this point recognize behaviors that will destroy it and confer upon those destructive tendencies the label, "unacceptable?" It is, of course, the latter.

The conformist homosexual in the closet agrees that his behavior is not society's norm. He or she works on his self-hatred in private. There may be thousands who have achieved inner peace in this way, who knows? Torie Osborn and the others who come angrily out, choose no longer to do that. They blame society and find professionals like Mercedes Harden to reinforce their delusions. These nonconformists are determined to make their behavior society's norm. When society resists, they see the resistance in the mirror of their own self-hatred.

This fits what CFV found throughout the campaign: everyone who opposed the homosexual agenda wore the "hate" label as a scapegoat.

If this continues, then perhaps it is simply helpful to understand where the hate label really belongs. This knowledge should inspire a measure of understanding for homosexuals, a measure of compassion and pity for these victims of self-hatred. But no one can be helped if society accepts the hate label where it does *not* belong. No one can be helped if society perpetuates a lie. True compassion, sincere love, begins with telling the truth, even when it hurts.

TRUE BIGOTRY

What of real bigotry? What of those who did not vote for the good reasons of the amendment? Perhaps some did vote out of hate for homosexuals. If so, it must be said that a number of homosexual activists voted with hate in their hearts as well. At least a few gays harbor an insane hatred for straight America. (A day on the CFV phones will remove all doubt about that.) But any study of real hatred must begin with the fact that only the homosexual lobby attempted to manipulate hate to their political advantage. Only gays painted signs, "Hate is not a family value," changing it to "Hate is NOW a family value," after the election. Only the homosexual lobby labeled Colorado the State of Hate. They were wrong on all counts.

So, how should real hatred be put into perspective?

First of all, it is an unfortunate part of the human condition. It has always been, and will always be. Thankfully, our civilization has found ways to keep it in reasonable check. (Morality, religion, traditional values, and police forces have historically performed this function.) A margin of hatred is also the risk one must necessarily find in the public arena. Coalitions of voters are not ideologically pure on either side of any issue.

So the battle in Colorado was not won or lost over hatred. (One befuddled voter asked, "What's hate got to do with it?") The election succeeded for the side with the better arguments, the one who told the truth more completely to the people. When the opposition labeled this a hate vote, they shot themselves in the political foot.

The most important aspect of this hate accusation then, is understanding that Amendment 2 itself, did not hate. Even if a few voters may have. The amendment itself possessed a voice of reason and did not give bigotry or hate a place. The amendment took no constitutional rights from homosexuals (except perhaps those invented by Colorado judges). The amendment merely removed the hand of government from forcing acceptance of homosexual values on the heterosexual majority.

Though often accused of it, CFV did not appeal to hatred or fear in its campaign. When homosexual behavior and health was discussed in seminars, brochures, the tabloid, or was made visible through gay pride parade footage, the opposition called this exposure hateful. But it wasn't. Perhaps it was painful, but not hateful. In an important debate, all of the facts are needed for an informed decision. Even the painful ones.

Many CFV critics said that the behavioral footage and statistics used may not have been hate motivated but they incited hatred in unstable voters. CFV could not find the evidence for this. Neither could just about anyone else. Most amendment supporters were family, salt-of-the-earth types, who used the behavioral information to get their friends and neighbors off the political fence. After realizing the serious threat of gay behavior, they could then say, homosexual rights laws are not values-free. They advance this excessive behavior and lifestyle, with real social and physical risks.

Will Perkins responded to the criticism of using gay pride footage with his deceptively simple wisdom. He shrugged helplessly and said, "You can't separate behavior from homosexuality. That's what it is."

Truth is the point. Consider the following list of names for events staged in our nation's Capitol during the homosexual march in 1993: A radical Faerie Circle (drumming and dancing behind the White House); The Sado/Masochist Fetish Conference (in which a photo of "fisting" was exhibited in a federal building and "master/slave" homosexual contracts were discussed); Drag Show Extravaganza on the Mall; Lesbutante Ball (in which observers saw mass nude dancing in public); Transgender conference; Queer Scout Cookie Sell-a-thon. No one is calling anyone names here. These are the homosexual organizers' own names for their own events.

From these descriptions it can be seen that behavior is central to the homosexual's perception of themselves. Why should behavior be off limits for Colorado for Family Values? Why should it be automatically hateful to bring it up? Even Gay and Lesbian mouthpiece Torie Osborn can't deny the community's antics after so many Washington marchers hung out their dirty laundry on C-SPAN TV in D.C.: "I love drag queens," she gushed after the weird show. "Queers are different. And I like using that word now . . ."[252] Of course she does. This thing is out of the closet and in our face. Its here for everyone to see and discuss—everyone that is, but those who oppose it.

Concerned people—the kind who will vote—are watching the nature of this debate carefully. The Colorado experience tells America that the side more committed to telling the truth in the fight over gay rights laws will win the people, no matter how the media distorts their voice.

THE KEY TO AMENDMENT 2

Months after their election success Will Perkins, Kevin Tebedo, and Mark Olsen huddled to put the CFV success formula into words. They emerged with a consensus. Partly by accident, partly by design, they had tinkered with a combination lock and unleashed the Amendment 2 victory. The key was simply this: they had fought unfair gay rights laws and defeated them with truthful civil rights arguments. It had yielded a political victory for fairness and justice, not a moral victory for the religious right.

The Colorado approach recognized the fact that, like it or not, America has retreated from its Judeo-Christian roots. Morals are not gone, but they have been banished from the public square where once they informed nearly every civic debate. Also, many Americans no longer accept a Judeo-Christian heritage as being worth any more than the cultures that spring from Hinduism, the Muslim religion, pre-Christian paganism, Native American rituals, or even Eastern Traditions. Many no longer appreciate Western Civilization itself.

Nevertheless, this same American public would not stand by as a rich sexual lobby seized the protected class status of real minorities. A sense of fairness still pervades this culture. Amendment 2 demonstrated it.

Political correctness is here too. It can blind even fair-minded people. Citizens have been intimidated by the peer pressure prevailing in education, politics, religion, and the media today. Because of it, nearly everyone fears a wrong label. A position against gay rights automatically receives the religious right tag in the press. Even with a civil law like Amendment 2, the religious right label is mindlessly applied. Michael Hudson of *People for the American Way* continues to throw it at CFV, long after the people of the state have spoken. Some people seem beyond learning.

The label would not stick to Amendment 2. The fairness arguments for the amendment proved superior, more reasoned and beneficial than the feel-good arguments of the politically correct crowd. The amendment's strong points were compelling enough that Colorado voted for it against a tide of elite pressure. They were not duped or tricked or manipulated by a slick campaign.

Will Perkins perhaps summed-up the amendment victory best in these words:

> We gave people a reasonable way to vote about what they feel is right or wrong. Nearly everyone feels that homosexuality is wrong, even if it is not a moral question for them. But in America, we hate to impose our versions of right or wrong on anyone else, especially if the standard comes from religious belief. So Amendment 2 gave the people of Colorado a truthful, honest, intelligent reason to vote the way they feel. The civil rights arguments formed a bridge of reason between their hearts and their minds. This was the key that allowed the majority to vote with us.

8

The near political future

The gay lobby and their allies tried in vain to raise the stakes of Amendment 2 to a moral level. They did this because they had always won the allegiance of city councils, governors, and legislatures by simply attacking the religious right. But against Amendment 2, the tactic wouldn't work.

For one thing, with Amendment 2 the homosexuals were not addressing the cultural elite, but grassroots America. The will of the people often differs from the will of elected officials. For another matter, Amendment 2 was not a moral issue. It could not be made into one, no matter how often the gay lobby beat the religious drum. Yet in this futile effort, they found many unwitting helpers.

A full twelve months after the election, even a thoughtful journalist like Bill Moyers couldn't see past the religious right. His hour long PBS documentary, titled *The New Holy War*, aired nationwide in November of '93.[253] In it he spent most of the hour interviewing Colorado Springs pastors, as if religious motivation explained the passage of the amendment. Furthermore, the evangelical pastors he featured had never publicly endorsed Amendment 2.

In this off-the-mark analysis, he was hardly alone. Colorado Springs' religion editor, Steve Rabey, who lived close enough to the campaign to know better, summarized the Amendment as a "conservative Christian" issue. In the prestigious national magazine, *Christianity Today*, he attributed the amendment's success to a handful of "evangelical laity . . . supported by Focus on The Family and other evangelical organizations." In this he, too, failed to give credit to the broad and sensible appeal of the amendment's civil rights logic. It's unfathomable that 53% (now closer to 58%) of Colorado's voters were primarily motivated by Christian sentiments, either right or left. Even the best journalists fall into this trap.

The biggest Colorado surprise, however, was Judge Jeffrey Bayless. This man dared to put the power of the court behind this previous error. In his injunction speech, his carefully chosen words "evolving standard of decency"—broadcast to the state on TV, radio, and print media—were designed to force Amendment 2 into a conflict of values, if not morals. (Any standard of decency requires that a value judgement be made by some authority. In this case, the Judge ignored the expressed will of the people and imposed his own value judgment on the entire state.) Perhaps Bayless, too, believed a moral crusade against Amendment 2 was the only way he could win.

But Amendment 2 had carefully dodged this moral ambush. Its language benefited the whole state, not just those who espoused traditional virtues. The sheer volume of moral aggression from the other side revealed that *they* would not let the amendment enjoy its blessed status of impartiality.

Why should this have been a surprise to anyone? A measure of irrationality had accompanied gay rights from the start. Forced affirmation of homosexuality had done violence to the standards of traditional morals in America for years. In fact, gay politics amounted to an inverted values campaign. When a neutral law like Amendment 2 put an axe to their civil rights agenda, gay rights defenders raised the specter of the religious right. It was their last, and only resort.

It now seems clear that politically correct Americans view themselves in sacred terms. They are moral revolutionaries—perhaps evolutionaries—shaping values for the rest of us. Amendment 2 provided a legal stop sign to their doctrinaire crusade. It told them to quit using civil rights laws for a moral quest. (But "questers" don't like being stopped.) Gay lobbyists promptly rounded up a bevy of religious leftists to call Amendment 2 itself an "immoral" law.

This charge revealed an appalling level of blindness. The homosexual lobby failed to see that Colorado had not provided them with a moral showdown—though Oregon's Measure 9 had. Perhaps it is not surprising that a group unable to discriminate between disapproval and hatred, would likewise dismiss the distinctions between Amendment 2 and Measure 9. ACLU lawyer Greg Walta, in a public forum following Bill Moyers' *Holy War* documentary, accused Will Perkins and his amendment crowd of forcing moral views on the rest of Colorado. (When will they give it up?) In any true moral contest, Amendment 2 will not even take the field.

So what had been Amendment 2's violation? Why had it attracted this level of antagonism? Why did the opposition seem driven to characterize it as a moral trespass?

The answer is that Amendment 2 stepped on the toes of their own moral crusade. Specifically, the amendment interrupted the evolution of America's standards of decency by the politically correct. Gay rights laws had been aggressively evolving family and traditional values across the land for years, deciding new standards of morality for Denver, Boulder, Aspen, and for any other government body that espoused them. Amendment 2 had stopped these zealots—and suddenly standards of decency were at stake? Whose? Theirs, of course.

The language of Amendment 2 had effectively confined morals, values, and opinions concerning homosexuality to the private sector. This made it a law in the best American tradition, the tradition of ordered liberty. According to Thomas Jefferson, laws and government should address actions only, *not* opinions or motives. Amendment 2 preserved Jefferson's idea of the separation of powers. Gay rights laws infringed it, imposing private opinions and motives concerning homosexuality on unsuspecting populations through legislatures, city councils, and the courts. Under Amendment 2, the government and the courts would be properly told to butt-out of the moral discussion.

In Oregon, the lessons of Colorado's law have found a newly receptive audience. Following the '92 Measure 9 loss, a local Oregon volunteer in the municipality of Cornelius took it upon herself to offer her town a new election issue in May of '93. The language used in this new contest followed the approach of Amendment 2. When the same Oregon voters came around and viewed the homosexual issue from the civil rights perspective, they rejected gay rights laws by a 62% majority.

Thus encouraged, Oregon's Citizens Alliance (the failed sponsors of Measure 9) initiated several new election challenges based on the Colorado model. Eleven percent of the state's population in four separate county elections responded. The Colorado model increased the vote against gay rights laws by 8% overall. In the two counties with the largest populations, the vote increased by an average of 11.2%.[254] This indicated enough new votes to win a statewide contest against gay rights laws in Oregon with an Amendment 2 approach.

Sensing this shift of voter opinion, the Oregon legislature quickly passed a law forbidding all local ordinances which banned gay rights laws. The hypocrisy of this action apparently never occurred to them. The courts had been used by the gay lobby to attack Amendment 2 because it supposedly restricted free access to the political process for gays; Oregon's gay alliance turned around and restricted the entire state from the same political access! Such duplicity may survive one election, but seldom two.

Oregon's Citizen Alliance properly challenged their legislature's ban in court. They continue to hold elections in defiance of it. This is the kind of political aggression required to break the grip of political correctness everywhere. The people will have to boldly *insist* that their leaders reflect their social standards. They will have to force the issue. "Asking nicely" will do nothing. This grassroots effort is growing in Oregon, where Citizen's Alliance is preparing an Amendment 2-style initiative statewide. Other states are mobilizing as well.

The Colorado vote revealed for the first time that the people of America will simply not support protected class status for homosexuals when given the facts involved. Some experts now say that Amendment 2 has defeated forever the number one goal of the homosexual agenda—inclusion under the Civil Rights Act of 1964. A recent poll in Colorado reveals that, not 53.4%, but a full 60% oppose the number one goal of the gay agenda now.[255] If President Clinton attempted to fulfill his promise to the gay lobby and give them the Civil Rights Act by executive order, the move would seal his fate to a one-term presidency. (Though he might attempt it in a second term, with less to lose.)

As Will Perkins asserted, "Anytime people have an opportunity to vote on this issue in today's political climate, we are confident this approach will win. It flushes the homosexual agenda out into the open where people can see it for what it really is. They know how to make up their own minds."

The final bastion of gay rights thinking remains entrenched in the courts. How will the voting majority fare there? With the current batch of Colorado judges, Amendment 2 should fail in all state trials. However, it seems destined to do well at the U.S. Supreme Court level (see Appendixes D & E). But the U.S. Supreme Court is fallible. It is possible that the nation's highest Justices would choose to evolve the Constitution yet again, expanding their powers dangerously. If they change court rules to include homosexuals as a protected class, then Colorado for Family Values has promised to come back with a new law that will meet the court's new criteria. A newly worded rejection of gay rights laws will likely win a much larger Colorado majority next time around. A new winning model will emerge for the nation to follow. In the meantime, the continuing will of the people, expressed in elections to remove gay rights laws nationwide, remains a more powerful force in the body politic than the decisions of Supreme Court Justices.

Lincoln's words are amplified by those of the framers of the Constitution, specifically Madison in The Federalist: "You must first enable the government to control the governed; and in the next place oblige it to control itself. A dependence upon the people is, no doubt, the primary control on the government."[256]

Be encouraged. The people, not the courts, will have the last word on the fate of gay politics in America.

Appendix A
DECplus Handbill

The following handbill circulated at Digital Equipment Corporation's Colorado Springs facilities during Pat Long's tenure. It illustrates the elite position the gay agenda seeks to establish for itself. (Punctuation errors are reproduced from original document.)

WHAT IS DECplus

- **An organization for networking and support for Digital's gay and lesbian and bisexual community.**

- **Opened to "self identified gay men, lesbians and bisexual people.**

- **DECplus stands for 'DEC P.eople L.ike U.S. This is a social group and support network for lesbian and gay or bisexual identified employees of Digital Equipment Corporation. To participate you should be a full-time, part-time or TAG employee of Digital. The group's purpose is to create a support group and professional network, and to provide a regular opportunity to socialize with fellow employees.**

- **Confidentiality: DECplus membership names or lists are never open to discussion or presentation to anyone not in DECplus. The mailing list is seen and used only by the holders. Participants in any meeting agree not to discuss with others, not in DECplus, who was at a meeting.**

- **DECplus is now recognized by the company,' and supported in the sense that we have received some funds from the EEO/AA/Valuing Differences corporate office and continue to meet offsite to ensure confidentiality.**

Note: The author of this handout had AIDS at the time. He has been on an extended sick leave and, in several calls to Digital management, is rumored to have died.

Appendix B
Ethnic Harassment Bill (H.B. 1059)

Fifty-eighth General Assembly

LLS NO. 91 0241/1 HOUSE BILL 91-1059 Judiciary

STATE OF COLORADO

BY REPRESENTATIVE Webb

A BILL FOR AN ACT

CONCERNING STRENGTHENING CIVIL RIGHTS PROVISIONS.

(Note: This summary applies to this bill as introduced and does not necessarily reflect any amendments which may be subsequently adopted.)

Declares that it is the right of every person, regardless of age, handicapping condition or disability, or sexual orientation, to be protected from harassment. Expands the scope of ethnic intimidation to include illegal acts based on a person's sex, age, handicapping condition, or sexual orientation. Increases criminal penalties for offenses that involve ethnic intimidation. Establishes a uniform reporting registry for complaints and convictions based on ethnic intimidation.

Permits the director of the civil rights division of the department of regulatory agencies to subpoena witnesses, compel testimony of witnesses, and to compel the production of books, papers, and records relevant to any unfair employment practice charge.

Defines the term "harassment" for illegal employment practice purposes. Provides that on-the-job harassment shall be a discriminatory or unfair employment practice.

Be it enacted by the General Assembly of the State of Colorado:

SECTION 1. 18-9-121, Colorado Revised Statutes, 1986 Repl. Vol., as amended, is amended to read:

18-9-121. Ethnic intimidation. (1) The general assembly hereby finds and

[1]Capital letters indicate new material to be added to existing statutes.
[2]Lines through the words indicate deletions from existing statue.

declares that it is the right of every person, regardless of race, color, ancestry, religion, [1]SEX, AGE, HANDICAPPING CONDITION OR DISABILITY, SEXUAL ORIENTATION, or national origin, to be secure and protected from fear, intimidation, harassment, and physical harm caused by the activities of individuals and groups. The general assembly further finds that the advocacy of unlawful acts against persons or groups because of a person's, A THIRD PERSON'S, or A groups's race, color, ancestry, religion, SEX, AGE, HANDICAPPING CONDITION OR DISABILITY, SEXUAL ORIENTATION, or national origin, for the purpose of inciting and provoking bodily injury or damage to property, poses a threat to public order and safety and should be subject to ENHANCED criminal sanctions. THE GENERAL ASSEMBLY THEREFORE FINDS THAT THE PENALTY FOR CRIMES MOTIVATED BY BIGOTRY AND BIAS SHOULD BE MORE SEVERE THAN THE PENALTY FOR THE UNDERLYING CRIME.

(2) [2]~~A person commits ethnic intimidation if, with the intents to intimidate or harass another person because of that person's race, color, religion, ancestry, or national origin, he:~~

(a) ~~Knowingly causes bodily injury to another person; or~~

(b) ~~By words or conduct, knowingly places another person in fear of imminent lawless action directed at that person or that person's property and such words or conduct are likely to produce bodily injury to that person or damage to that person's property; or~~

(c) ~~Knowingly cause damage to or destruction of the property of another person.~~

(2) [1]THE PENALTY FOR ANY FELONY OR MISDEMEANOR SHALL BE RECLASSIFIED TO THE NEXT HIGHEST CLASSIFICATION OF CRIMES, AND ANY CLASS 1 MISDEMEANOR SHALL BE RECLASSIFIED TO A CLASS 6 FELONY, WHERE THE COMMISSION OF SUCH FELONY OR MISDEMEANOR IS MOTIVATED BY BIGOTRY OR BIAS, OR EVIDENCES PREJUDICE BASED ON THE RACE, COLOR, ANCESTRY, RELIGION, SEX, AGE, HANDICAPPING CONDITION OR DISABILITY, SEXUAL ORIENTATION, OR NATIONAL ORIGIN OF THE VICTIM OF SUCH FELONY OR MISDEMEANOR OR ANY THIRD PERSON ASSOCIATED WITH THE VICTIM; EXCEPT THAT THE CLASSIFICATION FOR THE CRIME OF ASSAULT ON THE ELDERLY OR HANDICAPPED SHALL BE AS PROVIDED FOR IN SECTION 18-3-209, AND CRIMES CLASSIFIED AS SECOND DEGREE FELONIES SHALL NOT BE RECLASSIFIED.

(3) ~~Ethnic intimidation is a class 1 misdemeanor; except that a violation of paragraph (a) of subsection (2) of this section is a class 6 felony.~~

(4) The criminal ~~penalty~~ PENALTIES provided FOR in this section for ethnic intimidation ~~does~~ DO not preclude the victim of such action from seeking any other remedies otherwise available under law.

(5) THERE IS HEREBY ESTABLISHED A UNIFORM REPORTING REGISTRY FOR COMPLAINTS AND CONVICTIONS OF THE OFFENSE OF ETHNIC INTIMIDATION. SUCH UNIFORM REPORTING REGISTRY SHALL BE

[1]Capital letters indicate new material to be added to existing statutes.

[2]Lines through the words indicate deletions from existing statue.

MAINTAINED AND OPERATED BY THE COLORADO CIVIL RIGHTS DIVISION OF THE DEPARTMENT OF REGULATORY AGENCIES AND SHALL BE ADMINISTERED BY THE DIRECTOR OF SAID DIVISION. IT SHALL BE THE DUTY OF EVERY PEACE OFFICER IN THE STATE TO NOTIFY THE DIVISION IN SUCH FORM AS THE DIVISION SHALL REQUIRE EACH TIME AN INSTANCE OF ETHNIC INTIMIDATION IS BROUGHT TO SUCH OFFICER'S ATTENTION. THE NOTIFICATION SHALL INCLUDE, BUT NEED NOT BE LIMITED TO, THE SUSPECT'S NAME AND PERSONAL DESCRIPTORS, ANY KNOWN RESIDENTIAL ADDRESS, AND A DESCRIPTION OF THE SPECIFIC INCIDENT GIVING RISE TO THE COMPLAINT OR UNDERLYING THE CONVICTION. THE COLORADO CIVIL RIGHTS DIVISION SHALL COMPILE ALL INFORMATION RECEIVED AND DISSEMINATE SUCH INFORMATION TO ANY REQUESTING GOVERNMENT UNIT AND TO ANY OTHER ENTITY THE DIRECTOR OF THE COLORADO CIVIL RIGHTS DIVISION DEEMS APPROPRIATE.

SECTION 2. 24-34-306 (2) (a), Colorado Revised Statutes, 1988 Repl. Vol., as amended, is amended to read:

24-34-306. Charge - complaint - hearing - procedure - exhaustion of administrative remedies. (2) (a) After the filing of a charge, the director, with the assistance of the staff, shall make a prompt investigation thereof. If such charge alleges [1]AN UNFAIR EMPLOYMENT PRACTICE, AS DEFINED IN PART 4 OF THIS ARTICLE OR an unfair housing practice as defined in part 5 of this article, the director may subpoena witnesses and compel the testimony of witnesses and the production of books, papers, and records relevant to such charge. Any subpoena issued pursuant to this paragraph (a) shall be enforceable in the district court for the district in which the alleged discriminatory or unfair practices occurred.

SECTION 3. 24-34-401, Colorado Revised Statutes, 1988 Repl. Vol., is amended BY THE ADDITION OF A NEW SUBSECTION to read:

24-34-401. Definitions. (4.5) "HARASSMENT" MEANS ANY UNWELCOME CONDUCT DIRECTED TOWARD AN INDIVIDUAL ON ACCOUNT OF THAT INDIVIDUAL'S RACE, COLOR, RELIGION, SEX, NATIONAL ORIGIN, HANDICAP, OR AGE WHICH UNREASONABLY INTERFERES WITH AN INDIVIDUAL'S JOB PERFORMANCE OR CREATES AN INTIMIDATING, HOSTILE, OR OFFENSIVE WORKING ENVIRONMENT EVEN IF IT DOES NOT LEAD TO TANGIBLE OR ECONOMIC JOB CONSEQUENCES.

SECTION 4. 24-34-402 (1) (e), Colorado Revised Statutes, 1988 Repl. Vol., as amended, is amended BY THE ADDITION OF A NEW SUBPARAGRAPH to read:

24-34-402. Discriminatory or unfair employment practices. (1) It shall be a discriminatory or unfair employment practice:

(e) For any person, whether or not an employer, an employment agency, a labor organization, or the employees or members thereof:

(V) TO SUBJECT ANOTHER PERSON TO EMPLOYMENT-RELATED HARASSMENT, AS DEFINED IN SECTION 24-34-401 (4.5).

[1]Capital letters indicate new material to be added to existing statutes.
[2]Lines through the words indicate deletions from existing statue.

SECTION 5. Effective date - applicability. This act shall take effect July 1, 1991, and shall apply to all crimes committed on or after July 1, 1991.

SECTION 6. Safety clause. The general assembly hereby finds, determines, and declares that this act is necessary for the immediate preservation of the public peace, health, and safety.

[1]Capital letters indicate new material to be added to existing statutes.
[2]Lines through the words indicate deletions from existing statue.

Appendix C
Bill Armstrong's Letter

Colorado for Family Values
P.O. Box 190
Colorado Springs, CO 80901

Dear Friend,

As U.S. Senator for Colorado, I fought many battles in Washington. Today, as a private citizen, I am asking you to join me in combating a very grave threat now facing our State and its people.

As you are probably aware, militant homosexual activists and their liberal supporters have launched an aggressive statewide campaign to force you and me to condone and give our State's legal blessing to aberrant homosexual behavior and lifestyles. These tragically misguided people have one goal:

> *To secure for their "sexual orientations" the same legal (plus additional) rights, protections and privileges now enjoyed by legitimate racial, ethnic and religious groups.*

I am writing on behalf of Colorado for Family Values, to ask your help in stopping gay activists from achieving this goal. Colorado for Family Values, a newly-formed organization of concerned citizens, has already achieved major victories by:

1. Defeating a proposed Colorado Springs ordinance granting "protected class status" to gays, lesbians and bisexuals.
2. Halting passage of a proposed State "Ethnic Harassment Bill," which would, among other things, have made it a felony crime for church pastors to preach against homosexuality.
3. Devising America's first plan to stop special "gay rights" by voter initiative. A plan so innovative that it has secured the support of prominent Colorado civil rights leaders and gained national attention as a model other states are now following.

But militant homosexuals are not deterred by these setbacks. In fact, they have achieved victories of their own:

* In December 1990 Governor Roy Romer issued an Executive Order granting special status to gays in State agencies.
* Gay and lesbian activists succeeded in getting a special "gay rights" ordinance passed in Denver, similar to the one defeated in Colorado Springs. A referendum drive by Denver citizens failed, by a narrow margin, to repeal it.
* The Colorado State Civil Rights Commission (whose former head also chaired the State's most prominent special "gay rights" activist organization) voted to create and promote special "gay rights" legislation throughout this state.

How have militant gays made such inroads into our state and local governments? Claiming this is a "simple civil rights issue," gay extremists have played on the political sympathies of legislators to gain the reward of special rights and protected status. Their deceptive arguments boil down to this:

Gays have suffered emotional torment because society disapproves of their behavior. Therefore, society owes them protected class status to redress their injuries and make them feel better.

First, gays already have the same recourse under law as the rest of us against physical assault, libelous or slanderous verbal abuse and injury to their property. Second, to equate the self created miseries of pleasure-addicted gays—who sport average incomes of nearly $55,000 a year—with the innocent sufferings and crippling poverty of legitimate minority groups, is an insult to those who've struggled to achieve true civil rights in America. Third, sexual behavior alone has never been a reason to grant civil rights protection. Nor should it be. Tony Marco, one of the Founders of Colorado for Family Values, has put it well:

If having sex becomes all it takes to be considered 'ethnic' with full rights and privileges, the very concept of ethnicity will lose nearly all its meaning and value."

What will happen if gays achieve "ethnic" status and special rights? Quite simply, Colorado citizens of all kinds will be deprived of their civil rights. You'll lose your freedom of speech and conscience to object to homosexual behavior. Your church or business may be forced to hire gays. If you are a landlord, you will be compelled to rent to gays, regardless of your moral convictions. If you are a day care center owner, you will be forced to employ homosexuals and lesbians. Lest you think I'm overstating the impact of special "gay rights" legislation, consider the recent consequences of such laws in other states:

- In Madison, Wisconsin, two heterosexual women refused to share their apartment with a lesbian applicant. Under a city "gay rights" ordinance, the two women were fined a total of $1,500, requested to write letters of apology to the applicant, assigned to attend "sensitivity" classes taught by lesbians, involving graphic depictions of homosexual behavior, and were forbidden to ask later rental applicants about their "sexual orientation."

- In 1989, in Laguna Beach, California, a 9-year-old boy was frightened by seeing three gay men having sex in a public restroom. The City Council refused to act on the complaint of citizens disturbed by this outrageous event. Having a gay mayor, and a special "gay rights" ordinance, Laguna Beach did not see fit to investigate and prosecute this incident.

- Recently, the Minneapolis Roman Catholic Archdiocese was assessed $20,000 in damages and $15,000 in fines—for refusing to allow a homosexual club to hold meetings in church owned facilities.

Is it possible Colorado's people could face nightmares like these? It is not only possible, but probable if special "gay rights" laws are passed. Militant gays have made it clear in their writings that they have no use for the traditional family, for traditional moral standards, for traditional religion. Nor do they seem concerned about the health crises which may result if homosexual extremists succeed in forcing society to accept their promiscuous behavior. (Surveys of gays by gays show that homosexuals average more than 500 lifetime sexual partners.)

Gays are by far Colorado's most active communicators of sexually transmitted diseases. Though no more, probably, than 2% of our population, homosexuals are responsible for 85% of our State's AIDS cases. (More than four-fifths of these originate in Denver alone.) Caring for one AIDS patient from infection through death costs about $250,000. AIDS and its consequences will cost America billions of dollars in 1991 alone—of which Colorado will pay its share.

And you and I will pay, too, with higher health insurance premiums and hospital costs, exorbitant legal expenses and even higher taxes. Incredibly, despite their affluence, militant gays are demanding that taxpayers pay their health care bills—robbing the handicapped and true minorities of urgently-needed care and benefits as well.

But legitimizing special "gay rights" would exact a far greater price of our State than mere dollars. Doors would open for gays to make even deeper inroads into every public and private institution including our schools. Denver public school teachers and counselors are already being trained to teach our children starting in Kindergarten—that homosexuality is a normal, healthy lifestyle.

Clearly gays' influence will grow even more rapidly if responsible citizens like you and me allow militant gay activists to successfully promote civil rights protections for themselves.

What can you and I do to stop them?

Under Colorado law, citizens may gather petitions to place initiatives on election ballots, to be decided by public vote. This is the course Colorado for Family Values has taken to defeat gay activists. On July 31, 1991, Colorado for Family Values filed proposed ballot initiative language with our State's Legislative Council. The initiative was authored and reviewed by some of America's most noted Constitutional attorneys.

On March 20, 1992, CFV submitted more than 85,000 petition signatures in support of this initiative to the Colorado Secretary of State's office. If approved by voters in the 1992 General Election, this initiative will amend our State's Constitution to prohibit class status based on "gay" orientations. It will nullify all existing state and local laws giving gays special class status. It will make future attempts by militant gays to pass new special "gay rights" laws pointless.

Thus, one decisive move by concerned voters like you and me can eliminate the threat of protected states for homosexuals. But before achieving victory, Colorado for Family Values must still:

1. Enlist an "army" of concerned citizens to help carry out a massive, statewide educational campaign exposing the true aims of militant homosexuals and the impact of their legislative efforts. Public education is critical to the initiative drive's success.
2. Conduct a statewide drive to register and get to the polls enough Colorado voters to make sure CFV's initiative gets the YES vote into Colorado's Constitution in November, 1992.

To move forward toward these crucial goals, Colorado for Family Values must raise $100,000 in the next 90 days alone. That is why I am asking for your immediate financial support today. Colorado for Family Values depends solely on individual, voluntary contributions. Success or failure in this effort depends on people like you who will take a stand for family values. Will you please help?

You can contribute with confidence. I have known many of CFV's leaders personally for years. They are men and women of great integrity. Their intention is not to take away a single right homosexuals share with the rest of us. Their primary concern is protecting family values, traditional morality and legitimate civil rights for all Coloradans.

Please mail your contribution today. Your gift will help launch extraordinarily effective action, because CFV's special non-profit status allows this organization to directly interact with Colorado's system of government. Thus, you can take great satisfaction in knowing you have played a truly vital role in protecting those values which we cherish, and for which we have labored so long and so hard.

Sincerely,

Bill Armstrong

William L. Armstrong

P.S. Despite their claim to be "oppressed," gays are among Colorado's most affluent citizens. They have indicated they'll spend at least one million dollars in an attempt to defeat Colorado for Family Values' initiative. Our only hope for victory rests with God—and with responsible citizens like you and me. Thank you for giving generously.

Appendix D
BRIEF AMICUS CURIAE

MOTION FOR LEAVE TO FILE BRIEF AMICUS CURIAE OF COLORADO FOR FAMILY VALUES
in support of the *Petitioners*

Colorado for Family Values (CFV), by its attorney, Robert K. Skolrood, of the National Legal Foundation, moves this court pursuant to Rule 21.2(b) of the Supreme Court of the United States for leave to file a brief amicus curiae in the aforementioned action in order to present arguments stating why the petitioners' request should be granted.

The reason for requesting this action is based on Rule 10.1(c) of the Supreme Court of the United States. CFV spent thousands of dollars and numerous hours in obtaining the passage of the Colorado Constitutional Amendment at issue. It is in a unique position to illustrate the gravity of the Colorado Supreme Court's decision and its national significance.

The following parties, represented by counsel, have refused to consent to the filing of the attached brief amicus curiae:

Jean E. Dubofsky, Lead Counsel
Representing: Richard G. Evans, Angela Romero, Linda Fowler, Paul Brown, Jane Doe, Martina Navratilova, Priscilla Inkpen, John Miller, and Boulder Valley School District RE-2.
Refused Consent.

Edward M. Caswall, Esquire
Representing: the City of Aspen and the City Council of Aspen.
Refused Consent.

Joseph N. DeRaismes, III, City Attorney
Representing: the City of Boulder.
Refused Consent.

Darlene M. Ebert, Assistant City Attorney
Representing: the City and County of Denver.
Refused Consent.

The petitioners have consented to the filing of this brief amicus curiae.

Robert K. Skolrood
Robert K. Skolrood
Attorney for Amicus Curiae

The National Legal Foundation
6477 College Park Square, Suite 306
Virginia Beach, VA 23464
(804)424-4242

No. 93-453

IN THE SUPREME COURT OF THE UNITED STATES
October Term, 1993

ROY ROMER, as Governor of the State of Colorado, GALE A. NORTON, as Attorney General of the State of Colorado, and the STATE OF COLORADO,
Petitioners,
vs.
RICHARD G. EVANS, ANGELA ROMERO, LINDA FOWLER, PAUL BROWN, JANE DOE, MARTINA NAVRATILOVA, PRISCILLA INKPEN, JOHN MILLER, the BOULDER VALLEY SCHOOL DISTRICT RE-2, the CITY AND COUNTY OF DENVER, the CITY OF BOULDER, the CITY OF ASPEN, and the CITY COUNCIL OF ASPEN,
Respondents.

ON PETITION FOR A WRIT OF CERTIORARI TO THE SUPREME COURT OF THE STATE OF COLORADO

BRIEF AMICUS CURIAE OF COLORADO FOR FAMILY VALUES
in support of the *Petitioners*

Robert K. Skolrood
Counsel of Record
Barry C. Hodge, Esquire
The National Legal Foundation
6477 College Park Square
Suite 306
Virginia Beach, VA 23464
(804)424-4242
Attorneys for Amicus Curiae

TABLE OF CONTENTS

TABLE OF AUTHORITIES

INTEREST OF AMICUS CURIAE

Colorado for Family Values (CFV) is the grassroots organization which secured the passage of Amendment 2. Since CFV gathered approximately 85,000 signatures, spent thousands of dollars, and invested hundreds of hours educating the public about Amendment 2, it is interested in the continued vitality of the Amendment. CFV continues to educated the public concerning special rights.

CFV desires to maintain the integrity of our constitutional government, namely the sovereignty of the people. States have plenary power enabling them to pass a wide variety of laws impacting citizens. CFV is interested in protecting the rights of the citizens of Colorado who have expressed their will in Amendment 2.

The National Legal Foundation assisted in drafting Amendment 2 and participated as amicus curiae in this litigation at the state court level. The Foundation has participated as amicus curiae in several federal and state cases and has served as lead counsel in *Board of Education of Westside Community Schools v. Mergens*, 496 U.S. 226 (1990).

Counsel of record for amicus curiae is Robert K. Skolrood. He is licensed to practice in Illinois, Oklahoma, Virginia, the District of Columbia, the United States Supreme Court, as well as numerous U.S. Circuit Courts of Appeal and District Courts.

I. The Colorado Supreme Court Usurped Federal Judicial Power

The judicial power of the United States is vested in this Court:

> The judicial Power of the United States, shall be vested in one supreme Court, and in such inferior Courts as the Congress may from time to time ordain and establish.

U.S. CONST. art. III, § 1.

State judges are bound by the U.S. Constitution:

> This Constitution, and the Laws of the United States which shall be made in Pursuance thereof; and all Treaties made, or which shall be made, under the Authority of the United States, shall be the supreme Law of the Land; and the Judges in every State shall be bound thereby, any Thing in the Constitution or Laws of any State to the Contrary notwithstanding.

U.S. CONST. art. VI, cl. 2.

Since *Martin v. Hunter's Lessee*, 14 U.S. (1 Wheat.) 304 (1816), it has been established that state courts do not have federal judicial power but rather have only a duty to apply the federal constitution:

> It is obvious that this obligation is imperative upon the state judges in their official, and not merely in their private, capacities. From the very nature of their judicial duties they would be called upon to pronounce the law applicable to the case in judgment . . . .
>
> . . . .
>
> . . . In respect to the powers granted to the United States, they are not independent; they are expressly bound to obedience by the letter of the constitution; and if they should unintentionally *transcend their authority*, or misconstrue the constitution, there is no more reason for giving their judgments an absolute and irresistible force than for giving it to the acts of the other coordinate departments of state sovereignty.

Martin, 14 U.S. at 340, 344 (emphasis added).[1]

The justices of the Colorado Supreme Court are required to take an oath or affirmation by the U.S. Constitution,[2] and by taking this oath or affirmation,[3] they acknowledge their

---

1 *See also, Martin*, 14 U.S. at 338-42.

2 "The . . . judicial Officers, both of the United States and of the several States, shall be bound by Oath or Affirmation, to support this Constitution . . . ." U.S. CONST. art. VI, cl. 3.

3 COLO. CONST. art XII, § 8, COLO. REV. STAT. ANN. § 24-12-101 and § 24 12-102 (West 1988) provide that a Colorado state judge shall either swear or affirm that he will "support the constitution of the United States and of the state of Colorado . . . ."

duty to apply the federal constitution. Even the court below has recognized this duty.[4] The Colorado Supreme Court justices have no federal judicial power thus do not have the final say on issues concerning the federal constitution.[5] They have only a duty to apply that constitution.

Out of this duty arises an obligation to obey authoritative decisions of this Court:

> [W]hen a state court reviews state legislation challenged as violative of the Fourteenth Amendment, it is not free to impose greater restrictions as a matter of federal constitutional law than this Court has imposed.

Minnesota v. Clover Leaf Creamery Co., 449 U.S. 456, 461 n.6 (1981) (citation omitted).[6]

The Colorado Supreme Court has acknowledged this obligation[7] and other state appellate courts have as well.[8]

Despite this duty and its attendant obligation, the Colorado Supreme Court ignored its lack of federal judicial power and recognized a novel fundamental right not based in the language of the Constitution and one which has never been recognized by this Court.

---

4 *See People v. Western Union Tel. Co.*, 198 P. 146 (Colo. 1921) (in deciding whether a state trial court judge could declare a state statute in violation of the federal constitution (in light of the fact that Colorado had a constitution provision that allowed only the state supreme court to resolve such issues) the court, relying both on Article VI, clause 2 of the U.S. Constitution and on a state judge's oath, stated: "The answer is that the trial judge was bound by the mandate of the federal Constitution to *apply that instrument* upon all proper occasions and to hold it to be the supreme law of the land . . . ."). *Western Union Tel. Co.*, 198 P. at 148 (emphasis added).

5 U.S. Const. art III, § 2, cl. 2 (appellate jurisdiction of the U.S. Supreme Court). *See Pennekamp v. Florida*, 328 U.S. 331, 335 (1946) (stating that the Constitution had imposed upon it the final authority to determine the meaning and application of the "words of that instrument" in contexts requiring the resolution of judicial issues and that when the highest court of a state had reached a decision on such an issue the Court would give respectful attention "to its reasoning and conclusion" but that its authority was not final).

6 *See also, Oregon v. Hass*, 420 U.S. 714, 719 (1975); *North Carolina v. Butler*, 441 U.S. 369, 376 (1979).

7 *See American Federation of Labor v. Reilly*, 155 P.2d 145, 148 (Colo. 1944) (Even the Colorado Supreme Court itself acknowledges that "[t]he Supreme Court of the United States is the final arbiter in the field of Federal constitutional law and its decisions as to the meaning and scope of a constitutional provision bind state judges." In *Reilly*, before deciding whether a state trial judge had properly held that a state statute was repugnant to the federal constitution, the court announced: "In reaching its decision on the points now in consideration the trial court *properly relied* upon the pronouncements of the highest tribunal in our nation, which we think sustain the conclusion reached." *Id.*) (citations omitted) (emphasis added). *See also, People v. Berger*, 521 P.2d 1244, 1245 (Colo. 1974); *Wilcox v. People*, 104 P. 408, 409 (Colo. 1909); *Smith v. Farr*, 104 P. 401, 403 (Colo. 1909).

8 *Wuebker v. James*, 58 N.Y.S.2d 671, 677 (Schenectady County Ct. 1944) ("When decisions of the United States Supreme Court are based on a line of judicial precedents which have been accepted as correctly applying constitutional provisions on a subject, they are *entitled to serious consideration and respect* . . . .") (emphasis added).

The court below did so in the face of a sovereign act of the people of the State of Colorado. The means by which this was done has set a dangerous precedent. The judges of the Colorado Supreme Court should be reminded of Justice White's warning in *Bowers v. Hardwick*, 478 U.S. 186 (1986), regarding the discovery of new fundamental rights:

> The Court is most vulnerable and comes nearest to illegitimacy when it deals with judge-made constitutional law having little or no cognizable roots in the language or design of the Constitution.

Id. at 194.

II. The Colorado Supreme Court Violated The Standards Authoritatively Imposed By This Court For The Recognition Of A Fundamental Right

The issue before the court below was whether Amendment 2[9] violated an *existing* constitutional right:

> [W]e independently review the question of whether Amendment 2 has been shown to violate an *existing* constitutional right.

Evans v. Romer, 854 P.2d 1270, 1275 (Colo. 1993) (emphasis added).

According to this Court, the standard used to determine whether a right is fundamental is set forth in *San Antonio Ind. School Dist. v. Rodriguez*, 411 U.S. 1 (1973).

> It is not the province of this Court to create substantive constitutional rights in the name of guaranteeing equal protection of the laws. Thus, the key to discovering whether education is "fundamental" . . . lies in assessing whether there is a right to education *explicitly or implicitly guaranteed by the Constitution.*

Id. at 33 (emphasis added).

In *Rodriguez*, this Court refused to recognize education as a fundamental right because it failed to meet this standard.

A. The Fundamental Rights Cases Relied Upon By The Court Below Are Irrelevant To This Case

---

[9] Amendment 2 provides in pertinent part: "Neither the State of Colorado, through any of its branches or departments, nor any of its agencies, political subdivisions, municipalities of school districts, shall enact, adopt or enforce any statute, regulation, ordinance or policy whereby homosexual, lesbian or bisexual orientation, conduct, practices or relationships shall constitute or otherwise be the basis of or entitle any person or class of persons to have or claim any minority status quota preferences, protected status or claim of discrimination." COLO. CONST. art. II, § 30b.

The court below failed to conduct a textual and historical analysis of the Equal Protection Clause of the Fourteenth Amendment as required by *Rodriguez*. Rather it based its decision exclusively upon case "decisions [which] addressed entirely distinct questions and constitutional problems from those presented here." *Evans*, 854 P.2d at 1278. This lack of textual, historical, and authoritative case analysis makes clear that the court below has attempted to create, by fiat, the previously unrecognized "fundamental right to participate equally in the political process."

While the court below does cite fundamental rights cases[10] as authority, the cited cases have been held by this Court to demonstrate only "that a citizen has a constitutionally protected right to participate in elections on an equal basis with other citizens in the jurisdiction." *Dunn v. Blumstein*, 405 U.S. 330, 336 (1972). Simply put, the court below cites as support United States Supreme Court cases which recognize only that the right to vote and cast a ballot is constitutionally protected. The court below recognized the narrowness of the voting rights cases and concedes their inapplicability:

> The "precondition," reapportionment, and "candidate eligibility" cases are not dispositive of, or directly controlling on, our decision here, as Amendment 2 falls within none of those three categories of cases. Admittedly, those decisions addressed entirely distinct questions and constitutional problems from those presented here.

Evans, 854 P.2d at 1278.

B. The Court Below Extended The Hunter Doctrine Beyond Suspect Classification In Contravention Of This Court's Explicit Instructions

Aside from the previously mentioned non-dispositive fundamental rights cases, the court below based its holding primarily on *Hunter v. Erickson*, 393 U.S. 385 (1969), and its progeny.[11] Although the facts of *Hunter* and its offspring resemble the present controversy, those decisions were specifically decided with reference to suspect classifications, they in no way concern the fundamental rights strand of equal protection, and their principles cannot be extended beyond suspect classification.[12]

In *Hunter*, this Court struck down a voter enacted charter amendment preventing the city

---

[10] Reapportionment cases, *see, e.g., Lucas v. Forty-Fourth Gen. Assembly of Colo.*, 377 U.S. 713 (1964); *Reynolds v. Sims*, 377 U.S. 533 (1964); *Wesberry v. Sanders*, 376 U.S. 1 (1964); cases concerning minority party rights, *see, e.g., Williams v. Rhodes*, 393 U.S. 23 (1968); cases involving direct restrictions of the exercise of the franchise, *see, e.g., Dunn v. Blumstein*, 405 U.S. 330 (1972); *Kramer v. Union Free School Dist. No. 15*, 395 U.S. 621 (1969); *Harper v. Virginia State Bd. of Education*, 383 U.S. 663 (1966).

[11] *Washington v. Seattle School Dist.*, 458 U.S. 457 (1982); *James v. Valtierra*, 402 U.S. 137 (1971); *Gordon v. Lance*, 403 U.S. 1 (1971).

[12] The court below admits "[t]hat gay men, lesbians, and bisexuals have not been found to constitute a suspect class," nor do plaintiffs contend that they qualify as such. *Evans*, 854 P.2d at 1275.

of Akron from "implementing any ordinance dealing with race, religion, or ancestral discrimination in housing without the approval of the majority of the voters of Akron." *Hunter*, 393 U.S. at 396. This Court defined the aim of the Fourteenth Amendment:

> Because the core of the Fourteenth Amendment is the prevention of meaningful and unjustified official distinctions based on race, racial classifications are "constitutionally suspect" and subject to the "most rigid scrutiny." They bear a far heavier burden of justification than other classifications.

Id. at 391-92 (citations omitted).

In *James v. Valtierra*, 402 U.S. 137 (1971), this Court upheld Article XXXIV of the California Constitution which prohibited the development of low-income housing projects unless approved by a majority of the voters of the state. The lower court in *James* did exactly what the court below has done in this case: both courts improperly extended the principles of *Hunter* to include non-suspect classifications.[13] This Court reversed the decision and tersely restricted application of the *Hunter* doctrine to suspect classification, saying:

> The court below erred in relying on *Hunter* to invalidate Article XXXIV. Unlike the case before us, Hunter rested on the conclusion that Akron's referendum law denied equal protection by placing "special burdens on *racial minorities* within the governmental process . . . .
>
> . . . .
>
> *The present case could be affirmed only by extending Hunter, and this we decline to do.*

James, 402 U.S. at 140-41 (emphasis added).

Again, in *Gordon v. Lance*, 403 U.S. 1 (1971), this Court upheld a West Virginia state constitutional provision requiring approval of sixty percent of the voters in a referendum election before the state's subdivisions could incur bonded indebtedness. This Court clearly distinguished *Hunter*, explaining that its principles applied only to suspect classes:

> Unlike the restrictions in [*Hunter*], the West Virginia Constitution singles out no "discrete and insular minority" for special treatment . . . . We are not, therefore, presented with a case like *Hunter v. Erickson*.
>
> . . .

Id. at 5.

The only United States Supreme Court case cited by the court below which has actually

---

[13] The basis of plaintiffs claim in *James* was *identical* to the Colorado Supreme Court's reasoning here. The *James*' plaintiffs "suggest[ed] that the mandatory nature of the Article XXXIV referendum constitute[d] unconstitutional discrimination because it hamper[ed] persons desiring public housing from achieving their objective when no such roadblock face[ed] other groups seeking to influence other public decisions to their advantage." *James*, 402 U.S. at 142.

applied the *Hunter* doctrine in *Washington v. Seattle School Dist.*, 458 U.S. 457 (1982). In *Washington*, this Court struck down Initiative 350 which in effect limited the ability of the state to utilize forced busing to achieve racial integration. This Court stated that "[g]iven the *racial* focus of Initiative 350, this suffices to trigger application of the *Hunter* doctrine." *Id.* at 474 (emphasis in original).

Explaining the nature of *Hunter*, this Court stated:

> Hunter . . . rested on a principle that has been vital for over a century -- that "the core of the Fourteenth Amendment is the prevention of meaningful and unjustified official distinctions based on *race*."

Washington, 458 U.S. at 486 (emphasis added).

Surprisingly, the court below held that "the principle articulated in [*Hunter* and *Washington*] clearly is not one that can logically be limited to the 'race' context alone." *Evans*, 854 P.2d at 1281.[14] This blatant abuse of the *Hunter* doctrine usurps federal judicial power by ignoring clear precedent in derogation of the lower court's duty.

Aside from this abuse of power, the court below failed to explain how even an extended *Hunter* doctrine supports the existence of any fundamental right. No authoritative support for such a contention can be found. The words "fundamental right" are not mentioned once in *Hunter, James, Gordon*, or *Washington*, and the court below cites no authority in which any other court has interpreted these cases as supporting a fundamental right.[15]

Furthermore, it is illogical to use an extended *Hunter* doctrine to support the existence of a fundamental right. If the principles of *Hunter* really do apply to sexual orientation, strict scrutiny would then be triggered upon that basis alone, and the finding of a fundamental right would be unnecessary. Yet the court below went on to insist that an extended *Hunter* doctrine established a fundamental right: the right of identifiable groups to participate equally in the political process.[16]

---

[14] The Colorado Supreme Court defines the *Hunter* principle as one of neutrality. Neutrality, however, cannot be divorced from suspect classifications. *Washington* defines non-neutrality stating: "[T]he state allocates governmental power non-neutrally, by explicitly using the *racial* nature of a decision to determine the decision making process." 458 U.S. at 470 (emphasis in original).

[15] Quite to the contrary, the courts have consistently cited *Hunter* as a suspect classification case. *See, e.g., Flores v. Pierce*, 617 F.2d 1386 (9th Cir. 1980), *cert. denied*, 449 U.S. 875 (1980); *Arthur v. City of Toledo, Ohio*, 782 F.2d 565 (6th Cir. 1986); *Habron v. Epstein*, 412 F.Supp. 256 (D.Md. 1976), *aff'd*, 429 U.S. 802 (1976); *Parker v. Mandel*, 344 F.Supp. 1068 (D.Md. 1972).

[16] The only explanation for this illogical conclusion is that perhaps the Colorado Supreme Court realized that extension of the *Hunter* doctrine would, in effect, create a third strand of equal protection analysis if it were not somehow "stuffed" into an existing strand of equal protection. Since the Court refuses to admit that it is a suspect case, the only other basis upon which to employ strict scrutiny is by finding a fundamental right.

The Colorado Supreme Court failed to heed the warning of this Court in *Bowers* that a court is "most vulnerable and comes nearest to illegitimacy when it deals with judge-made constitutional law having little or no cognizable roots in the language or design of the Constitution." *Bowers*, 478 U.S. at 194. The illegitimate act of the court below was not without its price, and the people of the State of Colorado have borne the cost of this judicial inventiveness.

C. *The Decision Of The Colorado Supreme Court Paralyzes The Sovereignty Of The People Of The State Of Colorado*

> All political power is vested in and derived from the people; all government, of right, originates from the people, is founded upon their will only, and is instituted solely for the good of the whole.

Colo. Const. art. II, § 1.[17]

The right of the people to enact legislation through the initiative process is, in the words of the Colorado Supreme Court, a right "of the first order; it is not a grant to the people but a reservation by them for themselves." *McKee v. City of Louisville*, 616 P.2d 969, 972 (Colo. 1980) (citation omitted).[18] "Like the right to vote, the power of initiative is a fundamental right at the very core of our republican form of government." *Id.* (citation omitted).

This Court has acknowledged the paramount importance of the sovereignty of the people. "The referendum . . . is a means for direct political participation, allowing the people the final decision, amounting to a veto power, over enactments of representative bodies." *Eastlake v. Forest City Enterprises, Inc.*, 426 U.S. 668, 673 (1976). Although they are subject to the limitations of the federal constitution, "[p]rovisions for referendums demonstrate devotion to democracy, not to bias, discrimination, or prejudice." *James*, 402 U.S. 137, 141 (1971). Accordingly, the "Court will not lightly set aside the results of voter referendums." *Arthur v. City of Toledo, Ohio*, 782 F.2d 565, 573 (6th Cir. 1986).[19]

The court below, however, "lightly set aside" the results of the voter initiative Amendment 2 by ignoring *Rodriguez*. This Court has forbidden such actions which "discard these fixed principles in favor of a judicial inventiveness that would go 'far toward making this Court a superlegislature.'" *Mobile v. Bolden*, 446 U.S. 55, 76 (1980). As a result, the sovereignty of the people of the State of Colorado has been

---

[17] *See also,* COLO. CONST. art. II, § 2 ("The people of this state have the sole and exclusive right of governing themselves, as a free, sovereign and independent state; and to alter and abolish their constitution and form of government whenever they may deem it necessary to their safety and happiness, provided, such change be not repugnant to the constitution of the United States.")

[18] COLO. CONST. art. V, § 1 ("The first power hereby reserved by the people is the initiative . . . .).

[19] In *Arthur*, the Sixth Circuit Court of Appeals refused to strike down a referendum which plaintiffs claimed had violated the Equal Protection Clause.

crippled and their right to limit or control their state government has been paralyzed.

As this Court noted in *Gordon*, 403 U.S. 1 (1971), *James*, 402 U.S. 137 (1971), and *Washington*, 458 U.S. 457 (1982), application of the *Hunter* doctrine must be limited to suspect classes alone, not only because *Hunter* is based exclusively upon suspect classification, but also because there is no other limitation which would prevent the courts from granting this right to all "of the diverse and shifting groups that make up the American people." *James*, 402 U.S. at 142.

III. This Fundamental Right To Participate Equally In The Political Process Will Render Suspect Every Legitimate Limitation Upon The Power Of The Legislature

According to the Colorado Supreme Court, "Amendment 2 singles out and prohibits this class of persons [homosexuals, lesbians, and bisexuals] from *seeking governmental action favorable* to it and thus, from participating equally in the political process." *Evans*, 854 P.2d at 1285 (footnote omitted) (emphasis added).

Seeking favorable government action is an extraordinarily widespread practice. The political landscape of America is littered with interest groups whose very existence is predicated upon obtaining legislation favorable to the group of persons which they represent. If "any legislation or state constitutional amendment which infringes on this right by 'fencing out' an independently identifiable class of persons must be subject to strict judicial scrutiny," *Evans*, 854 P.2d at 1282 (footnote omitted), then all limitations upon legislative power which burden an identifiable group's ability to obtain favorable legislation would be suspect.

Failure to review now the decision of the court below will lend weight to an already dangerous precedent. A state could be forced to eliminate numerous "barriers" to the enactment of legislation regardless of how legitimate the limitation may be.

This Court expressed this same concern in *James* where the plaintiffs had relied upon *Hunter*.[20] This Court responded by stating:

> [A] lawmaking procedure that "disadvantages" a particular group does not always deny equal protection. Under any such holding . . . . [T]his Court would be required to analyze governmental structures to determine whether a gubernatorial veto provision or a filibuster rule is likely to "disadvantage" any of the diverse and shifting groups that make up the American people.

---

[20] Plaintiffs in *James* asserted the same argument which has been set forth by the plaintiffs in this case. The *James*' plaintiffs "suggest[ed] that the mandatory nature of the Article XXXIV referendum constitut[ed] unconstitutional discrimination because it hamper[ed] persons desiring public housing from achieving their objective when no such roadblock face[d] other groups seeking to influence other public decision to their advantage." *James*, 402 U.S. at 142.

James, 402 U.S. at 142.

Likewise, in *Gordon*, 403 U.S. 1, this Court refused to extend *Hunter* beyond suspect classification and upheld a West Virginia Constitutional provision which limited the ability of the state's subdivisions to incur bonded indebtedness. This Court noted the fact that "[t]he constitutions of *many* States prohibit or severely limit the power of the legislature . . . ." *Id.* at 6 (emphasis added). Such matter are *"more properly left to the determination by the States and the people than to the courts operating under the broad mandate of the Fourteenth Amendment."* *Id.* (emphasis added).

The decision of the Colorado Supreme Court sets a dangerous precedent that is unlimited in its applicability.[21] The scope of the decision is incredibly broad because the term "identifiable class" is virtually unrestricted and includes all groups organized on the basis of behavior. In contrast, suspect classification previously provided a logical, "bright line" limitation on the *Hunter* doctrine.[22]

The court below, perhaps recognizing the dangerous potential of its own decision, made a futile attempt to limit[23] the scope of its holding. The lower court attempted to restrict the definition of "independently identifiable class" while still including homosexuals, lesbians and bisexuals. Without any elaboration, the Colorado Supreme Court simply found the limitation set forth in *Gordon*, 403 U.S. 1, "both controlling and persuasive here." *Evans*, 854 P.2d at 1284.

---

[21] This Court has expressed this same fear in other cases as well. *See Jefferson v. Hackney*, 406 U.S. 535, 548-49 (1972) (citing *James*, this Court stated: "The acceptance of appellants' constitutional theory would render suspect each difference in treatment among the . . . classes, however lacking in racial motivation and however otherwise rational the treatment might be. Few legislative efforts to deal with the difficult problems posed by current welfare programs could survive such scrutiny, and we do not find it required by the Fourteenth Amendment."; *Whitcomb v. Chavis*, 403 U.S. 124, 156-57 (1971) (where this Court refused to recognize the "fundamental right" to equal group representation and stated: "[Such a] holding . . . is not easily contained. It is expressive of the more general proposition that any group with distinctive interests must be represented in legislative halls . . . . This approach would make it difficult to reject claims of Democrats, Republicans, or members of any political organization . . . . At the very least, [such a holding] would spawn endless litigation concerning the multi-member district systems now widely employed in this country."); *Mobile v. Bolden*, 446 U.S. 55, 77 (1980) (where this Court refused to recognize the "fundamental right" to participate equally in the political process, citing *Whitcomb*, 408 U.S. 124, and *Dunn*, 405 U.S. 330, and stated: "But this right to equal participation in the political process does not protect any 'political group' from electoral defeat."); *Parker v. Mandel*, 344 F.Supp. 1068, 1079 (D.Md. 1972) ("To hold that the strict scrutiny test applies to legislation of this sort would be to render automatically suspect every statutory classification made by state legislatures . . . .").

[22] Suspect classification is *the* limitation because it is a definite standard; it is also a *logical* limitation because unequal and burdened participation in the political process is a factor which suspect classes must demonstrate to gain such status. *See, e.g., Bowen v. Gilliard*, 483 U.S. 587 (1987). Thus, the rights of those actually burdened remain protected.

[23] Holding that a fundamental right is applicable only to certain groups is contrary to the very nature of a fundamental right. If the right is so "fundamental," certainly all should be entitled to its protection. This observation compels the court to recognize that *Hunter* is based on suspect classification as opposed to fundamental rights.

The limitation set forth in *Gordon*, however, cannot be understood apart from the contrasts and distinctions this Court was making.[24]

> Unlike the restrictions in our previous cases, the West Virginia Constitution singles out no "discrete and insular minority" for special treatment. We are not, therefore, presented with a case like *Hunter v. Erickson* . . . .
> The class singled out in Hunter was clear -- "those who would benefit from laws barring *racial, religious, or ancestral discriminations*." In contrast we can discern no independently identifiable group or category that favors bonded indebtedness over other forms of financing.

Gordon, 403 U.S. at 5 (citations omitted) (emphasis added).

The distinction *Gordon* makes is between racial or ancestral groups on the one hand, and groups which are not organized on the basis of race or ancestry on the other. Hence, *Gordon* clearly limits the *Hunter* doctrine to suspect classification.[25]

Aside from this misplaced reliance upon *Gordon*, the court below set forth no limitations and no criteria for recognizing what constitutes an "independently identifiable group."[26] Extending application of the *Hunter* doctrine outside of suspect classification and including groups organized on the basis of behavior,[27] such as homosexuals, bisexuals, and lesbians "will provide the basis to attack a wide range of routine federal and state legislation."[28]

---

[24] The opinion of the court below begins quoting *Gordon* in the middle of the paragraph at "In contrast . . . ," *Evans*, 854 P.2d at 1284, without indicating the contrast *Gordon* was attempting to make.

[25] Race and ancestry are the only two truly "suspect classes" recognized by this Court.

[26] The only meaningful distinction which *Gordon*, 403 U.S. 1, makes is that of suspect classification. Certainly there are "groups or categories that [favor] bonded indebtedness over other forms of financing," *Id.* at 5, but the distinction which *Gordon* makes is that there are no "*suspect classes*" which favor bonded indebtedness over other forms of financing. Except for this line separating suspect classifications from non-suspect classifications, there is no standard set forth in *Gordon* which separates "independently identifiable groups" (groups entitled to the fundamental right to participate equally in the political process) from non-"independently identifiable groups," (those not entitled to the fundamental right). Even if, as the Colorado Supreme Court believes, *Gordon* does not restrict application of the *Hunter* doctrine to suspect classes, there is no other meaningful limitation which can be found in *Gordon*. If the distinction in *Gordon* was not drawn on the basis of "suspect class," the Court in *Gordon* merely held that in this particular situation they could find no "independently identifiable class." *Gordon* then holds only that there is no "independently identifiable group or category that favors bonded indebtedness over other forms of financing." *Gordon*, 403 U.S. at 5. That is an extremely limited holding which does not exclude other "shifting and diverse groups of the American population" from the definition of "independently identifiable group."

[27] This Court has clearly held that sexual orientation "is primarily behavioral in nature." *Woodward v. United States*, 871 F.2d 1068, 1076 (Fed. Cir. 1989), *cert. denied*, 494 U.S. 1003 (1990); *See also*, *Steffan v. Cheney*, 780 F.Supp. 1 (D.D.C. 1991) and *High Tech Gays v. Defense Indus. Sec. Clearance Office*, 895 F.2d 563 (9th Cir. 1990), *reh'g denied*, 909 F.2d 375 (1990).

[28] Petitioners Brief at 13.

Homosexuals, bisexuals, and lesbians are groups which are, in a legal sense, organized on the same basis as any other political group. By pretending that gay men, lesbians, and bi-sexuals are a "so-called" "identifiable group" which can somehow be distinguished from other groups organized on the basis of behavior, the Colorado Court's decision grants, whether by design or inadvertence, suspect classification to "sexual orientation." This is contrary to *High Tech Gays v. Defense Indus. Sec. Clearance Office*, 895 F.2d 563, 573 (9th Cir. 1990), *reh'g denied*, 909 F.2d 375 (1990).[29]

IV. The Judgment Of The Colorado Supreme Court Is Final

Since the early history of this Court, the Court's decisions have recognized certain exceptions to the final judgment rule of 28 U.S.C. § 1257(a). *Radio Station WOW, Inc. v. Johnson*, 326 U.S. 120, 125 n.2 (1945). This Court's decision in *Cox Broadcasting Corp. v. Cohn*, 420 U.S. 469 (1975), categorized these exceptions. The first category encompassed cases in which the federal issue was "conclusive or the outcome of the further proceedings preordained" although state proceedings, including entire trials, were yet to occur." *Id.* at 479.[30]

The case at hand is closely analogous to two particular U.S. Supreme Court category one cases.[31] In those comparable cases, this Court granted certiorari.

In *Pope v. Atlantic Coast Line Railroad Co.*, 345 U.S. 379 (1953), a trial court, had sustained a general demurrer to the request for an injunction, but the Georgia Supreme Court reversed dismissing the petitioner's federal defense under a federal statute. The U.S. Supreme Court determined[32] that the state supreme court's judgment was final because the Georgia Supreme Court's decision, interpreting an important federal statute, was in conflict with U.S. Supreme Court decisions and the petitioner had no other defense. *Id.* at 381-82. These two reasons made the "federal question . . . the controlling question." *Id.* at 382.[33]

---

[29] *See also, Steffan v. Cheney*, 780 F.Supp. 1, 7(D.D.C. 1991); *National Gay Task Force v. Board of Educ.*, 729 F.2d 1270, 1273 (10th Cir. 1984), *aff'd*, 470 U.S. 903 (1985).

[30] Category two included cases in which the federal questions(s) would survive subsequent state court proceedings regardless of the outcome and was premised upon the fact that no other federal issues would arise in such proceedings. *Cox Broadcasting Corp.*, 420 U.S. at 480. This category has been argued to be the original historical exception to the final judgment rule. *See Johnson*, 326 U.S. at 126-6.

[31] For additional category one cases that are similar to the following two cases, *see American Radio Ass'n, AFL-CIO v. Mobile Steamship Ass'n*, 419 U.S. 215 (1974) and *Construction & Gen. Laborers' Union Local 438 v. Curry*, 371 U.S. 542 (1963).

[32] Only Justice Reed thought that the court's decision with regard to finality was wrong. *See Pope*, 345 U.S. at 387.

[33] *See also, Mills v. State of Alabama*, 384 U.S. 214 (1966) (the trial court sustained demurrers to the complaint based on state and federal constitutional rights of free speech and press, but the state supreme court reversed despite that the petitioners had no other defenses and only Justice Harlan disagreed that the

In *Organization for a Better Austin v. Keefe*, 402 U.S. 415 (1971), this Court held[34] that it had jurisdiction to hear the case even though a state appellate court had only affirmed the trial court's grant of a temporary injunction against leafleting and picketing. This Court stated that "[a]though the record in this case is not such as to leave the matter entirely free from doubt we conclude we are not without power to decide this case." *Id.* at 418 n.* (citations omitted). In light of that standard, it was crucial to the Court that the temporary injunction had been in effect for over three years holding the First Amendment rights of the petitioners hostage. *Id.*

Similarly, the court below decided an important federal question[35] and its decision is in conflict with U.S. Supreme Court decisions as in *Pope*. The petitioner-defendants have no other defense except to meet the burden of proving a compelling state interest. The judgment below is analogous to *Keefe* because there is no indication when the process of litigation regarding Amendment 2 will end. The preliminary injunction has already been in effect for over nine months,[36] and with the trial on the merits under way at the time of this writing and another state appeals process to come (regardless of the trial court's ruling), it is very probable that the injunction will be in effect for several years before a final decision is rendered. All the while, the sovereign power of the people of the State of Colorado is crippled.

V. Conclusion

The Colorado Supreme Court usurped federal judicial power in contravention of their duty, paralyzed the sovereignty of the people of the State of Colorado, and set a dangerous precedent that has no limits. The judgment is final.

Respectfully submitted this 22nd day of October, 1993.

Robert K. Skolrood

Robert K. Skolrood
Attorney for Amicus Curiae

judgment was not final).

[34] Although the decision was not unanimous, Justice Harlan's lone dissent was not based on the fact that the judgment was not final. Rather, Justice Harlan's dissent was based on the fact that the final judgement was not "rendered by the highest court of a State in which a decision could be had" as required by 28 U.S.C. § 1257. *See Keefe*, 402 U.S. at 420-23. Thus, on the issue of finality, this decision was unanimous.

[35] How state courts construe the Equal Protection Clause of the 14th Amendment is of great import.

[36] The preliminary injunction was granted on January 15, 1993.

Appendix E
Justice Erickson's Dissenting Opinion to *EVANS V. ROMER*

The following excerpts are taken from a 38-page dissenting opinion written by Colorado Supreme Court Justice William H. Erickson. The ruling involved the Amendment 2 case, known as *Evans v. Romer*. The State's high court upheld Judge Jeffrey Bayless's injunction against Amendment 2 by a 6-to-1 margin. These excerpts represent the view of only one Colorado judge involved with the Amendment 2 case. The full text of this document may be obtained as a matter of public record from any Colorado county courthouse law library.

Evans v. Romer, No. 93SA17
JUSTICE ERICKSON dissenting:

"I respectfully dissent." p.1

"The strict scrutiny standard of review was found to be applicable based on a *fundamental right* 'not to have the State endorse and give effect to private biases' with respect to 'an identifiable class.' The district court's delineation of the fundamental right supporting the preliminary injunction has never been identified or recognized by the United States Supreme Court or by any other court." p.1-2

". . . the only question open to [a lower court is] whether the Supreme Court has created a right, which, fairly defined, covers the case before [it] or whether the Supreme Court has specified a mode of analysis, a methodology, which, honestly applied, reaches the case [it] must now decide." (Quoting from the U.S. Supreme Court's decision in *Dronenburg v. Zech*, 1984.) p.7

". . . [i]f it is in any degree doubtful that the Supreme Court should freely create new constitutional rights, we think it certain that lower courts should not do so." (Quoting again from *Dronenburg*.) p.36

"The majority [of Colorado Supreme Court Justices] recognized that gay men, lesbians, and bisexuals constitute an 'identifiable group' . . . In fact, courts have consistently rejected claims that the identifiable group of homosexuals constitutes a suspect class." footnote 3, p.4

". . . the district court erred in issuing a preliminary injunction based on a fundamental right not to have the State endorse and give effect to private biases." p.6

"The Court is most vulnerable and comes nearest to illegitimacy when it deals with judge-made constitutional law having little or no cognizable roots in the language or design of the Constitution." [Quoting U.S. Supreme Court Justice Byron White, in the *Bowers v. Hardwick* decision of 1986.] p. 14

"In my view, the district court's [Judge Bayless's] underlying legal premise that the Supreme Court has recognized a fundamental right not to have the State endorse and give effect to private biases is erroneous. Similarly, the majority's [the six Colorado Supreme

Court Justices'] underlying legal premise that the Supreme Court has recognized a fundamental right to participate equally in the political process is erroneous. Because Supreme Court precedent does not support the evaluation of Amendment 2 under the strict scrutiny standard of review, I would reverse and discharge the entry of the preliminary injunction, and remand for trial on the permanent injunction.

Endnotes

1. Valerie Richardson, "Amendment 2, Act II: Gay-Rights Foe Builds Colorado Victory," *The Washington Times*, 2 June 1993.

2. Cathy Reynolds, "Gay Rights: Pro and Con," *The Rocky Mountain News,* October 23, 1991.

3. Associated Press, "Comparison of Polls Shows Coloradans can be More Tolerant on Gay Issues," *Gazette Telegraph*, 8 March 1993. Polls compared in this article were between a *Rocky Mountain News*/9 News poll of 426 registered Colorado voters coincided with the release of a similar *New York Times* poll of adults nationally. The news poll had a margin of error of 4.8% and was conducted February 26 through March 2, 1993.

4. Talmey-Drake Research and Strategy, "News Poll" (survey conducted 15-23 December 1992), *The Denver Post,* 3 January 1993.

5. Gallup, "Extend Civil Rights Laws to Include Homosexuals?" (GO 322054), *Gallup Poll Monthly,* April 1993, question #21.

6. "We Are In A Lot Of Trouble," *The Washington Blade,* 12 March 1993.

7. "Springs Gay Rights Backers Out Front," *Gazette Telegraph,* 22 April 1993.

8. Louis Aguilar, "Gay Rights Leader Takes Cause on Road," *Gazette Telegraph,* 7 May 1993.

9. Michael Booth, "Plans Made Early for Court Challenge to Anti-gay-rights Law," *The Denver Post,* 8 October 1993.

10. Denver Post/News4 Poll, *The Denver Post,* 27 October 1993, A1.

11. Jane Ostrow, "Sardella Got to Heart of Amendment 2," TV-radio, *The Denver Post,* 5 November 1992. (Note: Ostrow praised the only TV anchor who characterized Amendment 2 as the issue "that would legalize discrimination against homosexuals." She claimed this to be the heart of Amendment 2 and said voters were "hoodwinked into voting for the amendment.")

12. Digital Policy Paper, "Valuing Differences Work, CXO Manufacturing."

13. "What is DECplus," undated handbill distributed at Digital. Note: Pat Long requested that we remove the name of the author of this handbill. Calls to Digial management in December 1993 revealed that he had been placed on extended sick leave and was rumored to have died of AIDS. One is sadly reminded of Pat Long's Digital memo dated 13 April 1990 (see Endnote 14): "I believe I must love these people by confronting them with their sin. Failure to do

so could lead them to physical death and spiritual condemnation."

14. Pat Long, "SUBJECT: We should be valuing PEOPLE, not their sins," Memo to: Chuck Poe, Valuing Differences Committee, Digital Equipment Corporation, 13 April 1990.

15. Pat Long, "SUBJECT: Threat and Harassment," Memo to Dick Fletcher and Lisa Moore, Digital Equipment Corporation, 9 May 1990.

16. Ibid.

17. Pat Long, "SUBJECT: Summary on April 19th meeting, RE: We should be valuing PEOPLE, not their sins," Memo to CXO Christian Community, CC to Chuck Poe and Rochelle Patton, Digital Equipment Corporation, 23 April 1990

18. Michael Booth, "Log Cabin Pushes Conservative Plan," *The Denver Post,* 3 October 1993.

19. Berny Morson, "'Verbal Fist' Kills Gay-Rights Bill," *The Rocky Mountain News,* 8 February 1991.

20. "All-Out Battle Waged over Gay Rights," *Gazette Telegraph,* 17 February 1991.

21. Ibid.

22. Brian M. McCormick, Esq., "Memorandum of Legal Analysis; Colorado Springs Proposed Human Rights Ordinance," *The National Legal Foundation*, Virginia Beach, VA, 7 March 1991.

23. Tony Marco, "Operation Victory: End Run," working paper, ad hoc committee, Executive Proposal & Summary, 1991.

24. Sue Huck, "Post Script to Colorado's Amendment 2: A Salute to Will Perkins," *Conservative Review,* August-September 1993.

25. Tony Marco, memo to Will Perkins, 17 August 1992.

26. Huck, "Salute to Will Perkins."

27. Richardson, "Gay-Rights Foe Builds Colorado Victory."

28. Hall Clifford, "Why Is Gay Rage Targeting Aspen?", *Aspen Magazine,* Summer 1993.

29. Ibid.

30. Associated Press (Denver), "Lawmakers Draft Bills to Defuse Amendment," *Gazette Telegraph,* 15 January 1993.

31. Brian M. McCormick, Staff Counsel, The National Legal Foundation, letter to Tony Marco, Co-Chairman, Colorado Coalition for Family Values, "Re: Analysis of Language in Amendment Initiative," 13 June 1991.

32. Robin Miller, letter to Ms. Meyer, Colorado Secretary of State, Elections Licensing Office, (received) 19 September 1991.

33. Tony Marco, letter to CFV Board, 17 October 1991.

34. "From the Mouth of McCartney," *Gazette Telegraph,* 14 February 1992.

35. "Special Report: CU Coach Defends His Stance, 'I'm Not Going to Compromise,'" *The Rocky Mountain News,* March 1993.

36. Ibid.

37. Virginia Culver, "Armstrong Letter Called 'Tragic, Hurtful, Painful'," *The Denver Post,* 22 March 1992.

38. Karen Brunner, "Armstrong Shows Prejudice Toward Gays" (letters to the editor), *Grand Junction Gazette,* 25 March 1992.

39. Editorial, "Note to Bill Armstrong: Hate Is Not a Family Value," *The Denver Post,* 25 March 1992.

40. Editorial, *The Durango Herald,* 29 March 1992.

41. Ken Hamblin, "Mental Dinosaurs Spewing Bigotry and Hate," *The Denver Post,* 1 March 1992.

42. Culver, "Armstrong letter called . . ." (In this article Culver claims, "Armstrong . . . blamed the AIDS epidemic on the 'self-created miseries of pleasure-addicted gays'." Her accusation was a lie. Armstrong's quote about the "self-created miseries of pleasure-addicted gays" was lifted from a paragraph in the letter about the illegitimacy of gay civil rights claims. It compared their "self-created miseries" to the "innocent sufferings and crippling poverty of legitimate minority groups." The discussion of AIDS appeared seven paragraphs later on his letter's next page and cannot even be construed to apply to this quote-out-of-context.)

43. John C. Ensslin, "Blaze, Protest Hit Church that Fired Lesbian; 500 Forced to Evacuate First Presbyterian in Boulder; Demonstrators Cross-dress for Picket," *The Rocky Mountain News,* 18 March 1991.

44. Clifford, "Why Is Gay Rage Targeting Aspen?"

45. Aguilar, "Gay Rights Leader Takes Cause on Road."

46. "Equal Employment Opportunity Is The Law," poster of Federal Guidelines summary, posted in Perkins Chrysler-Plymouth dealership.

47. Nan Hunter, Sherryl Michaelson, and Thomas Stoddard, *The Rights of Lesbians and Gay Men: The Basic ACLU Guide to a Gay Person's Rights,* 3rd ed. (Carbondale IL: Southern Illinois University Press, 1992).

48. Maria Shriver, "The Gay '90s; Sex, Power and Influence," NBC News Documentary, broadcast 26 January 1993.

49. Al Knight, "Gay Rights Issues Multiply and Divide," *The Denver Post,* 21 July 1992.

50. Nan Hunter, Sherryl Michaelson, and Thomas Stoddard, *The Rights of Lesbians and Gay Men:* appendix C. (The appendix lists 7 states with comprehensive homosexual rights laws, 7 others have executive orders or hate or bias crime laws that apply.)

51. David Horowitz, "The Queer Fellows," *The American Spectator* 26, no. 1 (January 1993): 42.

52. Aguilar, "Gay Rights Leader Takes Cause on Road."

53. "1992 Denver Public Schools Health and Science Education Teacher's Guide: Gay and Lesbian Youth Tools for Educators," Denver Public Schools, 1992.

54. "Who Publishes those Pro-Gay Kids Books?," *Lambda Report,* February 1993.

55. Jay & Young, *The Gay Report* (New York: Summit Books, 1979): 275.

56. *The British Journal of Sexual Medicine,* April 1987.

57. *Psychological Reports,* vol. 58 (1986): 327-37.

58. James C. Coleman, *Abnormal Psychology and Modern Life,* 3rd ed. (Chicago: Scott, Foresman, 1964).

59. Masters & Johnson, *Human Sexual Inadequacy,* (Boston: Little Brown and Company, 1970): 180.

60. "Analysis of Punitive Homosexual Separations, Fiscal Years 1989-1992," *Memorandum For The Record: Department of the Army, Office of the JAG (Judge Advocate General),* doc. DAJA-CL 27-10, 27 May 1993.

61. *CFV Report,* Vol. 4 (May 1993): 3.

62. "No Place for Homophobia," *San Francisco Sentinel,* 26 March 1992.

63. Bradley Rose, editorial, *Bay Area Reporter,* 13 February 1992, 6.

64. *The NAMBLA Bulletin,* September 1992, 6.

65. *Insight Magazine,* 17 June 1991.

66. Tony Marco, "Special Class Protections for Gays: A question of 'Orientation' and Consequences," position paper, 1991, 1992.

67. David Thorstadt, editorial, *Gazette Telegraph*, 14 January 1983, E9.

68. *Newsweek,* 7 May 1979, 36.

69. *New York Post,* 20 Oct 1990.

70. Penny Parker, "Two Moms: A lesbian Couple Talks about the Joys and Challenges of Parenthood," *The Denver Post Magazine,* 10 October 1993.

71. "New York To Watch Over Sex Clubs," *Gazette Telegraph,* 29 April 1993, sec., National Briefings.

72. Dennis Prager, "Judaism's Sexual Revolution," *Ultimate Issues* 6, No. 2 (April-June 1990).

73. Katherine Dalton, "Privacy and the 'Lesbian Roommate' Case," *The Wall Street Journal,* 20 July 1992.

74. Marco, "Special Class Protections for Gays."

75. Ibid.

76. "Stop Special Class Status for Homosexuality," *CFV Tabloid,* 3.

77. Editorial, "Scuttling Scouts with Gay Rights," *Gazette Telegraph,* 29 March 1993.

78. "Stop Special Class Status for Homosexuals: Gay Rights Abuses Here in Colorado," *CFV Tabloid,* 5.

79. Ibid.

80. Ibid.

81. Ibid.

82. Ibid.

83. [Rutherford Institute Staff], "Court Declines Injunction Against Homosexual Rights Law," *Rutherford,* February 1993.

84. Hunter, Michaelson, and Stoddard, *The Rights of Lesbians and Gay Men.*

85. "Out Magazine Delivers Pitch for Upscale Gay Market," *Out Magazine,* 29 January 1993.

86. Space ad placed by WinMark Concepts, Washington, D.C., *Advertising Age,* 27 July 1992.

87. Marco, "Special Class Protections for Gays"

88. Ibid.

89. "The Shrinking Ten Percent," *Time,* 26 April 1993, 29.

90. "Overcoming a Deep-Rooted Reluctance, More Firms Advertise to Gay Community," *The Wall Street Journal,* 18 July 1991.

91. "Gay, Lesbian Groups Seek to Expunge Bias They See in Language," *The Wall Street Journal,* 3 May 1993.

92. Michael Booth, "Smoker-Rights Law Aids Gay's Lawsuit Over Firing: Lawyer Awarded $91,000," *The Denver Post,* 21 July 1993.

93. Ostrow, "Sardella Got to Heart of Amendment 2."

94. Shawn Mitchell, "A Clash of Rights," *The Rocky Mountain News,* 18 October 1992.

95. Richardson, "Gay-Rights Foe Builds Colorado Victory."

96. Mark Hartwig, "A Content Analysis of Amendment 2 Coverage; Summary of Results," *Citizen Magazine* (Focus On The Family), July 1993.

97. Joseph Sobran, "Objectivity Kept In Closet When Reporting on Gay Issues," *Gazette Telegraph,* 3 February 1993.

98. Angela Dire, "Survey Takes Center Stage in Debate on Gay Rights," *Gazette Telegraph,* 12 June 1992.

99. Al Knight, "Gay Rights Issues Multiply and Divide," *The Denver Post,* 21 June 1992.

100. Gale Norton (Attorney General of Colorado), "Opening Brief," *Evans v. Romer,* 1993.

101. Associated Press (Denver), "Nearly Half Denver Bias Cases Filed by Gays," *Gazette Telegraph,* 14 November 1992.

102. Based on $12,166 per four-person black American household, *Statistical Abstract of the United States* (1990).

103. "The Gay Nineties," *The Marketer,* September 1990, 12. Based on gays reporting a $55,430 annual income per household in this study, in households of the average size of 1.506, which yielded the $36,800 *per capita* figure. This compared to the average American income of $12,287 listed on p.13.

104. Based on $12,166 income per 4-person black American household, *Statistical Abstract of the United States* (1990). Thus, the individual black American's annual income is $3,041.50.

105. Dire, "Survey Takes Center Stage in Debate on Gay Rights."

106. "Overcoming a Deep-Rooted Reluctance, More Firms Advertise to Gay Community," *The Wall Street Journal,* 18 July 1991.

107. Ibid.

108. "Researchers Identify Gene Pattern Linked to Homosexuality," *Gazette Telegraph,* 16 July 1993.

109. Lawrence Ingrassia, "Fighting Words: Gay, Lesbian Groups Seek to Expunge Bias They See in Language," *The Wall Street Journal,* 3 May 1993.

110. Jonathan Rauch, "Beyond Oppression," from a reprint in The Australian, *The New Republic* (20 May 1993).

111. Hunter, Michaelson, and Stoddard, *The Rights of Lesbians and Gay Men.*

112. "Stop Special Class Status for Homosexuality," *CFV Tabloid,* 2.

113. Colin Powell, *The Retired Officer,* July 1992.

114. Associated Press (Washington), "Homosexual Rights Group Says Anti-Gay Violence Surged in '91: Task Force Cites a 'Message of Hatred'," *Gazette Telegraph,* 21 March 1992.

115. Hartwig, "A Content Analysis of Amendment 2 Coverage."

116. Associated Press (Washington), "First Look at Hate Crimes Finds Race Bias Caused Most," *Gazette Telegraph,* 5 January 1993.

117. Robin L., "Your Delegates-at-Large SOUNDOFF . . . on Membership Responsibilities," Calendar and Newsletter (Ground Zero), March 1993.

118. [Gazette Telegraph Staff?], "Justice" (sidebar, Source: Colorado Springs Police Department), *Gazette Telegraph,* 30 May 1993, A17.

119. Associated Press, "Hiring Grows More Quirky," *Gazette Telegraph,* 13 January 1993.

120. Ibid.

121. *The World Book Dictionary,* (New York: Doubleday & Company, Inc., 1983).

122. "VOTE NO ON #2" (Paid Political Advertisement), *Gazette Telegraph,* 1 November 1992, A22.

123. Equality Colorado: Colorado Anti-Discrimination Coalition, form letter to Colorado businesses, "Dear Business Colleague," *Equality Colorado,* June 1993.

124. Dr. Steven Sainsbury (guest editorial), "Condoms Assure Safe Sex—About Like Russian Roulette Assures Safe Roulette," *The Denver Post,* 18 July 1993.

125. Ibid.

126. Al Knight, "Gay Rights Issues Multiply and Divide," *The Denver Post,* 21 June 1992; reprinted chart from *Seattle Times* (Elizabeth Rhodes, 21 July 1991); figures from *Partners Newsletter for Gay and Lesbian Couples* (1991).

127. Rauch, "Beyond Oppression."

128. Associated Press (New York), "Breast-Cancer Risk Higher for Lesbians, Researcher Finds," *The Denver Post,* 5 February 1993.

129. Paul Cameron, Ph.D., William L. Playfair, M.D., and Stephen Wellum, B.A., "The Homosexual Lifespan," paper presented at Eastern Psychological Association, *Family Research Institute,* 17 April 1993.

130. Michael Booth, "The Man Who Sold Amendment 2," *The Denver Post Magazine,* 21 March 1993.

131. Glenn Tinder, "Can We be Good Without God? On the Political Meaning of Christianity," *The Atlantic Monthly,* December 1989, 69-85.

132. Isaac Kramnick, ed. *The Federalist papers: James Madison, Alexander Hamilton and John Jay* (New York: Penquin Books, 1987).

133. Don Feder, "America's Founding Fathers were Men of Firm Faith," *Gazette Telegraph,* 2 February 1993.

134. Proverbs 14.34 NIV.

135. Don Feder, *A Jewish Conservative Looks at Pagan America* (Lafayette LA: Huntington House Publishers, 1993): 112.

136. Genesis 19.4-5 NIV.

137. Anne Windishar, "Gay Rights Pit Pastor Against Pastor: Local Church Leaders Interpret Bible's Message Differently," *Gazette Telegraph,* 9 April 1993.

138. Ezekiel 16.49-50 NIV.

139. Dr. Ralph Blair, *The Bible is an Empty Closet,* pamphlet, (New York: Evangelicals Concerned). Pro-homosexual explanation of Genesis 19.

140. Leviticus 18.22 NIV.

141. Jude 1.7 NIV.

142. Romans 1.26 NIV.

143. John Stott, "John Stott Speaks Out," *Christianity Today,* 8 February 1993.

144. Matthew 19.6 NIV.

145. Blair, *The Bible is an Empty Closet.*

146. Booth, "The Man Who Sold Amendment 2."

147. Ibid.

148. Angel Hernandez, "Church Ducks Stand on Initiative; Colorado's Catholic Bishops, Archbishop on Sidelines over Effort to Ban Gay-Rights Laws," *The Rocky Mountain News,* 26 June 1992.

149. Tim Crater, "Reflection on Christian Citizenship Campaign," *United Evangelical Action* (National Association of Evangelicals), March-April 1993.

150. Dennis Pager, "Epilogue," *Ultimate Issues* (April-June 1990).

151. Reuters, "Vatican Endorses Bias Against Gays," *The Rocky Mountain News,* 1 November 1992.

152. Talmey-Drake, "Gay rights Fight to be Brutal Brawl in the Mud," *The Talmey-Drake Report,* Vol. 1, No. 1 (May 1992).

153. Matthew 22.39 NIV.

154. Gordon Muir, "Homosexuals and the 10 Percent Fallacy," *Gazette Telegraph,* 11 April 1993.

155. TV Previews, "Direct Gay '90s," *USA Today,* 26 January 1993.

156. Gary Massaro, "Poll Show Amendment 2 Going Down to Defeat," *The Rocky Mountain News,* 4 November 1992.

157. Henry Dubroff, "Colorado Business Leaders Square Off on Tuesday's Ballot Issues," *The Denver Post,* 1 November 1992.

158. Massaro, "Polls Show Amendment 2 Going Down to Defeat."

159. Michael Booth, "Gay-Rights Ban Narrowly Winning: Amendment 2 Opponents Stunned," *The Denver Post,* 4 November 1992.

160. "Protestors Decry Amendment 2" caption over photo, *The Rocky Mountain News,* 5 November 1992. Caption under photo: "Gov. Roy Romer, left, and Denver Mayor Wellington Webb, right, march Wednesday to the state capitol with about 400 people protesting passage of Amendment 2.")

161. Gary Massaro, "Angry Gays Vow to Keep Fighting: Lawsuits and Boycotts Appear to be Coming after Amendment 2 Wins by 100,000 Votes," *The Rocky Mountain News,* 5 November 1992.

162. Greg Trinker, "Shocked Gays Looking to Government for Victory," *The Denver Post,* 8 November 1992.

163. Ed Quillen, "Their Own Worst Enemies," *The Denver Post,* 8 November 1993.

164. Tom Gavin, "Here's a Soft Answer," *The Denver Post,* 9 December 1992.

165. Gary Massaro, "Gay Groups Assail State on Amendment 2," *The Rocky Mountain News,* 5 November 1992.

166. Trinker, "Shocked Gays Looking to Government for Victory"

167. *USA TODAY,* 4 November 1993, 4A & 5A.

168. Jack Lang y Marquez (Director of Colorado Civil Rights Division), *Memorandum to Colorado Civil Rights Commission,* Director's Report, December 1992, 18 December 1992, 4-5.

169. Kramnick, *The Federalist Papers.* Hamilton wrote: "The subjects of its [impeachment] jurisdiction are those offenses which proceed from the misconduct of public men, or, in other words, from the abuse or violation of some public trust." Governor Romer's sworn duty to uphold the Constitution as decided by the will of the people who elected him to office seems to be the specific public trust violated by his conduct of this meeting in which he conspired to overturn Amendment 2.

170. Angela Dire, "Amendment's OK 'Last Straw' for Troubled Gay Man," *Gazette Telegraph,* 11 November 1992.

171. Associated Press (Colorado Springs), "Gay Man's Suicide Note Cites Passage of Amendment 2," *The Denver Post,* 12 November 1992.

172. Michael Booth, "Coalition Files Suit Against Amendment 2," *The Denver Post,* 13 November 1992, 8A. (Including photo caption: "Protest: James Shiner endures a mock crucifixion at a gay-rights rally in Civic Center Park yesterday. Story 8A.")

173. Natalie Solo, "Clergy Lead Protest Against Amendment 2," *The Rocky Mountain News,* 16 November 1992.

174. Al Knight, "AIDS ACTIVISTS VS. THE CATHOLICS: Church Vandalism is a Poor Way to Express a Viewpoint," *The Denver Post,* 6 December 1992.

175. Ibid.

176. Associated Press (Denver), "Lawmakers Draft Bills to Defuse Amendment," *Gazette Telegraph,* 15 January 1993.

177. Dana Parsons, "You Don't have to Hate Gays to Keep Loving Colorado," *Los Angeles Times* (Orange County Edition), January 1993.

178. Denver Post Staff and Wire Reports, "Bradley Asks L.A. Council to Ban City Travel to Colorado," *The Denver Post,* 15 December 1992.

179. William J. Bennett, *The De-Valuing of America: The Fight for Our Culture and Our Children* (New York: Summit Books, 1992).

180. Denver Post/News4 Poll.

181. Associated Press (Denver), "Romer: Voters Who Said Yes Meant Well," *Gazette Telegraph,* 6 January 1993.

182. Mark Obmascik, "Amendment 2 Scuttles Librarian Meeting," *The Denver Post,* 24 January 1993.

183. Lynn Bronikowski, "Amendment 2 May Keep Ziff Out of State," *Rocky Mountain News,* 6 January 1993.

184. Associated Press (Denver), "Romer: Ziff-Davis Sure Thing Before Amendment 2," *The Denver Post,* 6 January 1993.

185. Jerry Mahoney, "Amendment 2 Won't Help the Economy," *Gazette Telegraph,* 10 January 1993.

186. Peggy Lowe, "Snow Wins Over Politics as Stars Hit Aspen Slopes," *Gazette Telegraph,* 25 December 1992.

187. Associated Press, "Heavy Snow Lures Skiers to Colorado, *Gazette Telegraph,* 16 April 1993.

188. Steve Caulk, "Ski Areas See Record Season," *The Rocky Mountain News,* 16 January 1993.

189. Chuck Green, "'Hate State' Rally Draws 32 People," *The Denver Post,* 24 January 1993.

190. Jim Buynak and Ray Flack, "Hispanic Group Votes to Move Convention," *Gazette Telegraph,* 10 January 1993.

191. Associated Press (Denver), "Librarians Join Amendment 2 Boycott," *Gazette Telegraph,* 25 January 1993.

192. Louis Aguilar, "Colorado Library Association Votes Against Holding Annual Meetings in Yes-on-2 Counties," *Gazette Telegraph,* 24 February 1993.

193. "Conventions Cancelled," *The Denver Post,* 7 February 1993.

194. Associated Press, "Gay Activists in New York Defend Products Boycott," *Gazette Telegraph,* 15 February 1993.

195. Renate Robey, "Tea Party to Oppose Celestial Boycott," *The Denver Post,* 7 February 1993.

196. Michael Booth, "Boycott's Bark Worse than Bite," *The Denver Post,* 7 February 1993.

197. Associated Press (Denver), "Convention Surge Seen as Making Up for Boycott/More Towns Urged to Defy Amendment," *Gazette Telegraph,* 9 February 1993.

198. Louis Aguilar, "Gay Group Defends Colorado Meeting," *Gazette Telegraph,* 3 March 1993.

199. Associated Press (Denver), "Ziff-Davis Decides Against Move," *Gazette Telegraph,* 13 May 1993.

200. Louis Aguilar, "Local Lawyer Group Rips State Bar," *Gazette Telegraph,* 9 March 1993.

201. Louis Aguilar, "Bar to Meet in Springs: Letters Help Sway Lawyers," *Gazette Telegraph,* 21 March 1993.

202. Associated Press (Denver), June 27, 1993, "Colorado's economic gains lead nation, report says," *The Denver Post,* 27 June 1993.

203. Michael Booth, "Colorado Shrugs Off Gay Boycott: But Some Effects are Painful," *The Denver Post,* 14 November 1993.

204. George Gilder, "Sexual Politics," *Men and Marriage* (Gretna, LA: Pelican, 1986): 104. Gilder adds the following endnote to his quote:

> 3. Stanley Rothman and S. Robert Lichter are directors of a continuing study of U.S. social and political elites conducted under the auspices of Smith College, the Research Institute on International Change of Columbia University, and George Washington University. Their findings show that elites in every area of American life hold social and sexual views far more "liberal" by usual standards than the rest of the population. The results are regularly published in issues of *Public Opinion*, American Enterprise Institute, Washington, D. C.. For example, "What are Movie-makers Made of?", *Public Opinion*, December/January 1984, pp. 14-18.

205. Hunter, Michaelson, and Stoddard, *The Rights of Lesbians and Gay Men.*

206. Ibid., Preface.

207. "Citizen's For Excellence in Education: Church State Debate," debate, Colorado College, Colorado Springs, January 1993.

208. "Gays in the Military," National Public Radio News feature, 26 November 1993.

209. Joseph Sobran, "An 'evolving' Constitution really means no Constitution," *Gazette Telegraph,* 2 June 1993.

210. Robert K. Skolrood (National Legal Foundation), "A Lawyer's Perspective on the Amendment 2 Trial," *CFV Report,* December 1993.

211. Louis Aguilar, "Educators Join Fight to Stop Amendment: Keep Injunction in Effect, Say Unions, Church Groups," *Gazette Telegraph,* 4 May 1993.

212. "White Supremacist Group Puts Off Rally: Amendment 2 Hailed," *Gazette Telegraph,* 6 January 1993.

213. Green, "'Hate State' Rally Draws 32 People."

214. Kathryn Sosbe, "Police End Probe of Therapist's Reported Attack," *Gazette Telegraph,* January 1993.

215. Al Knight, "Are Fundamental Rights Invented?", *The Denver Post,* 24 January 1993.

216. Ibid.

217. Jethro K. Liebermann, *The Evolving Constitution: How the Supreme Court has Ruled on Issues from Abortion to Zoning* (New York: Random House, 1992): 121.

218. Warren Epstein, "Judge's Decision Sparks Outrage: Residents Speak Out on Injunction," *Gazette Telegraph,* 17 January 1993. (Count taken from entire issue.)

219. Ibid.

220. [Denver Post Staff], "Colorado Springs: Ruling Foes" (sidebar), *The Denver Post,* 18 January 1993.

221. Robert K. Skolrood (Counsel of Record, National Legal Foundation), *Brief Amicus Curiae of Colorado For Family Values*, October 1993, 18.

222. Colorado Supreme Court Justices voted as follows: Chief Justice Luis D. Rovira, with Justices Howard M. Kirshbaum, George E. Lohr, Mary J. Mullarkey, Gregory K. Scott, and Anthony F. Vollack upheld Bayless's injunction. *The only dissenting voice came from Justice William H. Erickson.* Their terms will be up for renewal on the state ballot on: Justice Erickson in 1995, Justices Kirshbaum and Scott in 1997, Justice Vollack in 1999, Justice Mullarkey in 2000, and Justices Lohr and Rovira in 2003.

223. Louis Aguilar, "Court: Amendment 2 Flawed," *Gazette Telegraph,* 20 July 1993.

224. William H. Erickson, "Justice Erickson dissenting," *Evans v. Romer, No. 93SA17,* p.1,37-38.

225. Angela Dire, "'Special rights' Tactic Now Called Irrelevant, Amendment 2 Author Testifies," *Gazette Telegraph,* 19 October 1993.

226. "Norton Out to Prove Constitutionality of Measure," *The Denver Post,* 10 October 1993.

227. Joseph Nicolosi, *The Healing of Homosexuality: Case Stories of Reparative Therapy,* (Jason Aronson, Incorporated, 1993).

228. Richard John Neuhaus, "A New Order of Religious Freedom," *First Things,* February 1992.

229. Jane Grandolfo, "Businesses in Springs Fight Fallout," *Gazette Telegraph,* 14 February 1993.

230. Greg Walta, memo to Will Perkins, 27 December 1992.

231. "Lawyer Works to Restore Harmony," *Gazette Telegraph,* 8 February 1993.

232. Hunter, Michaelson, and Stoddard, *The Rights of Lesbians and Gay Men.*

233. Jeff Thomas, "Compromise Called Slap in Face," *Gazette Telegraph,* 9 February 1993.

234. Jeff Thomas, "Group Says Voters Were Misled on Amendment 2," *Gazette Telegraph,* 16 February 1993.

235. Matthew 5.9 KJV.

236. Ecclesiastes 3.1-3 KJV.

237. Grandolfo, "Businesses in Springs Fight Fallout."

238. Ibid.

239. Ibid.

240. Stephen Bransford, "An analysis of Greg Walta's 'Clarification' of Amendment 2," February 4, 1993.

241. Jeff Thomas, "Amendment 2 Compromise Falls: Walta scraps plan, cites lack of support," *Gazette Telegraph,* 16 March 1993.

242. Jeff Thomas, "Finding Middle Ground," *Gazette Telegraph,* 7 March 1993.

243. Thomas, "Amendment 2 Compromise Falls."

244. Ibid.

245. Talmey-Drake Research & Strategy, Inc., "News Poll."

246. Parsons, "You Don't Have to Hate Gays to Keep Loving Colorado."

247. James Dobson, PhD., "Dr. Dobson Answers Your Questions," *Focus on the Family Magazine*, July 1993.

248. Rosemary Harris, "Church Service is Interrupted by Gay Activists Throwing Condoms," *Gazette Telegraph,* 8 November 1993.

249. "Weekend Edition," *National Public Radio*, July 1993.

250. Aguilar, "Gay Rights Leader Takes Cause on Road."

251. Mercedes Harden, director, "El Paso County Department of Health and Environment Provides Therapy Group for Gay and Lesbian Youth," *El Paso County Department of Health and Environment,* Colorado Springs, December 1992.

252. Aguilar, "Gay Rights Leader Takes Cause on Road."

253. Bill Moyers, "The New Holy War," *Bill Moyers' Journal* (PBS Television Network), 19 November 1993.

254. Election figures composited from Beverly Maloy, *Oregon Citizen Alliance;* Louis Aguilar, "More Rural Oregonians OK Anti-Gay Rights Measures," *Gazette Telegraph,* July 1, 1993; and *The Seattle Post-Intelligencer.*

255. Denver Post/News4 Poll.

256. Kramnick, *The Federalist Papers.*

Index

Other books by Stephen Bransford

Riders of the Long Road (1984, historical novel)
High Places (1992, fiction)

Limited quantities available from the author, in care of:

Sardis Press
Box 11
Cascade CO 80809